LIVING
PRIESTHOOD

D1471282

MICHAEL HOLLINGS

McCrimm(
Great Wakering Ess

First published in Great Britain in 1977 by
MAYHEW-McCRIMMON LTD
Great Wakering, Essex, England

Revised and reprinted in 1994

This edition published in 2001 by
McCRIMMON PUBLISHING CO. LTD.
10-12 High Street, Great Wakering, Essex, SS3 0EQ
Telephone 01702–218956   Fax 01702–216082
email: mccrimmons@dial.pipex.com
www.mccrimmons.com

ISBN 0-85597-110-X

British Library Cataloguing in Publication Data.
A catalogue record for this book is available from the British Library.

Cover design by Nick Snode
Printed and bound by
Permanent Typesetting & Printing Co. Ltd., Hong Kong

CONTENTS

Preface ....
1994 Plus 3
Foreword 7
Introduction 9
1　Some Personal background 17
2　Priest: Person of prayer 43
3　Priest: Sexuality, friendship and love 54
4　Priest: Listener, counsellor, healer 81
5　Priest: All things to all men all the time 94
6　Neighbourliness unlimited 110
7　Community relations 124
8　Developing parish community 141
9　Liturgy: Eucharist 158
10　Liturgy: Sacraments 175
11　Open living 192
12　People in council 211
13　What must I do? 224
14　Prologue to the future 236
　　Epilogue 248

Appendices

1　Involvement of religious sisters at Southall 249
2　A recollection of Padre Pio 257

PREFACE

In 1978, a year after the publication of *Living Priesthood*, Michael Hollings moved from Southall to be parish priest of St Mary of the Angels, Bayswater; and he continued in this post until his death in 1997. During the 'Bayswater' period naturally there were developments and adjustments in Michael's handling of life and ministry. Nonetheless this remarkable figure held substantially to the perspectives and ways displayed in *Living Priesthood* throughout the rest of his career.

The current preface is not the place for me to explore what it was about Michael Hollings that occasioned his considerable impact on others. I voiced some brief thoughts on this in a homily at a Vigil Requiem Mass for Michael. The homily was printed in *The Month,* April 1997, and is reprinted in a volume of collected memoirs, *Press On!.*[*]

Among those liable to find *Living Priesthood* rewarding are people who possess any out of a range of initial interests. Some people's starting interest will be desire to learn more about Michael Hollings himself: what 'made him tick', how he saw what he was about in life and priesthood, and so on. Michael stated that the book was not meant to be an autobiography. Nonetheless as regards some of his guiding ideas and main approaches, the book is perhaps the nearest thing you will come across to an autobiography.

Some people's initial focus will be on how their own or others' lives as ordained priests might be conducted. A very great deal in the book at hand seems to me still strikingly fresh and relevant in connection with contemporary priesthood, and

---

[*] Edited by Jock Dalrymple, Joan McCrimmon and Terry Tastard (McCrimmons, 2001)

some associated issues and concerns. To pick out just one aspect of this, by way of example: in Catholic circles today charges are on occasion advanced that certain seminarians or priests carry on in a narrow, inward-looking fashion remote from the lives of human beings in the wider Church and world. In *Living Priesthood* Michael Hollings shows something of how a priest's whole orientation can be the very opposite of that: can be towards open contact and supportive engagement with all manner of person, and with innumerable dimensions of individuals' daily existence – albeit this may be at marked cost to the priest's own self.

Again, some people's initial interest will be in Christian spirituality, ministry and caring on broad planes, beyond ordained priesthood specifically. Much in the present book speaks to such interest, as is the case too with other books by Michael Hollings.

Whatever be the reader's starting preoccupations, by the time they have reached the end of *Living Priesthood* their awareness, reflection and personal attunement may very well have been fruitfully extended and enhanced. This can be so, whether or not the reader agrees with every point that the author makes. These colloquially written, easily perused pages, even if at certain moments a little loose or repetitive, contain abundant riches.

What of the very title of the book? Michael Hollings comments on the title in lines which were inserted at the beginning of an edition brought out towards the end of his life, and which are reproduced below, '1994 Plus'. When I myself originally suggested the words 'Living Priesthood' as the book's title, these words seemed to me to evoke at least three elements which held – though at the time I did not fully spell all this out and risk embarrassing the author by so doing.

First, the priestly ministry portrayed is not deliberately restricted to certain set hours of the week or certain spheres: it is, to a very great extent, coextensive, or identical, with the person's entire, concrete living – a matter of total involvement. Second, what is portrayed is not lacklustre or moribund: rather – and with God's grace – it can prove animated, laden with vitality, life-mediating.

The third element is this. A striking degree of harmony obtained between how the author himself actually lived as a priest and the portrayal of priesthood in the book. Michael Hollings talks frequently in the text about his falling short from God's will and from the ideals depicted. I would not dream of denying that Michael had his share of limitations, could in ways be difficult, could make mistakes, and so on. (Let me add that I myself, for instance, do not even aspire to proceed in every respect exactly as Michael set forth.) It remains the case that the present work is no abstract, theoretical discourse. The book is largely a reflection, an expression, of the author's own practical experience. It exhibits at once a particular person in operation and a fine vision of priesthood: and the degree to which the two mesh is very considerable.

September 2000
ANTHONY BAXTER

1994 PLUS

Throughout my life as a priest, one of the challenges – one could call them poverties – which fairly continually intervenes is that of being available. I always think of Jesus Christ in his public life being at the beck and call of those who were round about him, from a poor woman touching his cloak to a centurion of the pagan Roman occupying force. For the priest, it is possible to have office hours, to hide behind the door of the church house, to be unavailable for little chores like Mass cards or passport forms, for depressed persons on the phone, for a quick letter to a bereaved person.

This availability is for me the challenge of *Living Priesthood*. The original choice of the title was not mine, but a close friend's. I had been tossing round various ideas which included priesthood in one way or another. None was satisfactory, and he quite simply suggested *Living Priesthood*.

So what is the challenge of this title? I see it straightforwardly as the day–by–day, month–by–month living out of the commitment to the original call from Jesus Christ to come, take up the cross daily, and follow him. This was crystallised at ordination for me in 1950. It would be lovely to think that I had remained totally faithful, open, generous and committed from that day to this. But it would be untrue. It is not for me publicly to beat my breast. God, ordinary people and those priests to whom I have turned for advice and confession over the years know something (in God's case everything) in which I have failed in the commitment. St Ignatius, I think, said that the greatest battle in life is against self. And self dies half an hour after we do. Well, being still alive, self is still alive, so the battle to be faithful is still being fought out.

After over forty years of priesthood, I have received so much love, support, use and abuse, wear and tear of being about, that I feel like the experience of the Skin Horse in Margery William's delightful children's story *The Velveteen Rabbit*:

'It doesn't happen all at once, said the Skin Horse. You become. It takes a long time, that's why it doesn't often happen to people who break easily, or have sharp edges, or who have to be carefully kept. Generally, by the time you are REAL, most of your hair has been loved off, and your eyes drop out and you get loose in the joints and very shabby. But these things don't matter at all, because one you are real, you can't be ugly, except to people who don't understand.'

My worry about priesthood is the very large number of priests I have known over the years who have 'moved on and out' for various reasons. Many of these in my estimation were better equipped mentally, spiritually and pastorally than myself. As events unfold and numbers of ordained men come from the Church of England, the position of those who are now, all over the place fulfilling good christian commitment in the married state and longing to practise priesthood, must come up for consideration. But what worries me in 1994 is wider than this. It emerges in all walks of life that few now feel able to make a commitment 'till death do us part'. In married life, a large number seem to part after a mere five years, some carry on into middle life, and start a new 'marriage' in the forties or fifties. Sadly, this is seen all too frequently among priest, some not even lasting as long as five years.

Interestingly, in the world of work, it is becoming less usual for one person to remain in the same job for a lifetime. Mobility, part time, work–share and all kinds of variety tend to make permanent commitment more difficult. So I fancy that there are many ways in which the nature and scope of the priestly order will be examined and discussed very widely. I would not exclude married priest, part time priests (like the C of E stipendiary priesthood). I think the question of the ordination of women will not go away, but must be openly and freely examined biblically, spiritually and theologically. Meanwhile, I would like to see women, who have done so much teaching in the Church enabled to preach at Mass, I would like to see men and women, not ordained, permitted to baptise and lead funeral services and burials/cremations. If it were possible to allow certain categories like hospital chaplains, male or female un–ordained to anoint the sick, this would facilitate the ease of sick care and the shortage of ordained male priests. I will be dead and gone when this comes to be, but I firmly believe that there will be further development of doctrine and practice in the life of the Church towards and beyond the Millennium.

There have been a number of attempts in different parts of the world to care for the carers ... that is the priest. Somehow, these have not been very successful. It is easy to reach certain priest, but they are the least vulnerable. Those who are private in their lives, withdraw from 'interference', resist soul to soul contact, can live happily and be fulfilled. But there are those whom become isolated, can take to the bottle, can get into depression and so on. In a way, if priestly training could include rather more opening of students to some counselling and listening and even psychiatric skills, without become specialists, it might not only enrich the pastoral care by priest, but also help them in their own life to counselling and a 'soul–friend'.

I have been very privileged in the priestly living. God has been so lavish in his graces, though he has also been apparently very absent for long hard intervals. He has also brought into my life some very holy people, some of worldwide acclaim, some little people whose faith, love and service is deeply touching and challenging. It is in somehow achieving space for prayer, for listening, for reflection, that the riches become apparent. I can see that when I come empty–handed before the Lord, the just judge, I will be carried there on the prayers and love of many sons and daughters of the Lord, whose names I have forgotten or never knew, or who are vividly with me as I continue here and now to shuffle through my later days of ageing, in trying to continue living priesthood geriatrically. For a long time now, it has been my practice when the alarm goes off in the morning to turn it off and then to make a sign of the cross on myself, and say 'Thank you, God … for the past, for the night gone by, for the day to come … Thank you'.

MICHAEL HOLLINGS

FOREWORD

When deciding to write about priesthood, I thought that I had already produced a certain amount of material for different periodicals which I could now use for a book. It was a lazy thought, and when I looked through what I had collected, I realised that for a book there would have to be a re-writing of the basic material, with the addition of a considerable amount of new thinking. In this situation, I still want to acknowledge and thank those who made me write in the first place. These include the then editors of *The Catholic Gazette*, *The Upholland Magazine*, *The Month*, *Christian Celebration* (now *The New Sower*) and *Christian*. I would also like to thank the Provincial of the Society of the Sacred Heart of Jesus for agreeing that I should use a letter and paper which here form the substance of Appendix 1.

I live in a busy open house with people in and out, fellow clergy as my daily companions and a continually growing number of 'parishioners' of all ages, both sexes and a variety of ethnic and social backgrounds talking, listening, eating, sleeping or just being about. I would like to include them and everyone else who has been through parts of the experience described in this book—or has had to bear with me as I have struggled to write the experience down. I admit I would have given up long ago without the kindly but insistent pressure of Kevin Mayhew and Joan McCrimmon; without the interest, encouragement, criticism and prayer of Etta Gullick, and the patient typing-hours of Helen Chilton. Finally, I express my lasting gratitude to Anthony Baxter, whose conversations with me over the years, along with his insight and careful work on this particular manuscript, have tightened up my own thinking and clarified its written expression. Errors and stupidities are mine not those of my friends.

It is indeed good to have friends like these and to be able to say: "You are close enough to tell me what you really think—and to let me do the same; close enough to be patient and to continue in friendship through and beyond disagreements and differences of opinion—into a deeper level of intimacy, love and friendship. Thank you for being you, for loving and serving God, and for sharing your love."

Feast of St. Teresa   MICHAEL HOLLINGS
of Lisieux 1976.   St. Anselm's, Southall

INTRODUCTION

The Incarnation of Jesus Christ, God's supreme gift of himself to us, is a shattering revelation of Love given without restraint. For any one of us who is happy enough to have even a small realisation of that mystery, there is something of a death and resurrection. Nothing can ever be quite the same again. The wonder of it may wax and wane, we may even want to forget it, push it out of our lives—because the very fact of Incarnation makes our finite minds boggle and the challenge to respond seems too demanding. But if we are caught up with God, we have to become givers and receivers of love, without sin, but without restraint also.

The essence of this book is the need to share . . . to share with you what I have learnt, what I have fumbled at, what I still look forward to learning. At the time of writing, I have done more than twenty five years in the ordained ministry, the priesthood. For over fifty years, I have been a baptised person, and so a member of the more embracing body: "a chosen race, a royal priesthood, a consecrated nation" (1 Pet.2.9). Both are for me formidable lengths of time, though nothing to God, and not so much to any octogenarian-golden-jubilarian!

In these pages I am going to open up something of my past, my ideas and way of life, myself. In this I am both looking back in assessment and feeling forward towards the next twenty five years . . . though I hope personally for myself that long before that period has been lived out, the good Lord will have come and called me saying: "Come little worm-and-no-man, little sheep-brother, whom I love because you have been trying to be a shepherd—come, and I will give you rest." Of course, like His beloved disciple John, he may leave me to soldier on, and even to be as productive as he was in ripe old age. I do not know!

Anyhow, this is not meant to be an autobiography, nor a theological exploration of the essence of priesthood. It is not a philosophical treatise. It isn't quite anything except part of my response to the Incarnation of Jesus Christ. If I have any real outlook theologically it is an incarnational one, which at the same time as being earthy, basic and of this world is shot through with the mystery of the transcendent God, a mystery which is touched with the finger-tip in prayer: realized in deep contemplation.

There is a lot of "me" in the book. I cannot apologise, because what is good and what is bad in it comes from living experience, from intuition bound into, and stemming from, praying-reading-listening-talking-loving-feeling living. If you happen to live in this way, you will know it is a muddle. But at the same time, through the midst of muddle there runs a joy, a zest for living and serving, and a sometimes almost intangible thread. The thread is Jesus Christ, who also lived on earth, and the zest springs from contact with him, understanding of his role among us, reaction to his reactions as he walked and talked, prayed and worked miracles, preached and suffered in human living. I might put it that to me the importance of Jesus Christ is that he is God made man certainly, but also a man who is God; in looking at him, I can see and "feel" God's action and reaction among his people in the world. Nor is that mere observation, because I also am in the world, and am called to open myself to knowledge and love of him, not for selfish satisfaction, but for sharing all he gives and all I know, little as that knowledge may be.

The time of writing is not the most peaceful in the history of the Church. Vatican II has achieved a shaking up process, has opened windows, let in air and light . . . and also draughts and in the famous phrase of another context "the wind of change". The Council was never meant to be comfortable, any more than the life of Christ was comfortable . . . or the following he demands will be comfortable. So looking round there is a lot of uncertainty, disillusion, frustration and general loss of direction among priests and many others in the Church. True some are so completely set in their ways that nothing seems to move them from the straight path . . . not even the suggestion of Vatican II that the path is rather different from the one they are following. This deep-set traditionalism has its beauty and its part to play in the truth of the Gospel, just as the message of Christ sprang from the Old Testament. But it is not enough in itself, and part of the malaise which affects the development of God's work in this country is the over-tight clinging to the past, coupled with a fear of loss in venturing forward as urged by the Church in Council.

It is not just older priests or older people who are affected by conservatism in this sense. Some younger people including college, university and seminary students I have known in the past and others I know now, react against change and fortify themselves in a "tradition" which is not always living and tends to the romantic or nostalgic.

Somehow as we go forward in the world which God has created as part of an evolving universe, our various strands of thinking and feeling need to grow together. There will necessarily be tensions; the very evolution and growth comes from the interplay of these different forces. The peace that Christ gives is not a static silence and stillness but a music which blends all the different notes and the silences to form a single symphony . . . though in our limited appreciation at any one time it may seem that there are many symphonies and many discordant sounds. Only God sees all, hears all, knows all . . . and understands *how* it is "good".

I write from within this time and this tension, offering a view of life which combines in apparent paradox a rocklike faith, with a certain agnosticism and even times of sheer disbelief. It could be said that such a combination is impossible, but it is very real in the passing moods of life. Acknowledging at one time that I cannot "understand" God, his mystery is too great for me, at another my reason still revolts at accepting the "impossibility" of God, when I am faced with horror, violence, cruelty, or even the mere indifference of mankind. At one time, my whole being seems absorbed with inexplicable joy, trust and love in or out of prayer; at another time, emptiness, weariness and the whole irrelevance of belief sap my strength. Now I have a vision of the wonder of the Eucharist and the Word of God; then I have to face the apparently impossible demands of the Church in interpreting the Word. Sometimes I long for the "unshakeable" faith of others, sometimes I reject the rightness of faith expressed in that way.

I am brought back to the Incarnation, to the difficulties Christ had both in living our human life himself, with its frustrations and its failures, and in teaching others to believe and live. We today must face the same issues but at a different point of history. We now have centuries of Christian living behind us, with its own successes and failures. And we have a rapidly changing society, with the growth of technology, materialism and inequality more evident than ever before. We perhaps wrongly look back to the calm solid believing of the 19th century. We did not live through their problems, and so we over-emphasise their peace of mind. There is perhaps a mistaken sense of a church-going, believing nation, at least on the English scene.

That is past. Our own present will soon be past. We are to have vision, to read the signs of the times, work for the future. Future springs from past and present. Neither should be ignored or totally discarded, if present thinking is to be seen to have roots in true (or at least "imagined") reality, and not be mere *a priori* theorising.

I must remind myself I was not always as I am now, nor was I always where I am now, physically, mentally or spiritually. Indeed it is interesting and salutary to listen to the opinions of others as they give their run-down: "How old you look now", "How fat you've got", "You used to be way-out, now you're very trad", "Won't you ever learn prudence?" . . . and so on. Each of us is in this living predicament, some by temperament going ahead, others holding back. At times we are depressed, moody; at other times we soar poetically, with inspiration and vision, even mystically inclined. Sometimes we are just flat, slogging along.

When we are up, almost anything is possible—belief in God, the idea of priesthood, the hope of converting the world. When we are down, our former idealism seems not only impossible but mad, our hope crumbles in the face of disbelief: with gloom we look at falling numbers, loss of faith, broken marriages, laicisation of priests and a malaise of indifference.

I write because I am part of the problem trying to be part of the solution. This I believe to be the lesson of Incarnation, working from inside not outside. With Christ this meant working as a man among people—without sin; for me it means working as a man among people, very much subject still to sinning, but knowing it is worth going on, because I know God's forgiveness and love.

When I was a student for the priesthood, I used to visit a very remarkable elderly priest. Very prayerful, very austere, he had tried to refound the male order of Bridgettines and failed, so was living out his days as a much loved chaplain to the Little Company of Mary. As I listened to him, over and over again he spoke of: "The daily miracle of a holy life." If we have our eyes fixed on Jesus Christ, our will should be to follow him in doing the will of his Father. The outcome of following may be personal success or personal failure. In a world built on success, hungry for fulfilment, we are pledged to show forth Jesus Christ who in a worldly sense was a failure. Strange really, is it not, that the Church has seen fit to "reward" those who serve the Lord in the ordained ministry with titles and ecclesiastical garments, with privileges and positions of power? The inevitable climbing and politicking, jockeying for position and intrigue must seem incongruous and even scandalous to those on the outside, and has an uncomfortable way of distracting from the main purpose of serving God on the inside. Should it matter to us which way things go? The straight answer is that it should not, but we are human. We can turn inward, fester in discontent, swing between self-depreciation or self-aggrandisement. If we can see and live beyond concern for success or failure, yet be fully alive to development, we will go on doing what we can, centred on God—and the outcome will be the "daily miracle of a holy life". The miracle will be in the way that Christ draws us to himself, and others through us.

The first chapter of this book sets out my own beginnings and development in order to give background to what comes afterwards. The next two chapters (Chapters 2 and 3) deal with the life of the individual who is called to be a priest, especially in his personal relationship with God and other men and women. This I attempt in the light of my own experience of various kinds of living leading up to ordination and the subsequent years of pastoral work as a priest in England. This is followed (Chapters 4, 5, 6 and 7) by a broad look at priesthood as it can be approached today. The bias of the writing is incarnational, so the assessment of priesthood is related to total life, covering wide ranges of contact, activity and apostolate, rather than attempting a definition. The practical experience of a "kind of living" comes next (Chapters 8, 9, 10, 11 and 12). This is illustrated to some extent from the developments which have been happening in the parish of St. Anselm, Southall, Middlesex—since that is the area which at present I know best. This book is no blue print, but a sharing of experience, a reflection on the existing situation. It is not a success story, but an ordinary reality of living which contains elements of failure as well as success, victory and defeat, growth and decay.

The title *Living Priesthood* gives the sense that being a priest is as much a total life as being a Christian. But can any way of life be more total than being a Christian? This is an area of function and charism which is open for discussion. Only God knows the full answer. Subjectively each of us is asked to live out our particular "calling" to the full—totally—as Christians married or single, labourer or technician, professor or housewife—sometimes combining more than one calling. And one such calling is— priesthood. But it should not be defined and spelled out in neat phrases. It *can* be: I maintain it should not be! In a sense it can only be lived out as a witness. This means that the priest must be alive, vibrant, filled with the Spirit, ready to be used by the Spirit at any time, anywhere. As local leader and stimulator he is in a particular way "the light". This light is in a general way placed by Christ on a lampstand. So—the ideal is set high! It may seem impossible—perhaps even it *should* seem impossible, because it is the standard of Christ himself. But with Christ all things are possible. Therefore we should not hesitate to commit ourselves utterly to him, without counting the cost involved. He will do the rest, one way or another, if we accept him in his power. That is the totality of our commitment—the "impossible" *YES* of Mary to the "impossible" call that she should bring forth the Word.

It is natural for us to be unnerved by the challenge, to want to give up, to back out. But it is not right for us to hear the word of Jesus and be: "filled with sadness" (Luke 18.23). The beginning, living out and ending in the service of Christ is a full-time struggle, in which the going is hard and exciting, demanding and fulfilling, impossible and achieved in experience. It is a life of joy.

Because of the intricacy and paradoxical nature of what is being exposed, there is much interweaving of thought, understanding, hinting and expectation in this book. Partly this is muddled me, partly it is the nature of what I am talking about. I hope the apparently contradictory expressions of what I say will not confuse. Taken slowly with patience and openness, may they contribute to the understanding of living priesthood.

It is a tall order, but I would ask you to take what you read here in conjunction with the various things which I have written elsewhere in periodicals or in books. Since what we are involved in is living, being incarnate in this present world, we "preach" to others by the way we speak, write and behave day-by-day. We must take the revelation of Jesus Christ in the Scriptures over all, rather than editing our selected passages as his entire message. What is written in this present book may affect you favourably or adversely—but it should do so in conjunction with an objective assessment of me, priest, living, working, failing and succeeding in the task which God has set us all—"You must therefore be perfect just as your heavenly Father is perfect". (Matt.5.48).

Would that I were!

1

SOME PERSONAL BACKGROUND

This book is not meant to be an autobiography, but to reflect upon priesthood and priestly life. However, it has been my experience especially among students and younger people that they respond to the personal. By that I mean that I can try to give a talk on faith to a group of people who for reasons best known to themselves have come to listen to me. If I make the talk a little philosophical, a little theological and on the whole abstract, when question time comes, they will often say quite simply and pointedly: That's all very well. But *why* do *you* believe? Then I am put on a personal spot and have to become "real" by exposing myself with all my doubts and fears, as well as the strange strand running through me and my life which fastens me to the reality of God.

Therefore this chapter will be given over to a sketch of the background from which I came, the formation which family, historical events, education and the hand of God fashioned in me, and some personal reflection. It cannot in my opinion be left out because each of us lives in this world as a fact, as real. To write in abstract is to deny the lesson of the Incarnation. God became man so that man might learn how God lives in human living. I am a man. I live in God's world. I am real, and therefore I must be known as real if I am going to try to preach the good news of Jesus Christ. And real means human, sinful, unpolished, biassed, psychologically conditioned . . . you name it, I have it. Anyone can analyse me if I give them the background. That is terrifying, humbling and perhaps humiliating, but I take it as being part of what it is to be a follower of God-made-man, who emptied himself. There will be those who read this and react by saying it is an essay in pride. It may be, and if it is, it may become even more of a humiliation. Really, that does not matter, if it can help a few, or warn a few, or encourage a few. I cannot really make a judgment; I can only say that I have been told that some of the things which follow have already proved of help to individuals.

My origin was a mixed marriage. My father's side had built Church of England churches in Yorkshire and refused to have a Roman Catholic in the house. My mother's side in a peculiar way made me descend directly from a Cardinal of the Holy Roman church. Cardinal Weld as a layman was married, his wife died, and he was left with one daughter. He became a priest and subsequently a Cardinal. She married and the family generations continued through her. For me there was here an ecumenical background, though I never appreciated it in my early days.

Brought up as a Catholic, my early schooling was not in a Catholic school. I went to the local catechism classes in the parish on Saturdays. But I was later sent to a Catholic boarding school which I feared and hated, though I can see in hindsight it did me good . . . only I must say I often don't like things which "do me good"! In fact, the strict Jesuit discipline gave me something, much as I disliked it. I made friendships, some of which have lasted to this day, not only among the boys but among the Jesuits and lay staff. Interestingly one of the finest men and teachers was not a Catholic; from him I gained a sense of fairness, honesty, straightforward integrity . . . in a word goodness. But probably the chief influence was the Jesuit who was in charge of studies. In his wisdom, he took four of us who were somehow "oddbods" and gave us "a year off" at fifteen between exams, when we were left free to read widely, study with some intensity on limited subjects in a group and work on a tutorial basis. From him, I think, I learnt to read in my spare time.

When I was seventeen World War II broke out. I persuaded my mother it would be a waste of money for me to go back to school for a further year. My father had died some years before. She very nicely agreed I could try to get in to Oxford University. We were living outside Oxford at the time, and I remember soon after the declaration of war taking a bus into Oxford, asking at an information centre and eventually finding St. Catherine's Society, where they agreed to take me. My experience of life over the next two years varied from cooking and cleaning and gardening for my mother who was sick to wining and dining in college; from training by day in the army training corps to attending pacifist meetings in the evening; from going to Mass and working with the Catholic chaplaincy groups to endless socialist and marxist meetings in college rooms and odd pubs.

Almost in default of anything else coming up, I was a member of the Home Guard, and also gained experience of fear in the Commercial Road area of London, helping in warden work in the shelters during heavy raids on London. Called up, I was sent to Sandhurst. In-for-a-penny-in-for-a-pound, I was commissioned in the Coldstream Guards, and after strutting round on King's Guard at Buckingham Palace got the worst ever report from an assault course in Scotland, where the Commanding Officer said I should not have been commissioned as I lacked guts and had no powers of leadership.

Overseas service was thrilling, terrifying, boring and enormously maturing. God went out of my life. People came in. They were real and so was life. I had to face myself and know that I was a coward in front of danger, that I hated hardship, that I was selfish, but I immensely enjoyed friends and parties and being alive. I wanted so much to stave off facing a battle-weary self and battle-weary companions, the horror and indignity of men broken by shellshock and sheer terror. Oddly God did not come in here—just some kind of basic human instinct and concern. But one way and another God found me out again largely in the disillusion of the after-war period. It was then I thought of priesthood. Realising I had been reclaimed by God or more correctly—I had come home to his welcome and love, I wanted to help other people. The chaplain I consulted about going to try to be a priest asked me why I wanted to do so. I said to help people. He asked if I did not see Mass as being the centre of what a priest is. I simply said

I did not, I wanted to help people

Just as I somehow got into Oxford and Sandhurst by the back door, so with seminary training. Cardinal Griffin, when he interviewed me, thought I was thirty four, when in reality I was twenty four. He had already made arrangements to send me to the Beda College in Rome for late vocations. His face fell when I declared my true age, but to the Beda I went, paid for as further education by a grateful government!

It is difficult to know how much to put in about training in Rome from 1946 to 1950. It was hard, physically, mentally, socially and spiritually. After being a Company Commander in a Guards Regiment with respect, power, authority and responsibility I found it very hard to be nobody, with nothing. In a way, I did not know what I was doing; the philosophy books in Latin made me no clearer and nor did the lectures. The spiritual director was dry as dust, though learned and holy. The college life was interesting, but we were both cold and hungry in the first post-war year. Rather lost, feeling unguided and alone, I took to stringent living. My motive for joining had been to help others. Apart from those among whom I lived, there was no one to help.

Two things from the past kept me going. I had learnt fear in the East End of London as bombs fell and again especially in Italy. Psychologically I discovered that in fear, when all I wanted to do was run away, it helped to do everything exaggeratedly slowly; not only did this instill calm in myself, it encouraged reassurance in others. Secondly, mostly in Africa and Italy, I learnt that if you have cowardly instincts as I do, the only hope is to face the fear, the unknown, the threat. My spiritual help in this time was the passage in Luke about Jesus in Gethsemane. I was not learned in scriptural analysis; the translation I knew told me of Jesus: "being in agony, he prayed the longer". (Luke 22.44.). The Jerusalem Bible tells me "In his anguish he prayed more earnestly". At the time, that translation would not have been so effective as the one I had! I felt Jesus had gone out into the desert in his earlier days to face the evil one and himself in aloneness; later in the garden he had prayed the longer: this was language I understood.

My reaction very much on my own was to begin a life which put most of the weight on prayer and penance. To some extent I had been taught what discipline meant in the army. They had said no one gets anywhere without hard slog and self-discipline. I had learnt then the hard way. Now I had found it true. It now tied up with Christ and his life. So, I set myself a routine of observing the *magnum silentium*, the silence following night prayers, when we were supposed to go to our rooms and not to talk to each other. There was a lot of temptation to go to coffee parties; not going, I came to feel isolated. I made a bedtime for myself, introduced sleeping on the floor and getting up to pray in the middle of the night. I rose early before the bell to get additional time for prayer. I also took to slipping away in the afternoon when many had a siesta or went walking. I located two churches which had exposition, one of which, S.Claudio in Piaza S. Silvestro near the English church, kept open all during the afternoon. There I often literally sweated it out, in dull, dumb, boring knee-aching slog. I slept there often; I seldom had much sense of prayer. Yet I went back there again and again, day by day, like a drowning man grabbing at a lifeline.

I have often said since then that it was there and in the chapel of the Beda that I learnt anything I did learn. That is not to be unfair to the professors who tried to teach me. I know I did learn from them, from the student priests there, from my fellow students who were by and large older than me. I've not much humility; what I have, I learned basically from the men of stature who came in all simplicity for God's service late in life, often having served so long and well already, submitting to discipline and becoming as little children; I learned it from those who had belonged to other christian churches, had found their way from quite eminent positions, and now rubbed shoulders with me who was a mere babe in religion, yet took me as an equal and opened the door of friendship. I am sure it was here that I realised more than ever before the value of a friend older than myself who could be really close and really a friend, so that he could tell me off, teach me by example and lead me by his matured personality and wisdom, which was often so distilled by years, humility and suffering as to be as simple as the dove.

Though the course at the Beda was only a short four year one, I met so many people, I saw so many things, I sat through and tried to absorb so much philosophy, theology and spiritual discourse that something must have rubbed off. In the middle, because of trying to cope with what was meant by celibacy and how it fitted with sexuality and intimacy and friendship, I nearly packed up before I broke down. Later, during the diaconate oddly enough, I had more strain than at any other time and with the rector's permission fled to the solitude and peace of Assisi. Every now and then throughout the four years I leaned towards the monastery, silence, the life devoted totally to God in prayer. I even did my preordination retreat in the Trappist monastery of Tre Fontane outside Rome. At other times I wanted to run away altogether because of insecurity, doubts as to the church, the priesthood and God himself. Several times offers were made of lucrative jobs in the world, and there were two or three marriageable young women both in Rome and in England, whom I had known when I was more glamorously clad as a Guards Officer . . . though it is true that some women are more attracted by the challenge of the clerical celibate than the eligible bachelor! What a life! When the invitations to dinner came in, and were allowed by the Rector, accepted and enjoyed, the floor afterwards seemed rather harder and the night vigil very much alone. But there were ways and means of toughening oneself, some self-imposed and some just happening. And there were "types" of self-giving to be met in Rome and beyond, of whom Padre Pio was the shining and thrilling example.

Anyhow, one way and another I came to ordination in a ceremony at St. John Lateran at Easter 1950. It commenced at 6.30 a.m. and ended round 2.00 p.m. It was long, hard, glorious, triumphalist, splendid and something I would not have missed for the world. In a way, it was the climax to the long hours each day I had spent alone in prayer. I was not just alone there with God, but had now been brought to the position, function, office or anything anyone wants to call it, which left me committed—as I had first thought I was meant to be—to people. Tre Fontane offered something beautiful, deep, attractive but distant. I had lived the life and death of incarnation in World War II, and for me reality in all its joy and pain remained in the heart of the world.

There was little contact with or from the Diocese during four years in Rome. Perhaps it was for this reason that I thought I had been forgotten on my return to England. After several weeks I wrote and asked for work and the then Vicar-General sent me to St. Patrick's Soho Square in the centre of London's West End.

St. Patrick's presbytery was dilapidated, as were the Rector and the two housekeepers. On my arrival, I was sent up to the first floor, and found the ancient, almost blind, and delightful Parish Priest seated behind his desk. Without his getting up, or my sitting down, he greeted me with a five minute interview the burden of which was: "There's nothing to do here. I look after the school; the other priests look after the hospitals. Well, I expect you'll find something. Good afternoon!"

Indeed, there was plenty to do; gradually building up, through being about and getting to know people. Life inside the house was more difficult than out. My room had a leak in the roof, which kept me changing the position of the bed according to the way the wind blew. One night I woke to find a rat, which seemed to have come in from the roof, chewing my hair. I was on the third floor, the telephone on the ground, the nearest and only bathroom between the ground and first floor. Intercommunication within the house was by blowpipe. The hall wallpaper was black. My salary was 50 shillings a month. In my recollection we never had a fresh vegetable during the four years I spent there. Presently when very run down, I landed in the National Temperance Hospital with a carbuncle on my neck and a temperature of 104°.

I loved and hated Soho. It was the beginning of being at work with people as I had first hoped priesthood would be. During the Rome training, forced to my knees again and again, I came to understand that helping was wider and deeper than I could have imagined before. Soho had a bad reputation, with the police walking in pairs, but we were never troubled by anyone, except sometimes jokingly by prostitutes. It was in fact the kindest, dirtiest, most village-like and lovable area, full of challenges. God and the Devil seemed to walk the streets, with the assortment of people from different backgrounds, the barrow boys and wide boys, prostitutes, beggars who led us a dance, comi-waiters from Italy, actors often "resting", film producers from Wardour Street, the restauranteurs. Soho was a kaleido-scope of life—there were murders and knifings, a kind of Mafia life, and odd characters who suddenly became violent; I remember once being hit hard in the face by a slightly mad young man as I sat talking to him and his wife in their flat. But openness and incredibly deep and simple holiness lived in tenements and up dingy stairways; there doors opened in welcome; in the squalor of living, patience faith and joy in saying the rosary and receiving Holy Communion lit up faces in decaying rooms, stinking of urine from the bucket under the bed. Sometimes a rat would run from the bed as an old and lonely bedridden "leftover" greeted the Lord with ragged-toothed grin and muttered prayers.

In the house and church there was a kind of tension which could have gone in any direction. The lunch-hour and evening Benediction for the office and other workers was a nightmare of unaccompanied singing for me, and a near-miracle of meeting souls there and through the confessional afterwards who were living lives of un-spectacular heroism. It made me ashamed as I tried to keep up the prayer routine of early mornings and was warned off by my fellow clergy for being over pious and not sleeping enough. The "givenness" of those lunch-hour worshippers contrasted with the life behind the presbytery door. There during meals we were allowed no phone calls, nor was the door bell answered: for the priests must not be disturbed. It began to breed in me a determination somehow, at whatever cost, to open any place where I had some authority, and to try to live celibacy unselfishly. I suppose in looking back I would sum it all up by saying I have never been happier, lonelier, more tired or more enriched.

At this time, I came across some things which need airing. I had somehow quickly become a little known, probably because of my strange history of Oxford, Guards and Beda. There was disapproval from the parish priest that I was invited out to meals; was asked to give talks in convents, did film reviews for the then Catholic magazine on films called Focus. There were remarks. I was told bluntly that a young priest should be seen and not heard. It was hurtful and I resented it, and argued with God about it on many early morning sessions in St. Patrick's church. We lived in theatreland, and were forbidden to go to the theatre! But wonder of wonders, the law did not cover theatre clubs or rehearsals. I found a different apostolate among actors and actresses and playrights, and an invaluable link with another section of God's people. But largely this was done by going through the loopholes of the law, and it caused me to sit and question myself and the Church before I went off to see in a theatre-club (to which I was allowed to go) the kind of play which was not allowed in the ordinary theatres (to which I was forbidden to go)! I value from those days, as close and deep friends, a wide range of people who have entertained audiences in many countries, while at the same time retaining their faith and bringing up families and leading an extraordinarily good christian life. Thank God they saw the funny side, and the limitless love of God. Sadly, we who represented God's church did not always help them to maintain and develop the life they longed to live in service of God and his people.

I think it may be useful if I mention two kinds of relationships which were wished on me from outside the parish. I had always been fascinated by the work of ordinary lay people in the church, because basically I had come and gone and come again to the church as a layman. The first relationship was with the Young Christian Workers, with strong and active, young and committed membership. They led me into real discussions and actions which were enormously constructive in my life, introducing me to unions and shop floors, hard living, confined family life, great aspirations and expectations . . . and all among young men and women who had had none of the "advantages" I had had, but were solidly, happily, strongly faithful both to God and to the people. I wish I could feel I gave them anything comparable to what they gave me.

The other relationship, also wished on me, was much shorter, closer and more intimate. I have written a little of it before. It came through the St. Vincent de Paul Society, who had befriended a family in distress. Basically Irish with a father who was possibly ex-Caribbean, the eldest boy had got cancer at thirteen . . . carcinoma of the leg. He had his leg off at the thigh, got an artificial leg and played football and rode a bicycle with it. Then he developed secondaries. I was put in touch with him because his mother was dying of cancer in a London hospital; his uncle was looking after the other three children all under fourteen; and his father had disappeared. The boy, Ailbe, was in Westminster hospital, he was refusing to open up to anyone, he felt disowned, he was afraid. I was brought in initially to lend him a typewriter, because he said he wanted to type, and the friend of mine who was visiting him rang me in despair when no one would lend a typewriter. I visited him. For a couple of weeks he glowered at me, would not talk, except for yes and no. One day, a smile suddenly appeared; it was immediately wiped off, but I was "through". And there began an extraordinary experience. He grew. First he gave me all his pocket money for a Mass for his mother, after I had had to tell him she had died. Then he became more open when he was moved to a beautiful but awful home for cancer patients. Beautiful because everything was happy, friendly, open and well run; awful because he was the only boy (now fifteen) and the youngest other patient was in his fifties.

He had a period of respite, when he was able to walk about. My friends, especially those who had contact with the film and TV world, were wonderfully supportive in visiting him and taking him out. Gradually, by seeing him almost every day, and sometimes two or three times a day, I came to know him. His disease developed, through lungs, liver, stomach . . . with increasing pain, skin irritation and shortness of breath. But he came to pray and to understand suffering. He got to a point of refusing drugs as painkillers, so that he could offer his suffering. He wrote of himself once as "a very lucky boy", and each person who met him became both struck by him and attached to him. But I want to mention this relationship specially because I personally had never experienced anything like this before. In a way, though his uncle was about, he came to rely on me, I was a curate in a busy London parish, where the Parish Priest was not too keen that I should be all the time in Westminster Hospital or later in Hampstead. So I began to learn a pattern of "bilocation". I mean that I became ingenious about how I could be here, and there, and back again in the period of time when it was sensible only to be here! There are ways of cutting corners, getting the odd lift, looking in on a happening and soon leaving, turning up from nowhere to say hello, and then like the Cheshire Cat in Alice disappearing, leaving only the smile behind! Towards the end of Ailbe's life, the nursing home even asked me if I could spend the night there, as they had no one to keep on night duty, and they felt he needed someone about. So for a month I went up about ten in the evening and sat in a chair beside his bed, until I became so exhausted they suggested I pulled up a bed alongside his, and slept there so that he could stretch out his hand and wake me if he was in pain or needed anything. It was an extraordinary period when night and day intermingled and I played Jekyll and Hyde first with the parish and then when I was moved with Westminster Cathedral, doing day duty with them and unknown to them a night duty at the nursing home I don't know how difficult I was as a result. I went to sleep in odd places at odd times, but I survived. I remember one morning saying Mass for the Sisters of Charity and sitting down afterwards to say a few prayers, and finding myself gently shaken awake a considerable time later by the sister who was supposed to have given me breakfast and who found when she came to clear away that it was untasted and I was asleep by the chapel!

Anyhow, between Ailbe, God and me there was an understanding. And it grew. I have written before of the night near his death when I was lying and dozing in a bed next to his, and he was saying now and then "Jesus! Jesus!" And how he then turned and put out his hand and shook me and said: "I'm not swearing. I'm praying". Later, he was near death, and I had to go to say Mass, so I told him I was off to do this. He said: "Will you ask God if he will take away just a little of the pain?" And later still, when he had been unconscious and regained consciousness, he saw me distressed and with tears in my eyes: "Don't cry," he said, "there is nothing to cry about". Then I spoke of his father and his sisters and brother and asked him to pray for them . . . and also to pray for all those for and with whom I would be working for the rest of my life . . . "Oh yes," he said, "I'll do all that!" At one point, talking to him about dying, I talked of his mother being in heaven and waiting for him, and his reply was: "I don't think I'd mind dying if you were dying too". Telling him I could not lay that on, we went further into a depth of understanding which was amazing for a fifteen-year-old. So I was not surprised when at his death one of the sisters asked to be instructed in the Catholic faith and two older men turned from blaspheming-atheism to a humble acceptance of Christ.

This relationship made a profound difference to my life. I found a new possibility of living; though I do not think today, any more than I did then, that it could last long, it was evident that I could live for a period stretched beyond the limit of endurance. I had known this a little in the army, now I met and realised it in priesthood. The relationship not only pulled out all kinds of stops which had only been a little used in recent years, it also taught me the depth and beauty of belief to which a lad of fifteen can grow, given time, sympathy, understanding, patience and love. He grew quite enormously; I could not begin to doubt that he went straight to the Lord; he taught me about trust, human and divine; he taught me about the resurrection, because when he died it seemed inevitable the Lord would say: "This day you will be with me in paradise".

It was in the middle of this experience, as Ailbe was reaching the crisis between life and death, that I received a letter quite simply saying that I would report to become a chaplain at Westminster Cathedral two weeks later. No one asked me, and I loathed the thought of going there. The administrator told me the purpose of my coming was to sing the daily office in choir and take part in the cathedral ceremonies. Well, I couldn't (and can't) sing, and ceremonies appal me! Once I got there, I found that after Solemn Vespers or a Capitular or Pontifical High Mass, I was soaked in sweat and had to go and change everything I was wearing. The pontificals were, I am sure, wonderful ecclesiastical and liturgical ceremonies. To me and some other chaplains at that time they seemed largely to consist of dressing and undressing the Cardinal, to music. Apart from sometimes being roped in to carry the cross in front of the Cardinal when his regular cross bearer was away, I had little to do during the lengthy ceremonials, and began to discover it was possible to pray deeply in the midst of it all, albeit with the hazard of suddenly finding I was sitting with a biretta on when everyone else was standing bareheaded, or else was standing bareheaded when everyone else had sat down. Over a period of four years, it brought me near to breakdown, but the love and humanity of the administrator got me away before the crack came. Hours in the confessional were sweatbox hours, but enormously rewarding. I think sometimes in the modern church priests are almost arrogant in saying what people should put into and get out of confession. If you have sat, as I have sat, regularly each week for three or four hours a day in the confessional, with the tally going up to eight, ten and even twelve hours at Christmas and Easter, you will known what I mean when I say that the love of God extends far more widely, far less selectively and far less tidily than the legalists would say. I cannot go into details for obvious reasons, but I know from recent contact after twenty years that my semi-deaf, intensely irritated, but nonetheless available ear was the immediate reason for individuals to cease abandoning God and the church, to struggle on in darkness and to come through into 1976 as seasick but at least surviving sailors in the barque of Peter.

So I lived at the Cathedral, I "sang" in choir, I stood casually at the back of that vast edifice after ceremonies, I was dogged by beggars, I instructed endless people in "the faith". When I was half asleep, I went in and out of choir in the cathedral often feeling like a zombie . . . and I was taught how stupid I was, how insignificant I was, how the power of God went on working despite me and the cathedral and the church.

I felt then and continued to feel the appalling distance which can grow between the priest and the people. Because of this, I learnt to say "no" as well as "yes". Authority is always authority. I learnt that for me the only way in which I could help towards a development was to go ahead, gently keeping along with authority but not necessarily agreeing all the time. The main difficulty in this was always that there seemed to have been bred into the church, over a long period, an inability to accept criticism of the church herself or of authority without labelling the critic disloyal. For me it was a strange contrast to my relationship with senior officers and military policies in the army days. I found it all very stifling and personally embarrassing in that I have never had the ability to dissimulate for long, but have always felt the need in the end to bring out things which seem wrong or unbalanced or in need of reform.

The inner struggle was whether or not I was just being proud in thinking that some ideas which to me seemed better than those being put forward and practised were in fact better. I had to review this in prayer and confession, as I still do, because those in authority have told me I am both proud and wrong-thinking—and should stop. At the same time I have been urged by others to continue. Life has been like a tightrope walk, a balancing between that obedience which authority accepted and an obedience which seems almost like disobedience, a thinking out of attitudes and life style and the approach to people and their problems, and an abandonment to God. It has never been very popular to insist, as I have felt again and again compelled to insist, that it is Christ I am following and that the immediate expression of church at a given place and time may be a stumbling block to that following. At various times, I have been starry-eyed in regard to the church, only to be brought into contact in myself and others with cracks and artificialities, with rottenness and selfishness. It is of the very pattern of incarnation with wheat and tares growing up together, with the good and bad side by side . . . where sin abounded, says Paul, grace did more abound. It seems to be only by the day-in and day-out continuing that the tapestry of God's world gradually is brought nearer to completion. Christ beckons from the cross as well as from the glory of the resurrection; the path of life is through suffering and through death. I have certainly at times been too ready to dismiss or write-off something I could not see at the time, or somebody whose goodness was not immediately evident. Perhaps it is just increasing age which gives a mellower tone. In the years at Westminster Cathedral in a very different way from those in Soho some of the seamy side of life came through and also some of the amazingly deep goodness among individuals and groups.

In the Cathedral the choir duties were a mixture of slog and deep religious experience. Sometimes I wondered very much how this could be so. Living in it, there were high excitements of liturgy done beautifully according to the existing Tridentine rite. The music was at a point of excellence during those years. The cathedral hummed with activity. There were more or less non-stop confessional hours, the choir offices and all the ordinary administration of sacraments. There were special series of talks and preachers and services which crowded the weeks. It was a period of learning in which the memory was more of things learnt the hard way than of golden years of joy. I was

personally delighted when there was subsequent simplifi-
cation and change of rite after Vatican II. But in a strange
way, because the ceremonies had to be prayed and worked
through, the need for ceremony, for the great function and
for the occasional magnificence found a place in my mind. I
would not go along with the idea of just having groupings of
never more than a few, because the texture and value of
coming together in large numbers for certain times and
occasions seems to me clear. Variety there was at
Westminster Cathedral in those days; the pomp and
vastness and colour of the enthronement of a new
Archbishop or the burial of the old one was and still is
appropriate. But the small is also beautiful, and a Requiem
Mass in a side chapel for a cathedral parishioner was in its
way more moving and closer to the heart than much of the
high altar worship.

It was because of my stupidity on the sanctuary and my
inability to sing that I was put out of the way to be
commentator at the first big telecast by ITV. With this
there started a new and fascinating development. I never
was or will be a good performer on TV, but one way and
another I have been involved with this medium since the
later 1950's. Perhaps the strangest thing was that when an
adviser was needed I was given the job, but without a base
and without any offer of money from the church for my
support. Indeed, officially I was told I had better get the
companies to pay me, and it took me a year even to get a
small pittance from the two with which I was involved.
During this time nothing was forthcoming from the
diocese, except the kindness of the London University
chaplain who invited me to stay at the chaplaincy and share
his life and food, in return for helping out a bit with the
students. So I lived on his and their charity for a year, while
trying to establish a position in the TV world, and in a way
sadly, I found eventually that it was easier to get support
from TV than from the Diocese!

The people working in the two companies were delightful and excellently professional. Though religious TV did
not always appear to be of a very high standard, this was not

due to any lack of competence on their part. I am full of admiration at the care and skill and creative talent, which often seems almost denied by much of what appears. One reason for the bad quality of religion on TV was lack of money, and another the sense of restriction in the early days about what might or might not be shown. From the angle both of myself and the church, I think the most important aspect undoubtedly was the ecumenical teamwork which prevailed there before the great advances which have since developed in the ecumenical field. Certainly working with lay men and women of any religion or none among the producers, technicians, cameramen and staff was a great dimension for me, growing into lasting friendships at all levels. The long and often heated discussions we advisers had alone or with the TV personnel were enlivening, broadening and satisfying. I was very fortunate indeed to move into this world. It had its difficult and funny and fighting moments, but over all the sense was one of new developments, touching and reaching out to the unknown, certainly often to the non-churchgoer. The stringent concern of the producers and directors was most helpful in bringing the parson down to earth, because all too easily we can hold forth uncriticised from a pulpit. It is not so easy to get away with sloppy speaking and sloppy thought in front of a TV camera, with the team watching and listening and criticising freely, while the people in charge are thinking of the audience and the viewing reactions, to say nothing of audience figures! I would heartily suggest that each and every person, man or woman who is going to preach the word of God should go through the rigours of some TV training. It could liven up that part of our evangelism greatly.

At any rate, having just got myself settled to TV and to life in London University, I was told by Cardinal Godfrey to go as Chaplain to Catholics at Oxford University. I had only been there in wartime, and had never seen myself as in any way an academic. I was horrified at the prospect. But the Cardinal simply summoned me one day, told me his plan, and said he would pray about it, and that he knew I would do whatever he decided for me. I went off to Lourdes on my annual stint, and there had the news that I was indeed to move to Oxford. So I went.

Chaplaincy life was interesting. It led me from London into eleven years of very varied work. In London I had no financial backing, but at least I did not have the Chaplain's headache of providing funds from nowhere to run the chaplaincy. In Oxford, there were both problems—no money and the need to find funds. There were no knives, forks, plates or cups to take over, or indeed anything except some furniture and a building of antiquity and beauty. It is no part of my intention to spend a lot of time moaning about finances. It is enough to say that my experience of university work made it clear to me that on the whole the hierarchy were not much in favour of universities or those who went there; chaplains were perhaps necessary evils, but did not have to be fully supported; furthermore, the emerging students were liable to be awkward, rebellious and probably lapsed! The Oxford chaplaincy was a bit better off than some, but to keep it going necessitated the chaplain finding a thousand or two a year from his own pocket or by his wits. I had nothing in my pocket, so relied on wits. It was a nagging grievance but one I accepted— and the situation even proved useful, because I had to get out and about, give retreats, continue TV work, write and so on. The outcome was that I learned a good deal about England, I gained great experience in preaching and talking. One point stood out. It can be of benefit to a priest not to stick slavishly to his parish, but to have the scope to move out, look back and observe, gain information and know-how from others, and generally grow in breadth.

One of the things which I have always counted as a great blessing has been the ability to fit in reading. In the army I was frequently frowned upon, because I used to go about with a book under my arm, even in uniform, which was not the done thing. But an enormous number of man-hours in life are spent waiting. I developed a policy of filling such waiting with reading. And it has stood me in good stead ever since. Some say they must have time and peace to read in. This is not essential. Time can be picked up out of the day. It is vitally necessary to learn the habit of reading in snatches, without having to go back to the beginning again after a break. It has been another part of my policy not to have a car of my own or to drive but often to use public transport. (I am not condemning cars or driving. Both are essential today especially in the country). This has meant a wide field lying open every time there is a journey from A to B. The habit of devouring of books in buses, trains etc., is a first class investment. It also helps to calm nervous agitation when the tendency is to champ up and down the platform, simply wasting more time till the train comes!

The continuation of reading over the course of life is, I have always urged, essential. Titles for me would be wide-ranging. Bloods, science fiction and ordinary novels are fine for certain times, especially for going to bed, or sometimes in trains or on aircraft. More serious stuff has to be done also by choosing a definite time allotment . . . possibly against the pressure of fellow priests to stop wasting time reading and get out round the streets. There is such a mass of material from the daily paper through to theology; there is all the children's book world and the magazine aspect. For years, I read the Economist every week, until it got too expensive for me to afford. Then I was given it.

Oxford furthered the challenge of reading, because there were so many areas about which I knew so little. As time went on, with discussion groups and with talks to be given, it was important to know what the undergraduates and graduates were reading, as well as what they were seeing at the theatre or in the cinema. I grew in the habit of never going to sleep however late it might be without reading a few pages. The whole process has paid off remarkably, but most especially the discipline of reading in snatches.

I was very fortunate in that at thirty seven I had a fairly free hand. Officially I was appointed by the hierarchy; actually I was a priest of Westminster living in Birmingham diocese. The result was that no one from anywhere paid much attention to us, unless we really boobed over something. Given a free hand, while my contemporaries were still being assistant priests in many cases, I partly continued the life style of previous chaplains and partly evolved my own as we all went along together. The only preconceived ideas I had were about availability and keeping the house open. What pattern there was developed of itself, and it is hard to say whether it was I or the university situation which fostered the "system".

A friend of mine who was a great student of Newman, and of the Oratory used often to say that he thought life at the Old Palace (the chaplaincy) really came very close to the ideal set by St. Philip Neri for his oratories. It was a wide open community; the chaplains lived together, with a secular institute for women (the Society of St. Teresa from Spain) looking after the house and helping with the people who visited; normally there were also some student priests, from almost anywhere, together with the odd under-graduate or two who could not find lodgings, or had had a breakdown, or was lonely, disturbed or unable to settle down to his or her essay writing. Again, there were often one or two non-university misfits who had fallen on evil days, through gambling, drinking, drugs and even sheer bad management.

The keynote and centre was prayer, round the liturgy and extending into colleges. But hospitality ran this a close second. I am a great believer in the "meal" for gathering different people. Most unexpected types find each other quite nice when they have wined and dined together! So the open house system grew, and seemed so obvious once we were living it, because all types and kinds came along. Old learnt from young, rich from poor, dull from the learned. It did not matter whether they were rich or poor, black, brown or white, intelligent or stupid. We shared, and sharing taught the lesson of availability. A question-naire covering the chaplaincy, the chaplain and his work brought in some very interesting as well as some ribald comments. The most delightful two, and in a way the most pointed, were answering the question: What should the Chaplain be? One reply said, "Christlike". The other said quite simply "About". The main difficulty, I fancy, is in the fact that there is no one perfect way to run anything. There is untidiness, overlapping. But the Chaplain is essentially there for those in residence, his whole life is beamed towards them. Therefore it is essential to be many different people, yet always the same. It is different from being in a parish and the standards of living, the openness, the young approach all have to be reckoned with. One of the previous chaplains had said "No undergraduate lasts more than three years". This is not quite accurate, but it underlines the constant in and out nature of students, which demands particular qualities in the chaplain.

With this area of work, the chaplain must be prepared to stick his neck out, which may offend the bishop; but he also has to keep his head down a bit, and this may offend the students. He cannot just "go along", because he is leader. But he cannot just stand still. Gradually he has to learn what he is prepared to go to the wall for, and what he is not. I remember a particular incident when Charles Davis left the priesthood and the church. I had known him and learnt much from him. The undergraduates asked him to come and speak at the Old Palace. I mentioned this casually in the presence of an Archbishop at a TV meeting. He was very upset, and said unless I cancelled the meeting he would get the Cardinal to do so. Faced with that, I rang the Cardinal, and got a firm refusal to allow Charles Davis to speak in any Catholic church or building. For me, though the students were annoyed and thought I should fight the decision, it simple was not worth while that for Charles Davis' visit I should lose the chaplaincy job or something silly like that. Charles Davis, of course, did come to talk. He and his wife came first to have a meal with me, as an old friend, and then the meeting, which was ecumenically organised anyhow, took place well away from Catholic premises at the Baptist college.

I can see that there could be ecclesiastical nervousness over an incident like this. Concern about the development of intellectual freedom and the ability to treat people as grown-up are however important qualities. They do not always seem to be shown in catholic-authority decisions.

After all, despite the 1870 repeal of the test Act it was only in the 1890s that the Bishops even allowed young Catholics to go to University, so much fear was there of danger to faith through the intellect in the "open" university atmosphere. I suppose this kind of outlook emphasises the very real differences which background, upbringing and education creates in the mentality of different groups. I have always felt much more sympathy towards the sense that truth will prevail in the end, and that confinement, censorship and frightened protectiveness do not really help any of us through to truth in the long run. Truth we must teach and preach and live. But truth must take its chance with untruth, with lies, with evil. It does not grow in a hothouse, because it is an open air plant born of God himself capable of living in the open where untruth and darkness will not overcome it—in the end!

It would really take a whole book to compass all the remarkable, human, dull and emotional aspects of Oxford life. But at this point I want to mention one very important area—the psychiatric. That is a generalised term; I mean that being and living with undergraduates is being and living with men and women in the late teens and early twenties who are developing, maturing, meeting new experiences. They are at the same time fighting for existence in a world of ideas, where there will be final examinations, but where status, boy/girl relationship, sport, politics and so on all pull and jostle, until it takes a fairly solid person to come through without danger of going off at a tangent. Some of the actual problems involved failure to communicate with parents, tutors or even those in their peer group. Partly from past experience, partly from prayer, partly because God blessed me that way, I had grown fairly good at listening. Gradually, I came to be used by individuals who were lost or could not work. They came along, talked, sometimes stayed all day or for a few days. Gradually too colleges, psychiatrists and doctors also began to accept me as useful. I was called in. I suppose one of the important facts in my regard was that I was available day or night, if necessary for most of twenty-four hours.

There were others also in the house. Together we formed a warm, welcoming background, of some security, where there could be refuge. When psychiatrists and social workers ended the day or the week, one of us was still about. We went to the hospitals, especially the psychiatric ones, we accepted young men and women undergraduates who needed to go somewhere; we gave them space to read or write essays, watch TV, or just sleep. And they knew they could literally come at any time of day or night.

Let me give you one rather amusing illustration of this, which was tragic too, but eventually worked out. I was woken about three one early summer morning by violent ringing on the doorbell. I looked out, saw two huddled figures by the front door, and went down to open up. One was a young man I had been trying to help through a bad patch of drink, drugs, muddled up sex, work trouble and so on. He was dressed for a ball and stood weeping on the ball-gown-bareness of his girlfriend's shoulder. He had collapsed at the ball, demanded to see me. We went up to my room and I sat them on the settee, while I put on an old mackintosh over my pyjamas and made them tea. Eventually about four-thirty I told his girl that I would let the young man sleep in the chaplaincy till morning, and suggested she went back to the ball. They agreed, we let him sleep. She went down to the front door, and being (as I thought) polite, I went with her out to the corner of the main road, some yards from the house door. There I said goodnight, and was about to go, when she said: "It's very cold! Can you lend me your mackintosh?". And I had to strip it off, stand in my pyjamas while I put it round her, and then hurry back indoors before gossips or the police arrived on the scene! There is no knowing what you may be asked as chaplain at a university.

There are memories of so many things and people . . . the lovely girl I instructed in the Faith, who learnt in her undergraduate life to pray three or more hours a day, to do her work and yet to be thoroughly liked and "in" college life, got a good degree and for years now has lived as a professed Carmelite nun. There was the average of three or four each year to train for the priesthood; or the talented young man who in the course of treatment for depression was given a sedative which sent him into a coma, and whom I tried to help back into health and maturity during hours, days, weeks and years of developing friendship, as he gained physical, mental and spiritual strength; the down-and-out who was one of the first members of the Simon Community set up in the chaplaincy rooms, but when others grew rough, fled to our part of the house, subsequently lived permanently with us—alcoholic, out of work, in and out of a mental home, once threatening his social worker he was going to kill us and her with a stolen gun—yet all the while thoroughly lovable! The African student who slit himself from navel to breastbone with a knife in his despair at failure; the orphan girl whose sad background history and subsequent long and tedious hours to maturity cannot be told, but makes all who knew her story feel gladness; the joyful talks with young men and women on politics, God, sex and love. There was punting and cricket, music, dinners in college; the Masses in college rooms and chapels, some of which had not been used by Roman Catholics since the Reformation; the consultation asked by heads of houses; the distinguished guests at the Old Palace from Cardinals to Heads of State who came to meals and to talk. There were Borstal camps each summer, and a string of ex-Borstal boys who came to stay, ex-prisoners too, trying to get set up in the world again. Sometimes there was marriage-advice for senior members as well as preparation for young couples. We cooked and ate and washed up, feeding, baby-sitting, praying, doing all-night vigils.

The very variety of University life covers up the reality of ordinary life which as usual had long, boring periods with much wasted time. I have no idea how it is possible to get across the light and shade which seems to be a necessary ingredient to real living except by real living. There is no short cut, no substitute. I certainly know that towards the middle of every term such a black mood of tiredness, feeling of failure and disillusion came down that I personally felt like packing the whole work up. Failure and tiredness are hard to cope with. The weight seems to come back on personal inadequacy. The few successes get totally obscured by the suicide incidents or the apparent falling away of good young men and women. The tragedy of a broken romance or a broken mind cloud the whole view. But in the life of the university there were definite terms and between them the recuperative period of the vacation. Life at the parish level is very different. There is no regular term and vacation, but the continuance of life. The rhythm is not the same.

After nine years at Oxford, I had no doubt that I should be moving. When I said this in my annual report, the kind chairman of the meeting said I should not leave that in, as I might be held to it and regret it. I left it in, and planned to leave. I believe basically that each of us will give more if we do not spend too long in any one work. Ten years in the slightly rarified and particular atmosphere of the university seemed to me enough. In fact I finished eleven. I was happy that there was a fine and able successor on the spot, with whom I had been at work for some years. I think we had gained from each other; I know I gained from him. The development of the chaplaincy buildings was already in progress at this time, and though I was conscious of leaving him with many possible future headaches, I felt that he was well able to go ahead and cope with them. The financial side of the chaplaincy was also in a healthy condition for the foreseeable future, provided everyone worked together and nothing calamitous occurred.

Looking back, I suppose the chief lesson of the whole period, was the delight of knowing and loving human beings personally and individually, being allowed to be involved in their development, admitted to their inmost thoughts and desires; trusted and used and known and loved in return by a cross section of people from teenagers through to the very elderly, from dull and struggling to the brilliant. There were people from almost every race under the sun, of every shade of political opinion, religious belief or school of philosophy. I felt at the time full of alleluias and I still do. This was very real, very much alive, now up, now down; loved, hated, accepted and rejected in the midst of mankind as incarnate—for God. It took prayer as well as reason to bring me to the point of decision to leave, because kind people said I was mad or that I would be so missed. People are kind in this way, but they may well be encouraging the pampering of self rather than the release of the Spirit.

When I asked Cardinal Heenan what he wanted me to do he said that when the time came he would put me into parish work. The prospect was fascinating. I often used to commute between Oxford and London on British Rail for TV and London meetings, always passing the well known landmarks Didcot, Reading, Slough, the Southall gas-works, Ealing Broadway and so to Paddington. Now and again my slight knowledge of people in the Heston/Southall area and some interest in the social setting of much immigration, poor housing and many other of the problems of mid-twentieth century urban development had led me to think that it might be a wonderful place to live and work in. Just the night before going to see the Cardinal, I was having a heart to heart talk with a deeply-aware head of one of the colleges. I outlined my leaving Oxford and was asked where I might go. Without hesitation I mentioned my preference for something urban rather than country and instanced the range from the East End to the edge of Middlesex and from the Thames to the top of Hertford-shire, naming Southall among other places. The immediate reaction from my listener was to urge Southall. Next day, the Cardinal spoke of possibilities and gave me the choice of three parishes which he said he had to fill. The first was Southall, the others I should not name, because I had no hesitation in saying at once that I would like to go to Southall, if he agreed. He did, and some of the life in Southall will find its way into subsequent chapters.

2

PRIEST: PERSON OF PRAYER

There are many questionings about the nature of the priesthood—its functions, limitations, about the difference between a priest and any other baptised person and so on. I do not intend to go into all this in this chapter, but rather to put one positive function of the priest which cannot be over-emphasised . . . the priest as a man whose whole life is deeply spiritual.

We can speak of the priest as a man of prayer, but, I think we need to be clear that what we are talking about is not the mere necessity for a priest to "say his prayers" . . . that is get through his daily office of psalms and readings, say the rosary perhaps, spend some time in meditation and even do a bit of spiritual reading . . . though that is a list which sadly would prove too exhausting for many a priest who is nevertheless slaving away for the greater glory of God.

So what do I mean here? I mean that the centre and core of the whole priestly life is the relationship with God—Father, Son and Holy Spirit. I mean that this relationship is to be so deep, strong and all-pervading that it is the very pulse, life-blood, heart of his whole being. Without it, he is empty, a functionary only, wrongly balanced and so ineffective.

To this you could well say—Yes, but that is what every Christian should be, where every Christian should have his life centred. And I would agree with you, and say that this is why all the baptised are to a lesser degree or in a lesser kind of priesthood. And I would sing many an Alleluia if we could find this attitude in the average Christian.

In one sense, in these latter days, there is so much to learn about God and man, the Church and so on, there is no time to get to know God and man! I find myself in difficulty, because writing so briefly I may well give the impression of being anti-intellectual, or against the study of theology, philosophy, scripture, pastoral care and so on. In fact I am not, but I do have serious reservations about the amount in one gollop that any student can or should take. I am all for living out and continuing to read, to listen to explore new avenues, to keep the mind open, alert, inquiring, interested.

Because life is what the human being is all about, the old cliché that "holiness is wholeness" fits well, and is deeply true. That the whole man should be taken up in priesthood is self-evident, because THE priest is Jesus Christ, and our share of priesthood takes its origin from him. He was entirely given up to the will of his Father, and no part of him was not committed to his inherited Old Testament role of prophet, priest and king. In a sense, all three are encompassed by priesthood.

For the priest God must be central to his whole being. God's will is the priest's touchstone; God's love is his driving force and inspiration through the gift of the Spirit; his greatest desire is to be so one with God that it is God who lives and loves through him and so does the work. Once this centrality is lost, once another love or interest pushes God to the periphery, the whole balance and texture of priestly life is altered. It could be said that he had not only lost direction but lost the "essence" of priesthood. Yet today how often the average priest sees his life in pastoral terms. His work for God is immediately in visiting, meetings, administration. He is fully, and generally energetically, engaged from morning till night on "the things of God", with very little time for God himself, because "someone had got to do them". Prayer is fitted in as and when possible so as not to interfere with the business of life. Such priests are good men, hard working men. They are devoted to their parishes and their parishioners. They are doing their very best for them.

The sad fact is that the weight of work has thrown them off balance. The priest is nobody, has no power, is empty no matter how hard he works, if he is not given over to God in the Spirit. So the point of this chapter is to re-emphasise the primacy of the spiritual in the life of the priest. It is not my intention to cut out or deny the amount which has to be done with and for God's people in all directions. The thesis is simply the need to allow God the first place in the mind, heart and strength of the priest.

If the basis and mainspring is the relationship with God, my thesis goes, then it is essential that God is given time out of the priestly life in a regular and deep and particular way. Outwardly this will seem like a curtailing of time for other Godly purposes to do with his people and their welfare. But if the priest faithfully commits his time to prayer and himself to God in an open and self-abandoned fashion which may even seem exaggerated or foolish, then many important things will happen. In the first place, he will manage to have more time: or if that is not true in an actual extension of twenty four hours, it will appear true in the relative use of time. Then he will find that the depth of help which God can give through him is very different from that which he gave when working on his own. Even his tiredness, or his sense of being empty and having nothing to say and nothing to give, will react upon people in a fruitful way. In himself he will realise that the relative importance that he was giving to "his work" is now in better perspective, and he can be more selective and more sensitive.

However, it is only by taking hold of this theory and living it out that the practice proves the theory. The living out is itself tough. It demands a firm discipline and determination against a constant assault from all round and even from inside one-self suggesting that it is all a waste of time. So long as anyone pays lip service only to prayer by acknowledging its importance and then allowing other busy-ness to shoulder it out, the theory will remain only a theory. It will be ineffective in that person's priestly life. So the wonder of the things which happen in the prayer-centred, prayer-lived life will not be experienced, and (remaining unreal) will seem indeed a bit of imaginative thinking which is irrelevant to the main body of day-to-day parochial living.

Quite simply then, the life of prayer for a priest has to be lived out come hell or high water in whatever situation he finds himself. Because he is utterly given to God he is in no position to indulge himself by saying that he can only pray, he can only serve God, he can only be fulfilled in priesthood—IF . . . ! This sounds harsh. There is clearly room for some questioning and some adjustment. Those in authority can jeopardise a priest's spiritual growth by not treating him as a human being, but rather as a pawn. However, a degree of toughness is expected in facing the trials and challenges of particular situations which arise in different postings. There has been a tendency in recent years for considerable restiveness among younger clergy, especially in regard to living with and under an older man who is stubborn in refusing to update his way of working in his parish or living in his presbytery. It is in this kind of situation that a deep commitment to prayer is more than ever essential if the younger man is not to begin to get frustrated and lose heart. If he is given in prayer, there is more likelihood that he will both gain from the experience, and also win through one way or another for the way of development which he is seeking in the post-Vatican II church to which he has been ordained.

What I am writing here may seem to be asking too much, to be perfectionist. I would stress that each of us is individual and at a different personal stage of our own development both in regard to the world and to our relationship with God. Therefore, it is not easy to say anything sufficiently positive without rather depressing some people or making others write off the whole issue. I hope very much that reading this will give you a sense of "the possible with God" . . . not on our own, but with him. Through the years, I have experienced and do experience failure and darkness, moods of depression and elation, a sense that none of it is worthwhile. But the extraordinary and uncomfortable feature of our life in relationship with God which I want to open up is that there are these varieties of "feeling". We should not be oppressed, depressed or repressed! God's ways are not ours. They often seem circuitous; then sometimes they seem too direct. We need to learn to listen to God. I have in other books tried alone and with help to put some of these ideas on prayer, relationship, union, and love of God, in the more general context of all men and women. Here specifically, I am writing briefly of the relationship of the man who has been ordained by the church to the special ministry of priesthood in the ecclesiastical sense. Whatever else may come your way, be of good heart. The Lord has overcome the world. Though we fail and fall and tend to be disheartened, there is every reason for confidence in God. He is our strength . . . if we do not assume strength in ourselves.

In order that there should be a proper balance and a proper wellspring for priestly living, it is my contention that day by day, summer, winter, spring, autumn, rain or fine, time must be given lavishly to God. By this I do not mean simply the total giving of life in a generalised way, but also solid giving of personal time each day. The how, where and when and for how long are not so easy to legislate upon. Indeed, it would go against ideas of individuality and God's purpose for each one of us to specifiy too closely. This has, perhaps, been one of the failures of the past . . . there was a certain rigidity of Mass, office, meditation, rosary and so on. If the rigidity cracked, the prayer life often disintegrated.

I always remember and quote the famous Dr. Sangster, the great Methodist preacher, with whom I spent many hours talking of prayer. He used to say (a fact I fear I have not checked) "John Wesley and John Henry Newman, two great men, and both of them used to spend four hours a day in prayer". Such a demand may seem out of this world for many clergy. Perhaps it is. But then "Be perfect as your heavenly Father is perfect" is also a bit out of this world, but nonetheless is at least a counsel if not a command of the Lord whom we are following.

It is no very easy task to steer between laxity and overintensity in what I am writing. If we are prepared to "get away with" the phrase *laborare est orare* (even those who utterly refuse Latin in liturgy seem to know what that means!), then many a priest knows that it is possible to edge prayer more or less totally out of life. I presume it could also be true that a demand for four hours a day could turn some off, and could seem to be a source of neglect of pastoral work.

My thesis is that the latter—neglect of pastoral work—is not in fact the outcome, because the deepening knowledge and love of God through prayer drives the person out from the solitude and depth of union to a zest for spending himself on God's people. Time and again, I have come across just such a person—not only among priests—and their impact is electric.

What practical things, then, can be said about the time schedule, if it can only be a generalisation? I fancy the first is that there needs to be a regular daily encounter, beyond the Mass and beyond the Hours of the Day. How that is put in depends largely upon an individual and the demands on his time. Personally, I have found no substitute for early morning. Varying constantly, I have looked to my proposed time of rising, my sleep requirements and so back to the necessary hour at which to go to bed. Naturally, different people need different sleep patterns. My own, learnt to some extent on split watches during World War II, have been subject to lengthening and shortening, to earlier getting to bed and later rising according to surroundings. First, at Soho, it seemed fairly easy, except for the odd occasion, to go to bed around 11 and to get up at six or seven. In Westminster Cathedral, which was my next stop, little happened after ten, unless one was out, and consequently I went to bed earlier and got up earlier. The first Mass there was at six-thirty, and an attempt to pray for an hour beforehand meant a switch of timing. But both London and Oxford Universities which followed had very different patterns, and at Oxford particularly, it was impossible to tell when anyone would come, undergraduates are temperamentally late-comers, and the last post out of Oxford from the G.P.O. up the road went at midnight. As a consequence, with the first Mass at seven forty-five, a six or six-thirty rise went well. And so on.

I only put this in as an autobiographical exercise, because

within the pattern of each place there was obviously a variety of demand upon time at various parts of the day or night. I came to find that the only way to remain consistent, whether I had been kept up till three or four in the morning by an undergraduate love-affair-gone-wrong, or a sudden schizophrenic, was to get up at the same basic time I had previously decided. Demands, particularly of book work have made me find ways of subsequently catching a nap in mid-afternoon, but still resisting the temptation to lose prayer-time. This is admittedly a difficult balance which each person must work out.

Of course, prayer could and can often be sleepy-stupid, but it is important to remember that it is God who is doing the work, and that the brightest of my thoughts pales to insignificance in the light of his revelation. My part is to be there, to be willing, and to try to be open. A man is often most vulnerable to God in tiredness and on the borders of sleep. My feeling of stupidity is no good excuse for postponing prayer.

So, once having established the necessity for a good length of time to be given, and leaving it to the individual to locate that time and length within his own day, it is to be emphasised that this is the source, together with the Eucharist, but that the extension of prayer into every nook and cranny of the day is as vital as the air we breathe. Again, there are methods explained in many books. The essential is very simple. By practising short or ejaculatory prayer at different points of each day, it is possible to build a web of prayer which takes some spinning, but is then embracing and pervading. "Contact" with God is then of such a consistency that though work, play, conversation and many other occupations seem to drive the thought of God from us, his abiding presence is made clear by the ease with which he returns to our minds and hearts at moments of stillness, waiting or rest. As with a person deeply in love with his wife, who will feel a closeness and warmth, without even first consciously adverting to her, so this experience of loving and being loved wells up from the depth of being.

For the priest, such a habit is of real practical and

pastoral service. All too frequently, we miss the opportunity of asking help as we approach a house, a person, a
moral or social problem, asking for a few words which
could and should speak the Lord rather than speaking
ourselves. But, if the name of the Lord is ever in our hearts
and on our lips, he himself comes into conversation easily;
we can slip into a prayer without embarrassment, using the
presence of people and problems as an outlet to our love of
God and them. It is fruitful to suggest to a marriage-
preparation couple or someone sick or bereaved that we
pray with them immediately or that they join us in a short
prayer. This is much better than promising we will pray for
them and then parting on a prayerless word. This is even
more true when we are trying to come close to those who are
sick or dying. Praying with them, laying our hands upon
them unselfconsciously, using the anointing of the sick
with faith, hope and love—all this is far more possible if we
are ourselves deeply given to trust in God through prayer.

And, I suppose it is by a development of this mentality or
atmosphere of God's presence that gradually every action
can truly be said to turn into a prayer.

There is no doubt in my mind that meeting with others
for prayer, home masses or even discussion groups is a
valuable contribution both to the development of a holy
priestly life and to the holiness of all who take part. Here I
think the priest has a very priestly and serious duty in his
role of spiritual leader. His own life has much to gain from
knowing about different ways of prayer and growth in God.
There is an immense field here, from ancient to modern,
and across the world from West to East. In a way, though
he may be personally more attracted to one way than to
another, and for that reason more able as a leader in
particular "school", the variety of Christians and Christian
approaches should make him eager to try to know
something, to appreciate something of schools, methods
and systems which do not attract him. In so opening
himself, my impression is that he is going to gain spiritually
himself even though he may not use or may even discount
the information and methods he has freshly encountered.

Something rubs off, if only the sense that there is great variety in human nature as it reflects the simplicity of God.

He is also, the more able to point out to others who may come to him for advice some of the paths and the leaders and their writings which are available for the seeker. So frequently, spiritual direction has really meant making another person follow the way the director knows, trusts and possibly uses. There is much to be said for the director using himself and his experience for helping another. But there is also much room (or should be) for freedom in the Spirit, where the director can only have the humility, openness . . . and personal experience . . . to know that there is no single way, except Jesus . . . and he seems to reveal himself to us differently in his Spirit.

The advantage of groups is that they bring people together to share prayer and experience in a way they may never have experienced before. Being together, listening to the thoughts, hopes, prayers and insights of others, and getting the courage to speak out one's own fears and thoughts, emotions and desires in regard to God . . . this is powerfully useful. The content and character of the group and its prayer may be very varied, from almost total silence to almost total noise; from well-turned phrases and well-thought intercessions to inarticulate groanings. The freedom of the Spirit has not always been present in the more stylised and conventional methods of praying. Yet the Spirit blows where he wills, and he speaks and moves and fills according to no law except the very being of God. Therefore when we know that Christ has said that he is present when two or three gather in his name, we can be sure that his Spirit is there. What we can never be sure about is how the Spirit will manifest himself. He is not a tap of spiritual energy to be turned on as soon as I gather with a few others, or even pray by myself: "Come Holy Spirit, fill the hearts of the faithful and kindle in them the fire of your love!" It would be wrong if God was at our beck and call like that . . . yet his presence is certain, because without God we do not exist.

This passage is trying to spell out that any person, but

especially the priest in his leadership position, should be aware of God's presence always and all the time. This is no more than saying again what I said at the beginning of the chapter . . . for the priest God must be central to his whole being. That centrality, that presence is in reality the person—priest or any human being—opening and awaking to the presence of God which is true and objective without this awakening, but which is powerful through the awakening. Much of our time we are quite simply asleep . . . spiritually if not physically. No wonder St. Paul shouts at his audience through his writing that the time has come for them to awake. For too long we have been sleeping, dreaming of building the city of God in bricks and mortar, in numbered persons who have been categorised Christians by baptism or named "practising" by mass attendance on a Sunday. For too long many of us have been deaf to the movement of the still small voice breathing in the wind of change, to the groaning of the spiritual prisoners which is part of the unspeakable groaning of the Holy Spirit. Too long prayer has been shelved and the "good priest" accepted as the master planner and master builder.

The time has come for every priest to understand that his purpose is to be another Christ, an inspirer, a leader . . . not to political revolution, though that may come on the way; not to social betterment of conditions, though that too may come on the way—but to a spiritual revolution in which each Christian can be inspired to take his motto: All for Christ. What this will mean in terms of political commitment, social involvement and style of life is anybody's guess. In the complete commitment to Christ and the gift of self to Christ in the Spirit no one knows what God will ask or demand. That is why the main burden of any following of Christ in the priesthood today must be openness to the Spirit of Christ whether he is silent or whether he calls to an apparently impossible task. Unless the leader, the inspirer is given over to God in this depth and reality and totality he cannot hope to be the channel God will use for communicating His Word and His Spirit. Like the prophet he has to be prepared to be seized by God, with all that means in the life of the prophet: from fear, degradation, stupidity, being a fool before men to the dazzling realisation and communication of God's presence.

3

PRIEST: SEXUALITY, FRIENDSHIP AND LOVE

Of all the questions, heart-searchings, private discussions and public controversies which today surround the priest and priesthood in the Roman Catholic church, the most argued is probably celibacy. This is partly because of its demand which to some seems unnatural, partly because the church makes it an absolute requirement for any man who wishes to be a priest. From some people the celibate meets an un-thought-out feeling almost of revulsion. This reaction implies that no thinking human being could possibly accept celibacy as a way of life, and so is open to the criticism of being itself unthinking. There are other attitudes which range from questioning whether celibate life is a practical possibility to questioning whether it could have any real point. There is the very wide questioning among many people whether a celibate could reasonably be considered a person fit to guide others who are "fully using" their natural sexual drive in marriage.

No book by a Roman Catholic priest trying to cover some of the joys and sorrows, frustrations and fulfilments of the calling to priesthood could possibly ignore the issue. The subject is controversial and therefore thorny. Lines have been drawn which seem to polarise the position between the ruling of the church and those who are critics. There is not much flexibility, and this to some extent is due to the apparent rigidity of the basic teaching about sexual morality by the church.

This chapter sets out to consider celibacy in the context of human nature by looking a little at the make-up of man. It is not an exhaustive treatise on sexual morality. At the same time it will try to look at the freedoms and the necessary disciplines which are available to the human being, accepting that both are present as possibilities but that freedom or discipline may be differently interpreted by groups or individuals, and also that one or other may be inappropriately rejected, curtailed or ignored.

There are wonderful varieties in God's creation, even within a particular species. He has made living things with a capacity for reproduction. Mankind is not different in this, but has been created male and female: the same species but differently sexed, able to reproduce and basically enjoying and being fulfilled by reproduction. But sexuality has a wider purpose than reproduction. It is woven into the very texture of the human being so that if it did not exist in a particular individual he or she would be less than fully human. In the use of the various faculties and powers of our body, mind and will in the pursuit of balance and fulfilment, a great deal of freedom has been left to us. Indeed, so great is the freedom that we can maim or even kill ourselves and others by a variety of excesses, mis-applications or deprivations. Over the course of the centuries there has been an endless amount of experimentation. As a result, and through developments in many departments of human knowledge and experience, there have been changes of view, different emphases in different ages, modifications in law and even about-turns in medical treatment.

The basic Christian stand is that through all this the human being is essentially the same human being, a creature of God, made by and for God. God's revelation to man comes in various ways through the study of nature in general and the human species in particular. The greatest revelation, in itself unique, is the revelation of Jesus Christ, God and man. We learn from his living among us, from his example and from the teaching which his followers have handed on. We know from them that he says the first and greatest of all commandments is to love God with heart, soul, mind and strength. The second is to love your neighbour as yourself. He goes so far as to say that the whole law and the prophets are summed up in these two. We see how Jesus himself lives them out; we pick up various direct and indirect teachings. But we have not got a full textbook of christian living to cover every eventuality. We have gone to work therefore, with the freedom God has given us, to interpret his meaning and even develop it.

We understand Christ himself never married. His immediate followers he seems to have chosen from both married and unmarried. The early church assumed the possibility of marriage for the "president" and the deacon (cf. 1 Tim. 3). As regards sexual morality, there are clear lines in Christ's firmness and also in his gentleness, in instances like the woman at the well and the woman taken in adultery. His outline of general morality has the same marvellous but difficult combination. He is clear, downright, strict in his upholding of God's law. Principle is definite. Knowing man as he did and facing the experience of his own life he seems to underline the necessity for mankind to have clear principles. It is very easy as I personally know to my cost to become thoroughly woolly. But the difficult balance that Christ leaves for us to follow is the clarity and definiteness of principle, and the way he interpreted the application of the law in generality or in particular cases.

For instance, the disciples ask him about forgiveness, and he gives them a very high standard . . . seventy times seven. He is criticised for breaking the sabbath and chides them on getting wrong the relation of sabbath and man. As regards anger he says that anyone saying "thou fool" is worthy of condemnation; he warns sharply about lusting after a woman. In these and other instances he seems to be saying that the teachers of the day can fall into the trap either of laxity or of undue severity. Then when he comes to individual cases, while condemning the sin he is wonderfully understanding and uplifting to the one who has failed.

Whatever we say and do we have a duty to live by the mind of Christ, so that our interpretations and reactions keep the same balance. He always treats human beings as human beings, but he wants us to go forward into a state which seems out of reach—he tells us to be perfect as his heavenly father is perfect. We are all to seek this perfection, but we do this as individuals living in society. The seeking can be very much alone and individual, or we can come together for our development. Amidst the wide possibility there can be many variations. There can be two people together in marriage, or again married couples joining a community for mutual support; there are individuals who live totally alone as hermits, others who do not marry but live in the world as single people, and there are those who have vowed themselves to celibacy.

It is important that the variety is seen and accepted. With such variety it is narrow to assume that one way of life is the only way. Though statistically it can be said that the majority of people marry, the minority cannot reasonably be written off as unfulfilled, crossed in love or any other epithet. Anyone who has had contact over a period of time with members of both sexes, married and unmarried, knows only too well that there is no guarantee of "fulfilment" in or out of marriage, but that fulfilment can be reached in either state. Probably it would not be as beautiful as we might first think if everyone lived in total harmony as soon as they were married. Single or married we live in tensions of various kinds which are part and parcel of our existence and—like the grit in the oyster— form the pearl.

To turn directly to the person who for reasons of service of God has vowed himself or herself to celibacy, I want to distinguish various different backgrounds from which the call is heard. There are some who come from the beginning with a complete acceptance of the reality and purpose of being given so totally to God that there is no place for such a close relationship between two individuals as marriage demands. For such persons there is from the beginning a single-minded, single-hearted commitment. It could be said that their vocation is celibacy for the Lord, and that had they not felt the call to his service in priesthood or religious life they might well have been among those who would remain single anyhow throughout life. For there are those who live single lives and often work for a high calling of charity, welfare, nursing or teaching for instance, but do not necessarily have much if any relationship with God. Others who seek the priesthood have been known to "slip into" celibacy because they have become committed to the idea of priesthood early in life, have gone into training equally early and have simply assumed that they will be celibate. Some of them have not come to any real sexual awakening. If such awakening takes place during training, some of them leave and some work through it to a deeper understanding and commitment; if it comes after ordination to the priesthood, the crisis of awakening can be more acute because the decision to be made is already weighted by the celibate status of priesthood.

Finally there are those who go into training knowing something of the tugs and pulls of their sexuality. Some may have faced and suffered what awakening and self-discipline mean in terms of overwhelming attraction and genital desire, and yet gone forward without any actual genital relationship with another person. Others may have had the experience of orgasm and intercourse, and so have had to face a different experience of rejecting sacramental fulfilment of this way of life. (Some like my forefather Cardinal Weld have made this choice after marriage itself). Such people are then in a different category from those who have not experienced physical genital union.

I am stressing here differing factual situations because it is not always plainly said that the background of priests in regard to sexual experience may vary. On the whole, perhaps more in the past than today, there was I think a general assumption that all priests were totally ignorant of what the textbooks used to call "carnal knowledge". This is not so, though it does not mean that clergy go round publicly saying "I am a virgin" or "I had intercourse before I became a priest and know all about it". In any case, the strong basic rule of the church which is accepted by each person going forward to ordination is that the man ordained to priesthood is ordained to a celibate priesthood. Though the understanding of this may vary with experience, and though some may say they would like to see the possibility of a married clergy, the fact today is that all asking for priestly ordination must agree to live celibate lives. This cannot be stressed too strongly, because woolly thinking could lead to a very muddled and rather self-indulgent outlook.

That said, I need to go on to more basic principles.

"Every high priest has been taken out of mankind and is appointed to act for men in their relations with God, to offer gifts and sacrifices for sins, and so he can sympathise with those who are ignorant or uncertain because he too lives in the limitations of weakness" (Hebrews 5.1). The passage goes on (and you must read and absorb it) to liken *our* living and suffering and learning to the living, suffering and learning of Christ.

Each young man or woman who is called is a human being. I must write from the male angle, but this will not exclude certain relevance to female attitudes, desires and problems because again we are all basically human. The importance of what I am saying is this . . . the person training for priesthood or religious life, the person subsequently taking vows or being ordained is still human. Any training or future way of living remains within the human-being context. Certainly there are demands and asceticisms, disciplines and functions which will call heavily upon the spiritual, upon the gift of God who is behind the calling. But it is vital to the true expression of Christ in the world that bishops, ecclesiastical authorities, colleges, religious orders and the students themselves recognise their human nature and train it to reality and not some esoteric and unreal dream picture of a de-sexed and so non-human creature. Christ came into the world that we might all be more fully human, not less.

Every training college and every clergy house or convent or monastery really needs a large sign over the door which would read something like: "You are human. Be real, and give your real self to God and each other." We each of us live "in the limitations of weakness". With St. Paul, we need to revel in this, rather than fearing all along the way. But also with St. Paul we need to remember to bring our bodies into subjection. It may be a bit of a digression, but if it happens that I am giving a retreat say to enclosed religious women and a sister obviously well into her old age pension period asks to see me; and suppose that further, in fear and trepidation, she confesses to having "bad thoughts" or perhaps "bad feelings"—my reaction, after talking to her, might well be to say "For your penance go out into the cloister and dance round it two or three times saying out loud: 'Alleluia, praise the Lord: I'm still alive; I'm still a human being: I can still feel, I can still love: Praise the Lord Alleluia!' But being still human, remember you still need a life of prayer, penance and self-denial".

My plea is . . . let us face our human nature. Let us not be afraid of it. Let us accept (and I mean really accept with our guts) that Jesus Christ was human, that he had human feelings and emotions, and that he was like us in all things except sin . . . so that our facing up to our nature is equally true and real, and does not halt and hesitate at every step for fear that sin lurks everywhere.

A student for priesthood then, or an ordained priest is a man; a human being. As such, he is flesh and blood, mind and body, spirit, emotions, conscious and sub-conscious. He is sexed, he is made by God for relationship with others, of both sexes, in knowledge, affection, friendship and love. He comes normally from a family background, has the ordinary mixture of joy and sorrow, hope and fear, ambition, pride and division between the part of him which is full of self, and the part which feels unlovable and unloved. He desires to be loved, he fears being loved, he desires to love, he is mixed and sometimes torn . . . he is real. So, he also knows what it is to be alone, and in being alone, knows loneliness. He suffers, he laughs, he is brought to tears by family grief, by pain, by desolation, and many other ways. He is a man. And because he is a man, he can also reach down into that wondrous depth, into the mystery of being, into self; and he can soar up in the spirit, through the material and the temporal in a vivid and vital pulse which seems to lift him beyond the human.

Too often the training for priesthood and for lay living has been too narrow. I personally grew up in a household where my father had already died by the time I needed or wanted to know the facts of life. At school, I learnt quite a lot fairly early on and a bit from my sister and brother at home. Later, not through school teaching but through school living and talk I learnt a great deal more. If it had been left to school teaching (and I hope my memory is not maligning the staff) I would still have been pretty ignorant by the time I went to University. There I entered the first really secular society of my lifetime and discovered ideas and situations which shook me, even given what I had come across in various ways in school days. But the most different and sophisticated arena into which I suddenly found myself pitched was the London life of a young Guards officer in wartime. I have no idea what it was like in peacetime, but certainly the proximity of bombing and the expectancy of a short London posting before going overseas to fight, opened the way to a riotous kind of life for anyone who fancied it. I was not properly of the Guards background. Most other officers seemed to be of well-heeled families from famous public schools who already knew their way round London. I was a "country bumpkin" in that respect; and also a very poor one. I had only my pay. They were kindness itself; I had known many of my fellow officers vaguely at Oxford and better at Sandhurst. They showed me round London night-life, introducing me to a night-club existence filled with wine, women and song, which often had us literally staggering onto parade the following morning. It was a strange life of irresponsibility with little or no belief in God in the midst of responsibility, an experience of "eat, drink and be merry, for tomorrow we die". And this extended in a lesser way to the few-and-far-between leave periods which we subsequently had during the fighting in North Africa and Italy.

I know this situation I outline was my own, but for my age-group, caught up in war, this was a familiar enough pattern of life in those years. Subsequent generations have had the after effects in education, loosening of moral standards and so on. In this development of society, priestly training has not always taken into balanced perspective the very many aspects of human personality. The result has been that those who went through the system of the seminary have developed in different ways, some very normally, balanced and human, some over rigid and frigid and somewhat withdrawn from humanity, some breaking loose in an emancipation which can easily become personally self-indulgent. Now the purpose of the training is training for the future. No one is saying that celibacy is an easy way of life. But the training is for the whole man, and like Christ each of us is expected to grow "in wisdom and grace before God and man". Within this, the difficult balance in sexual development is a part, and it depends upon the mind and will as well as upon the physical. There are those who would say that a vow of celibacy should not be taken before a person has had a sexual awakening, an experience of love in friendship, intimacy and affection which has reached to the depth of his being and included genital experience, and in this way given him an understanding of what he is giving up. I could not agree with this and the Church has certainly never taught or held this. There is no evidence over the centuries that those who have, in their millions I suppose, taken the vow without such experience have in fact been unfulfilled, failures or incapable of a true vow. I realise that such a statement could be questioned or some evidence brought forward of clergy who have gone wrong or even gone mad! But at the same time the general rule, the general stand and the general run of clergy living has been based on the teaching and practice of a fulfilled life of celibacy, reaching to a depth and truth of relationship, intimacy and friendship which does not necessitate sexual union. All I want to underline here again is that such depth of relationship between human beings inescapably includes some sexual element, because we include sex essentially in our make-up.

It is clearly the genital aspect which can here get out of proportion and dominate thinking. Instead of the realisation that there are very varied levels of relationship, but that it is an acceptable and non-sinful fact that each of us is sexed and that some even slight genital reaction may involuntarily enter most relationships, the atmosphere has been to cut off or shut down as soon as the genital enters the scene. But to cut off relationship as soon as this aspect emerges is to castrate the reaction of the normal human being.

I wonder if it would help some priests and some who are considering their way forward to celibate living if it could be said and accepted that each and every one of us is sexed, experiences sexual thoughts and feelings, is moved some-times to a surge of emotional and sexual awakening which is true, authentic, naturally human and good. There is too much fear about. There are too many inhibitions, taboos, sin-fears. To be sure it is necessary to realise the true nature of the human being, and also to appreciate and live towards the perfection to which Christ calls us. We must be disciplined.

One of the difficulties is in realising that we do not suddenly, by a statement of vow, enter a "state of perfection". Rather we have entered by our vow a "novitiate" of perfection, in which imperfect as we are, we try by all God's help, our own purpose and endeavour and the support of the church to live within the "perfect way". On the whole, only those who hear confessions, counsel clergy or are in close relation to them know just how far some of us fall and how far some of us climb, and how much rough ground there is in the process of fulfilling the commitment.

This is not to belittle a vow of chastity, it enhances it. After all, the general teaching of the church is that all, male or female, have a condition of chastity up till the time that they enter marriage or pledge themselves in another personal way to chastity in priesthood or religion. This "natural" engagement to chastity still has to be lived out, especially during the time of puberty and young adulthood. It would be a person totally out of touch with reality who said that the average teenage boy or girl went through this period of living without some sexual awareness. It would still be totally out of touch with reality to believe that the average teenage boy, at least, went through these years without any sexual exploration, and more particularly, without masturbation. This is not to say that every young man masturbates. It is to accept that the greater majority, including those who have subsequently vowed chastity, have in all probability masturbated in their lifetime, at least once, but on average more often.

The vow of chastity is a very real giving to God, and a giving which goes as deep as it is possible to go. If anyone were to think of it as superficial he would be out of touch with the reality. The married man should always and everywhere in his life live as a man vowed to one woman in the depth of his being, and therefore at no point act in a way which would infringe the fullness of the gift he made of himself to the one he loves. This is the ideal; the fulfilment varies, but the whole of our moral fibre and the strength of human fidelity gets weakened when we accept as normal and natural that there will be unfaithfulness. It is today more than ever necessary to restate the ideal and to encourage men and women to live to it. With the celibate, he is always and everywhere vowed to a love of God which is to take up his whole heart, soul, mind and strength. The fact of failure, the fact of selfishness entering his life, the fact that he may be caught by human love . . . these are facts which cannot be ignored. But the vow remains, and the whole of his life, which includes all his work and his relationship with others, must be orientated to God. It is not as a loose term that mystics speak of spiritual marriage for the soul taken by God in the depth-love of prayer. Nor is it surprising that St. Teresa of Avila has to speak to her nuns of the fact that there can be sexual feelings aroused in prayer. The whole person is taken up and committed and plunged into love.

In writing of celibacy and priesthood, I am concerned with the whole human being. The whole thrust and emphasis is the fulfilment of the human person in accordance with the plan of God, till in Christ we build up the perfect man. But, let it be stressed, the perfect man is not a-sexual. He is a fully sexed man, but one who has worked through his very manhood to realise relationship, love, friendship; to know and live with the urge to genital involvement; to have grown through this urge to know that, important as such involvement is and seems, it is not the totality of loving, it is not necessarily the fullest expression of friendship. One who is married has accepted that, difficult as it may seem to be in practice, the unique commitment is something to which he is pledged *in love*; he is also sane and balanced enough to admit the attractions of the genital, even away from his pledge union in love . . . and somehow, not necessarily without a failure, he has come to live that life "beyond" which is the flowering of true, deep and lasting love, in sickness and in health, for better or for worse, for richer or for poorer . . . till death do us part.

Similarly, the celibate as a human being needs to come to full maturity. I could not possibly specify all the ways that this person or that, this school or that, might suggest as psychologically right, emotionally right, morally right and so on to achieve this end. (I repeat however my rejection of the claim that genital sexual expression is a necessary condition of full maturity). But I must in justice and in love say that normally each person should be led to admit sexuality, rather than denying or suppressing it, or feeling it "wrong in itself ". It is good in itself, it is God-given, it is of the essence of our human nature. But to say that is not to deny that sexuality presents challenges. Decisions, options, the knowledge and choice of what is right and what is wrong belong to the *use of sex*, not to the *fact of sexuality*. The point is, there is decision to be made. There is right as well as wrong. Not everything is wrong.

In addition, it is really important that each person comes to know, preferably with assistance and down-to-earth teaching, that there are stages, growths, pitfalls and goals. For instance, there is much to be known and faced about the areas of development between one person and another; how meeting a person, of either sex, does not necessarily mean any immediate attraction, but may mean a violent "fall into love"; how acquaintance may grow to common points of view, to frequent meeting . . . e.g. for political reasons, because we are both studying art, because we take to friendship. Each should know that in the growth of intimacy, often almost drowning every other aspect, may come the genital. But that this is *not* so basically and supremely important to developing relationship as the ability and willingness to share, to open up, to be committed and accept commitment, to love and to be loved.

All this is vitally important to the growth of the individual concerned, but how much more necessary is it again if this person is setting out to be the guide, philosopher and friend of others. Certainly it is possible to teach from a text-book knowledge, provided that the textbook itself is full, competent and humane. Experience is not, and must not be said to be essential; but empathy and sympathy are essential, and these are difficult to come by, if the tone of one's textbook is hostile and condemnatory, and no other compensating angle has been available in reading, conversation or experience.

The human child is born into a society which by its very nature is sexually mixed. I mean that female and male combine to bring the child into the world and society. Though sadly it does not always happen, it would be considered normal for a child to have a background of father and mother after birth. Indeed the child is such a beautiful, delicate creature in so many ways, especially psychologically, that damage can occur if the balance of parenthood is not maintained. From the very earliest moments of existence influences are being felt unconsciously, and later as the child becomes aware there are conscious feelings as well. The tragedy of broken families and the "destruction" of persons which often follows such a breakdown is more common in the present age, though not enough highlighted or studied. Not only are the two, man and wife, emotionally involved, but also frequently another man or woman or both, with perhaps their partners, and then the children of all parties. The child is particularly vulnerable because particularly impressionable during the stages of growth which themselves are delicate.

Even where the family is intact and happy, there are still influences which may occur like the over-dominance of father or mother. Children themselves being individual and developing may have physical or mental or emotional problems of their own in addition to general growth. There are also the outside influences of street, friends, school and so on. And it is with all this potential for good and possibility of harm, within and part of natural growth that sexuality itself develops or is stunted. In this area there may be ordinary growth, or distortions and inhibitions may take their toll. Today much more is known about the complexities of the period of growth as research has gone forward. The priest who is going to cope with himself and also to act as counsellor needs broader and deeper study of the whole area so that he may be aware of possible differences in sexing, growth, development of attraction and orientation. Previously much of this knowledge has been only scantily passed on in training, to the extent that it has not always been acknowledged in ecclesiastical circles that the human being is a mixture of male and female, that this ambivalence, this hetero- or homo-sexual attraction which is already present latently, will emerge more definitely towards one or other sex in the ordinary course of development.

I am not knowledgeable enough to go properly into the complicated field of sexual development. It is normally taken for granted that this development will be hetrosexual. But at this time there is much more being said and written about the origin and nature of homosexuality. I personally am convinced that much more has still to be done in exploring human nature and sexual orientation. Homosexuality is a state of being. The fact of homosexuality cannot be ignored. Whatever arguments there are about its genesis, in the upshot some human beings are homosexually orientated. The church has clearly and consistently condemned genital homosexual relationship as unnatural, and therefore tended to "write off" homosexuals in a pastorally unhelpful way. It has followed, I am afraid, that very many clergy have been closed to the pastoral needs of a certain percentage of their people. This in itself is wrong and has and still does cause intense suffering. This situation led to my being asked to write on the pastoral care of the homosexual because, as the editor of a pastoral care series told me, "no one else would do it". The result was not only the rather bad little book I wrote, but also a wide involvement with the hopes, fears, bitternesses and relationships of homosexual men and women. This has convinced me that they must continue to press moral theologians, scripture scholars, doctors and psychologists to study their situation exhaustively. In all that I have been saying I want it to be quite clear that sexuality in itself is good, and that sexual development and feeling are natural. The use or misuse of it is what counts morally. Because a person grows sexually to be more attracted to the other sex this neither gives license towards genital activity in that direction, nor does it mean that the person should be repelled by contact with a member of the same sex, nor feel it strange or unnatural to have intensely deep and serious relationships with a member of the same sex, even to feeling some sexual inclination. In this situation, as with all sexuality, discipline is necessary. It is important to stress that there is far more to human relationship than just sexuality. In the case of those who are "sexed" so that the main or even exclusive attraction is towards their own sex, suffice it to say here that such attraction is not in itself evil: it can be used beneficially for the individual and society, and it needs to be understood, not only by celibates who may themselves be sexed that way, but also by any counsellor, clerical or lay, who hopes to help the full development before God and man of such a person.

To conclude this particular line of thought, it must be re-emphasised that the complexity of human relating is such that it cannot be easily fathomed and must not be lightly dismissed. Each of us, in our own way, single or married live through personal experience. And some of us, more than others, leave ourselves open not only to guiding people in developing Godward and manward relationships, but also to trying to guide others out of pitfalls and corners into which we personally have never been. Some reading, some listening, a great deal of patience and the acceptance of the need to relate very deeply indeed in prayer to God who is responsible for this human nature . . . all these are facets of the training which allows a human being to grow firmly from God-roots, and openly in human living, so that he or she may encourage and help others forward on the beautiful dangerous, exciting and joyful development of man before God and his fellow men.

What I must now try to do is set out a few thoughts on the actual living out of celibacy.

I want to make a clear assertion. It is fairly normal for the modern psychological approach to lay down that the only possible fulfilment for the human being is when there is sexual fulfilment, normally seen in terms of marriage. I would contest this as too absolute, and as putting too much weight upon the genital. This is not to say that the greater number of people in this world will not find fulfilment through sexual union . . . and please God the increasing problem of marriage breakdown, which is reaching plague proportions, will be tackled so that there may be more true fulfilment and less destructive associations. I repeat that nothing, genital or non-genital, *guarantees* the fulfilment of any one or two people.

Without going into the ups and downs of personal development and relationship within marriage I simply want to speak from my own experience of the many remarkable people in different walks of life who have lived singly, vowed or simply singly, and have been developed, rounded, caring, loving, warm and wise people. I have known them in most caring professions . . . medicine, nursing, social services, probation, law, local government, teaching, the church and so on. Some have been "religious" people, some have been humanists, some have been left, some right, some centre in politics.

I hope this will be some reassurance to those, especially in the student body, who find themselves pressurised by learned and professional writing and lecturing which may over-emphasise the genital. I well remember, for instance, a very fine consultant psychiatrist who professed himself an agnostic and humanist. At a public talk and discussion I shared with him, he referred to the celibacy of Christ and also had quite a lot to say about the value of "the celibate" in the world of today, when this was a deliberate and full stand and a witness to the world. However, later on, in questions he said how much happier he would be about Christ if he knew he had had an affair with Mary Magdalen. In talking to him, it was clear that he could not really accept fulness of relationship without the explicitly genital act, even in a person such as Jesus. I suppose we ought to admit the difficulty of accepting Jesus as truly God and truly man, and go on from there to the difficulty of accepting that if he was truly man, in the fulness of man it is not necessary to experience marriage. Given Jesus' acceptance of the contemporary Jewish condemnation of fornication and adultery, he could not gain full genital sexual experience in that way. If genital experience were necessary "to become a full man" he could not have been a full man. However, I and all the followers of Jesus Christ accept in their minds and hearts his complete human nature . . . like us in all things other than sin. To marry is not to sin, but can be to find fulness. To be celibate is not to sin, but *can* also be to find fulness. That is the thesis!

Let us again face the fact that we are all human beings, and it is of our very nature to be sexed. This is a state we must all live with, whether celibate by vow, single or married. Let me put plainly that I am sure we can confuse and magnify the difficulty of being sexed if we too quickly leap from total-remote-living to marriage or genital expression of affection. A very-wise very-human very-spiritual very-real priest born and bred in one of the Caribbean islands had a long discussion with me one day about sex and its problems in the Caribbean. He told me of his personal concern that for the young people relationship between sexes went straight from "acquaintance to steady"; the implication was that very soon after they met a particular girl was "this boy's girl" . . . she was not free. The result, he said, was that there was no real opportunity for moving from acquaintance to openness to intimacy and through to friendship. If the marriage prospect was "out", then the girl was no longer the boy's girl, and the possibility of friendship at a deeper but less "engaged" level did not exist. He was very concerned that boys and girls could not develop *friendship.* His is an instance from a special area of the world, which has its own local problems in regard to marriage. But we too have had the difficulties, because we have been very scared at any "physical contact". Embracing, kissing, even holding hands can be felt to be "an occasion of sin". Frankly, the further out from contact the line is drawn, the more likely we are to jump the line. I am not trying to advocate license. I want people to open their eyes to the goodness which is in the expression of friendship by affection expressed in physical contact. To be close to someone, to kiss them hello or goodbye, to hug them in joy or hold them weepingly in distress—these surely can be human, good and affectionate actions. It is a mistake for a human person to try to be too a-physical. It is also a mistake for a human to swing to the other extreme of "anything-physical-goes". If we accept physical contact as all right and indeed good when it is disciplined and affectionate rather than an expression of sexual indulgence, then we need to live a life which is disciplined and controlled.

Moreover, there is strength and sensitivity built up by insistent return to prayer each day and for a prolonged period. There is no "plain sailing" in human life. To live safely we have to live at risk; to live as Christians is to lose our lives in order to gain them.

Every one of us has the exciting, though sometimes daunting and almost overwhelming task of working out ourselves and our salvation as we live through our life. No one can live my life for me, though almost inevitably (and indeed often rightly) there will be plenty of people about to tell me how I should be living it! It is important for me to be open to advice, to try to learn from others, but day in and day out, it is I who have to work out my salvation.

In this, each of us has a public and private sector in life. For me, this has perhaps been the most difficult to work through in any kind of balance. In another part of this book, I write about clergy difficulties we have experienced in trying to live an "open" life in a clergy house. When I was young, I was immensely shy, blushed when spoken to, was never trusted to appear on any stage or show because I either tripped up in nervousness or broke down and cried. We lived a very close family life, and I hated with a deep hate being sent away from home to a boarding school. I liked to be alone quite a lot, and though I had deep and happy friendships, we were not a family who went away much, except as a family. All this was broken into by war, and as I have already said I found myself pitch-forked into the open life of the army, where there was little privacy, a great deal of sharing especially in the war areas and a kind of intimacy of fear, relief, excitement, death-closeness, pain and loss, wild "letting down of hair" between battles and on leave.

I don't know that anyone teaches us directly about public and private in our lives. It is something we learn, or go ahead in living without consciously putting a name to it. There is and always will be in each of us as an individual a private sector which will be incommunicable except to God. Only he reads the inmost heart. But additionally, there can be quite a wide range of thought, feeling, desire and even activity which I can keep and regard as private. When however I accept the call to priesthood I am by definition accepting a call to public office, I become a public servant. I must stand up officially, represent the church officially, be approached as "the priest". It is here that a person can get a real kind of schizophrenia. The old rule was that the priest in public always appeared garbed as a priest. There was no doubt of identity. On a golf course, in the street, in the cinema, having a meal in a restaurant, the clerical collar was worn. Even in the priests' house or in the seclusion of one's own family, the same was often true. To some extent it was a kind of tangible safeguard and mindcheck of status, of being a public person. This situation in part led to the very "enclosed" life for clergy within the house. It was their place of privacy, the only situation in which they knew they were not being watched (except of course by the housekeeper who therefore had to be taken in on the side of the priests, as it were, as a defender of their privacy.)

For some years now there has been a revolt against this rule and habit, an emergence into civilian clothes, a desire to be called by Christian names rather than referred to always as "father". The distance between priest and people has been whittled away. The immediate reaction from some in authority and some ordinary clergy has been to deplore the movement as very dangerous, the first sign of a priest who is "on his way out". This shows insecurity and a reliance on the safeguard of the collar, but it has behind it a real and deep sense. The blurring of public and private is all very well if a person has been trained to it. But there can be no doubt that the collar was a visual and psychological safeguard and a distance maker. To take it off makes me, in an unknown place, just another unknown person, a face in a crowd, topping trousers and an open-neck shirt. It may help me to get close to people; it can also help me to be as alone and lonely as many ordinary people find themselves. But psychologically it can also release me from inhibitions. It is easier for me to feel less conspicuous drinking in a pub, going to places and doing things which are not wrong in themselves but cause people to stare and mutter to each other if I am in a collar.

In many ways, the liberalisation is excellent and beneficial to both clergy and laity. But it is also dangerous in that the possibilities and the difficulties of living in this way must be seen and faced. I am not wanting simply a safe life detached from the possibility of temptation. I am wanting priests and students to understand that we are human as priests and that if we do not have the safeguard of the collar we need to have a much stronger and deeper training in our commitment to Christ—Christ not in our neighbour but in himself. By that I mean we need to know hours of prayer, personal asceticism in food, drink, sleep and availability which are the "new" safeguards for celibacy. It is a wonderful idealistic picture that I can vow myself to Christ utterly and then give myself openly and fully to all people just like that. No! Anyone who thinks this way should read Henry Suso:

There came a hostile thought in the guise of a friend, counselling him thus: "It may be as well that thou shouldst amend thyself, but do not exert thyself too much. Begin in such a moderate way that thou canst carry it through to the end. Eat and drink in a reasonable measure and be comfortable, but at the same time guard against sin. Be in thyself as good as thou wouldst, but do not be so abstemious that people are horrified at the very sight of thee. As people say: 'If the heart is good, all is good'. Thou canst quite well be cheerful in society, and yet remain a good man at the same time. Other people want to go to heaven too, and yet they do not lead such an austere life".

In this and similar ways he was sorely tempted, but Eternal Wisdom refuted this false counsel thus: "He who hopes to catch a slippery eel by the tail, and he who hopes to begin a saintly life with a lukewarm heart, are both deceived. For when they think they have caught it, it escapes. Moreover, he who hopes to overcome a pampered and rebellious body by gentleness, lacks common sense. He who would have the world, and yet serve God perfectly, strives to do the impossible and will falsify God's teachings themselves".

(Henry Suso: *The Life of the Servant*, p.17)

So I suggest that the way forward in this balance of the public and the private in the new mode is to live that kind of commitment to Christ which really does dig deep into each of us in our time alone, our discipline of prayer and reading, our willingness to be available to everyone (not just our friends) at all times. I suggest this will demand a training outside as well as in the seminary which is a realistic forecast of the demands which will be made emotionally, physically, mentally, spiritually and ascetically if we are to be the kind of priests of Jesus Christ in our day who can preach his good news not only in terms of his humanity but also in terms of his divinity.

For me personally, I realised that if I was going to spend so much of my time public, it was essential that somehow I also had the opportunity to be private. The first and quite simple way, and often the hardest way of all, was to be alone, to spend a good long time in prayer and to throw myself on the love of God which unfortunately for the human-me was frequently quite intangible, and in moments of real emotional-pull also unreal. I needed to escape to human privacy as well, to intimacy, understanding, relaxation, love and friendship. Perhaps I should have been able to find it in the presbytery. Well, I couldn't always. And I expect this is where danger can lie. I have no doubt that it is essential, if a priest is to remain human, approachable, interested, loving and unafraid working in the world, that he should have access to personal and intimate friendship . . . the friendship with God in prayer, and the friendship with human beings who will take him as he is, treat him as a human being, accept intimacy, friendship and love, and give in return.

Now all that could be dangerous, depending on choice of friends. It may sound too ordered and stylised, but I have found that for me personally the fulfilment at an individual level has variety to it. For instance I mean that if I did not have good priest friends, I would find it very difficult to relate and share at a certain common level of experience, demand, vow and so on. There is also as it were a "professional" quality to relaxation among those committed in the same way with or without full development of an individual and particular friendship. Now this may well sound a contradiction of most seminary and religious training in past centuries, where there has been strict censure of "particular friendships". The point is why were they considered wrong. Firstly they were thought, I fancy always to incline to the genital and so be disorientated. Secondly they were felt as disruptive of general balance and relationship within the community where they occurred.

Both these fears might be realised in individual associations, but the generalisation from there on is fairly typical of the extreme position which has sometimes repressed and desiccated otherwise human approachable and warm priests. In advocating the goodness and value in close, real and particular friendship, I am only responsible if I point out the dangers which possessiveness, cliquishness, exclusiveness and exaggeration of the sexual factor bring to such a relationship. However, rather than moving from realisation of that danger to banning of such a possible friendship, we would be better and more positive if we set out to work as religiously inclined, Godfearing, human and disciplined men to face, work through, enjoy and benefit from that depth of relationship which is "life-giving" to the two people concerned. The repercussions of such experience and character-building can also be invaluable for those beyond the particular friendship with whom "the friends" are in contact, because non-cliquish relationship helps to build community.

For me, in addition to priest friends, I have found a wonderful companionship in sisters of religious orders who often give a more civilising inspiration, as well as warmth and a reason for the male to tidy himself up from his bachelor existence. One's own family is normally a great source and resource, but beyond this there are those men and women who both ask and give in friendship.

It would be wrong to instance such friends here, but suffice it to say that I do not think I could really have survived, without the availability of families and individuals with whom I could go away from the "centre" and find peace and joy, time for prayer and reading, and a precious friendship. The fact that these were men and women, old and young, intelligent and slow, sick and well made no difference. Individually or in pairs or groups they were real—they were sometimes in need, and they could give. Thank God for real sharing . . . thank God for men and women who will share! And I was very fortunate early on in having three or four people, of both sexes and different ages, outside family, with whom I could give and receive deeply, without fear or charges of favouritism or scandal or jealousy.

I fancy it would be a common experience of development in priesthood, counselling and all the giving-side of this calling that the more each of us gives, the more we need replenishment and refreshment. It is basic and vital that each of us should seek much in and from God. Without that, not only the essential message we have to give, but also the very foundation of our ability to live this rather strange kind of life of a celibate lover to me becomes humanly impossible. How each gears himself to this relationship and what it means in time, prayer, aloneness, reading, thought and so on . . . this I cannot lay down, because it is a personal relationship and development. I can only say, most strongly, neglect this at your peril; it is the life blood of your celibacy. This I cannot spell out; live it and you will know what I mean.

But, the other side is also very deeply important, and here I think we can meet ignorance, fear and even a tilted moral outlook in training and upbringing, which can be destructive and limiting, rather than energising, renewing and releasing for battle-weary and battle-scarred clergy who need all the human and divine support they can get, and all the encouragement to get it, without some terrible cloud of guilt hanging over them when they are human, relax, and revive in the morally acceptable atmosphere of friendship.

All this has to be within the context of regular prayer, single-minded and single-hearted service of God, and a frequent examination of way of life to check that the relationship is not destructive of prayer or God-centredness, or of the pastoral work inherent in the calling. Note too, that such relationship is either between the same sex or opposite sexes, or preferably for any one individual in both directions.

At this point, I do not think I can enlarge more, beyond urging that the bald, shorthand way in which I have skated over very delicate and deep areas of our living should not be taken as a reason for dismissing what I am trying to say.

Think about it, discuss it: for our basic attitude to these matters, and our ability to live out celibacy in a positive way is the only way to help others, and the only way to give the lie to those who are so ready to pounce upon individual example of failure to condemn or dismiss not only a whole way of life but also some very remarkable men and women who are doing much to encourage and promote harmony, service, fulfilment, joy and love among their fellow men and women.

And from that point, I must go on briefly to touch on one or two other practical things. In the first place, to live open to feeling, growth in relationship and the development of love is to face the inevitability of suffering, tension, the necessity for decision-making, the probability of "falling in love" and of others "falling in love" with you. There is also the likelihood of "heart-break", and that not once but many times. None of this is evil, sinful or necessarily destructive. I expect all of it could be all those things.

Secondly, and I think this is very important, one of the teaching roles of a priest counsellor will be to "teach people how to love". This sounds a tall order, and it may also sound very presumptuous. What I am getting at is that over and over again in pastoral work, I have come across young men and women, grown men and women too, who for one reason or another in their psychological make-up or because of problems in the home environment find great difficulty in relating to others. This was especially true in the period I spent as a university chaplain, when the age range was narrower, but I came across the problem both before and after, and still do.

The situation which then faces the priest counsellor is that of being available in the maturing and development of the other person. It is something which needs prayer, patience, reading and talking to those skilled in people, a real interest, a willingness to "use" a lot of time in apparently useless silence, or outpouring etc. It demands the possibility of being available not just as "the priest" but as oneself, who is a priest, so that a relationship can be allowed to grow; for very often the barriers which are up concealing the person "inside" are there because of fear of self-revelation, or inadequacy, of losing personal identity (which is probably an unknown quantity anyhow). There is also fear of being hurt, let down, disliked on deeper knowledge, and so on. To some extent, the role of priest can be that of a "safe" person with whom, perhaps for the first time, a deeper and more trusting relationship can grow. Once a real relationship can be experienced with another it is often that much easier for the "shut-in" to have the confidence to open up towards other relationships.

However, this is a risky business, and the priest needs to be very clear, especially in his attachment to God in prayer and his regular and prolonged facing God alone in silence. For growing friendship can and indeed often should lead along the path in which all the aspects of the human being become emeshed in the one-to-one relationship. Here is danger, but I suggest necessary risk, if the development and the self-giving of the priest is to allow the other to grow in such a way that he or she finds it possible to move on into other one-to-one relationships, enlarging the personal character and so becoming fitted either for the permanent one-to-one of marriage, or a considered election of the single life. What I write is only sketchy, without space to enlarge. It is testing on the priest's character, patience, unselfish love and real desire for the growth of the other, whatever the cost to himself.

Because the material we are working and living with and on is the human being, there must be care, sensitivity, a clear understanding of the possible hurt and the possible development, and the experience knowledge that no one other than God is capable of doing more than poorly in attempting to be "all things to all men". Without God, the healer and source of life, we are unlikely to do much, but if in the Spirit we take seriously the healing element in our ministry, them we must know that far more important than physical healing is the coming together in one of the whole man.

The kind of thing I have been trying fumblingly to put down here is something of a way of life which I have learnt over my own lifetime. The experience of it is an extraordinary mixture; the validity of it's suggestions rests largely on the premise from which everything begins and the goal to which everything tends—God, creator, named in a letter of John as LOVE.

4

PRIEST: LISTENER, COUNSELLOR, HEALER

Rightly, beautifully in the ordination celebration comes the invocation hymn to the Holy Spirit. For us he personifies so much that can be most lovely in the human being. He is the expression of Love who is the unifier, the healer of all that is broken or dishevelled. He is the strong fire cast down upon the earth that we may all be set alight; he is the cool clear water of understanding, who heals through peace. He is the rushing wind who blows the needed changes in us and in the world; and he is the gentle breeze, ruffling the hair of the child of God with a caress more tender than that of any human mother. He is strong and sweet; he is supple and hard as rock.

And so the hands are laid on the head of the ordinary man who is being given by God a different kind of function in His body. This man is filled with the Holy Spirit and is given a work to do for Christ: minister to Christ's body the church by ministering Christ as word and sacrament.

I wonder how many priests-to-be at some point before or at or after ordination opened the Gospel for their meditation and like Jesus himself found the scroll of the prophet Isaiah:

> The spirit of the Lord has been given to me,
> for he has anointed me.
> He has sent me to bring the good news to the poor,
> to proclaim liberty to captives
> and to the blind new sight,
> to set the downtrodden free,
> to proclaim the Lord's year of favour.
> (Luke 4.18;cf.Is.61.1,2.)

Frankly, I think I went round the streets and alleys and tenements of Soho after ordination with this background feeling. I had been sent. This was the place to which I had been sent, and I had the words of eternal life. I set off to change the face of the world. I was different; under my lead, all would be changed, by the power of the Spirit of course, but because I was there. It reminds me in hindsight of an occasion soon after my arrival as chaplain at Oxford when I was approached by a deeply good and committed group of people. I asked them what they were doing in Oxford; they said they were in Oxford to look after the spiritual welfare of the Catholic undergraduates. I said I thought that was what I was supposed to do. Ah yes, they said, but you cannot do it in the way we can do it!

The gloss and glow and charism of ordination is with us like the glow of honeymoon love . . . true, real, important and useful . . . but to be scarred and dirtied and dried up and watered again in the very ordinary life of living. None of us is Christ; each of us has to be "another Christ"; we can only be that if we are putting him forward and not ourselves or our cause. It is Jesus who is the good news to the poor, not my smile and charm; it is Jesus who can give liberty, not I. And so, again in myself, I think I had great hopes that not only Isaiah 61 could apply to me but also Isaiah 11:

> on him the spirit of Yahweh rests,
> a spirit of wisdom and insight,
> a spirit of counsel and power,
> a spirit of knowledge and of the fear of Yahweh . . .
> He does not judge by appearances,
> he gives no verdict on hearsay,
> but judges the wretched with integrity,
> and with equity gives a verdict for the poor of the land.

The struggle I had then and still have now comes most forcibly in trying to realise that without Christ and his Spirit, I can do nothing; with him I can do all things. It is much easier to feel that I can do all things, and he will back me up! Frankly, there is no guarantee of that.

Over and over again, I write, and preach and come back to the fact that Jesus himself spent a long time learning to be man, and it was only after that that he came face to face with himself and evil in the desert, and then came back to teach. It is most interesting that Luke tells us: "Filled with the Holy Spirit, Jesus left the Jordan and was led by the Spirit through the wilderness" (Lk.4.1.). Later he says that after the temptation: "Jesus, with the power of the Spirit in him, returned to Galilee". It was in his preaching and teaching there that he openly read out the Isaiah passage and claimed for himself the fulfilment of the prophecy, a prophecy which he then further drew out in his conversation with those whom John the Baptist sent to him: "Go back and tell John what you hear and see; the blind see again and the lame walk, lepers are cleansed, and the deaf hear, and the dead are raised to life and the Good News is proclaimed to the poor; and happy is the man who does not lose faith in me". (Matt. 11.4)

Where is this leading? To the fact that the priest as follower of Jesus is meant to be follower in a close sense. The classic spiritual writing *The Imitation of Christ* is not at present in the "top ten" spiritually popular books, I imagine, but the following of Christ does demand such an openess to his will and his way that the priest should be closer than imitation, because Christ living in him does the work. Now, to me one aspect of the development of the message through the course of scripture is that Isaiah shows the work of the spirit of Yahweh in Ch. 11 as completely "spiritual". By that I mean that it is wisdom and its outflow of power rather than any physical healing which is put forward. In Ch. 61 it is still almost entirely healing work of the spirit in the non-physical sense. But when it comes to the testimony of John the Baptist the weight seems to be upon the physical manifestation of healing much more than upon the spiritual.

It is true that quite an amount of the text of the Gospel is given to miracles. Physical healing and healing from possession receive much emphasis, but this is nothing compared to the spiritual effect that seems to be an essential outcome of all his miracles. Perhaps the most important piece of the puzzle given to John the Baptist is: "happy is the man who does not lose faith in me". Time and again the lesson of Jesus is one of freeing from sin, commending faith before and continuing faith after the cure. Because, after all, Jesus is concerned with "the whole man", of whom the physical is a very real, immediate and, sometimes in sickness, dominant part. But the mind too is often sick, and one can prey upon the other. The "soul" can be sick, if we want to make a further division in the wholeness of man.

What it is not easy for us to know, though it is sometimes suggested that it is, is the full measure of God's will in suffering. Acceptance of this lack of knowledge is crucial if we are to live a balanced, full life in Christ, who himself suffered and implied in the command that we take up the cross and follow him that each one of us will also suffer. Without excluding the role of the priest as a bringer of physical healing by the power of the Spirit, I want to fill out a bit the more important role of the priest as healer of the whole man.

In discussing this, the first point from my angle and the life that I have been through myself and with others is that suffering has its part to play. I am sure the medical profession should pursue research and work its hardest, along with all the auxiliary services, to relieve pain and to heal. But always the whole person has to be considered, rather than the removal of *this particular illness* at all costs. In some cases physical and even mental handicap can produce in the person concerned a beauty of character and a fineness which is remarkable. We cannot judge in any particular instance what would have happened in character development had the individual not been handicapped, and we can produce instances of others similarly afflicted who seem to have been warped. But over-all the building of the character with or without sickness, the healing . . . that is, the making whole . . . is something with which we ought all to be involved. In this the role of the priest can be most efficacious.

Inevitably I come immediately to the priest himself. So far as training is concerned and the development of his own character and personality he needs to be opened to the gift of the Spirit, especially as shown in Isaiah 11. The more it is accepted that a major role for the priest is counselling and so working with others for wholeness the more the priest must give himself to deeper and more pervasive prayer-life. This is not to exclude the importance of studying and training in techniques and methods which are known and available. Very serious consideration must be given to the relationship between the role of the priest and the realm of the psychologist and psychiatrist. For myself, I really "fell into it", because I was working first in London and then at Oxford with young people, middle-aged and old who seemed to me to be needing the help of the "medico" as much as the help of the "padre". Probably interest had begun with me when I used to spend long sessions in Italy trying to work out with our medical officer the way we could help officers and guardsmen who were being gnawed with fear and becoming quite "bomb-happy". In ordinary life, every priest will have his quota of individuals who have their personal mental, spiritual and psychological problems. I was very lucky in my "fall" because I came to know some excellent and Godly psychiatrists, who developed my understanding and widened the possibility of my being of use. This was especially so in Oxford, where a good number of undergraduates and graduates, to say nothing of senior members, faced psychological problems. I found that I was able to work in with psychiatrists in the area, and was very heartened (to blow my own trumpet) when a committee, which was set up to examine mental breakdown and mental care in the university, asked my help as the person most involved in this field among the student body. But my know-how was based on a certain amount of reading, a considerable amount of listening to and observing psychiatrists at work, and a great deal of living and moving among all ages and kinds of caught-up individuals. It is the kind of competence which any priest can obtain by giving time, patience, interest and love. It is full of failure, as well as being full of the joy of watching a frightened, cut-off being become a real, happy and useful member of society. It is a priestly role of building the body of Christ. It is in some degree the work of each and every priest, on the non-professional scale, the ordinary, every day caring of the pastor. Only a few priests will go through to proper professional qualification; that they should do so is excellent and their role in the more highly trained field of competence is most valuable. But the greater number of clergy are probably far more useful if they work within the limits of their competence and do not try to be amateur psychiatrists.

The limits of competence depend a great deal upon the degree to which the priest can be both fully a man and fully spiritual, which is of course what the whole or holy man means. As Jesus Christ spent a long time and a great degree of mortification or self-discipline in learning to be man, so we have this task as we live day by day. That is why the actual living of the life of prayer combined with the actual living in contact with men, women and children in all kinds of conditions is the best training possible. But the actual living contact with people has to be a real one, and by that I mean that we can be detached from reality by the safeguards which surround us, by the cushioning we have against many of the trials of ordinary life. The effort to remain open and in touch is a demanding one. The possibility of remaining open and becoming more open I do not doubt, but the cost of it is not only in what I describe in the chapter on Open Living, but in the expectation of being laid open by God. I cannot underline sufficiently strongly the value of living deep in God and deep in mankind. There may be other routes to "detached" wisdom through an enclosed life of prayer, and these I would not at all want to minimise, because I have myself felt the benefit of this distilled knowledge and love of God overflowing from within convent and monastery to the visitor from outside. I would strongly press for the validity of such a vocation. But what I am getting at is the idea which is summed up best in the Dominican motto: *"contemplari et contemplata aliis tradere"* . . . contemplating and handing on to others things received in contemplation. This motto is normally, I think, understood to refer principally to the things of God contemplated, whereas the stress I am making would include the vital importance of receiving also into the contemplation the things of people and the world.

From Christ we learn directly how utterly given he was. We can read about him being "spent" on people. Not as it were in second place to the will of his Father but utterly *part* of that will was his love for mankind and therefore his service of mankind. The service was built on love, the two loves which are really a single love . . . of God and man, the second flowing from the first. So that the priest must really love people. He is not seeing them, listening to them, teaching them, learning from them, helping and being helped as a professional duty. It is his way of life, and his life is to be a life of love. It is necessary therefore to be clear that love costs, pains, suffers, endures. It is as much caught up with boredom and weariness as it is with joy and fulfilment.

The life of the counsellor is a draining one. The draining is in the demand which the person asking counsel makes. This is in time, mental alertness, attention, interest and patience as much as in advice given. It can be a drain which is in fact a surfeit; facts, symptoms, moans, despair and every kind of thing are poured out onto the counsellor. They cannot just be allowed to wash off like the proverbial water off the duck's back. They have to be received—I think suffered is the best word—and somehow there has to be the balance of detachment from and commitment to the person, to be involved and yet not involved. The life is draining because there is no clue as to how long an individual person will be there, not in terms of half an hour or an hour—I mean a week, a year, a lifetime. It is inescapable that we may die before a particular person is liberated from whatever it may be that they suffer. Learning to live with "a problem" may be the only teaching which we can offer them; but then we may have to learn to go on living with the need to boost morale and to inject our time and interest and hope . . . it sometimes seems "till death us do part".

The object of the counsellor-priest is to make it possible as far as he can for the person who is being counselled to grow in every way. That is an overall statement. There can be a small point for which a person seeks clarification which will not seem to be very momentous and may be the only occasion this person comes for advice. It may seem to be isolated and useless, with no follow-up and no future knowledge of whether growth has taken place. But no point, however stupid, however small can be fully measured. This in itself is draining. If you do not know the individual, you do not know what is important and what is not. Coldness, abruptness, irritation, a sense that the counsellor "has not got time for me"—these are all attitudes which each of us is liable to show occasionally over a lifetime of meeting people. It is impossible to estimate reaction. I once thought I had really messed up a situation with an Italian law student who came to England, as he thought to study, and found he was meant to be washing dishes for a religious order. He came in tears of frustration to me. I suggested he left there and came to stay with us. No, he could not afford to pay for lodgings. He could come free. No, he would not do that . . . and so it went on. Eventually I hammered my desk, almost literally threw him out of the room saying I could not care less what he did; the offer to come was there—take it or leave it! A few days later he took it! Later still, he came shyly in to see me, he wanted to talk. At once he said how *wonderful* I was! Why? "Because you lost your temper with me; in the religious house no one lost their temper; they were not real—you are real, you are wonderful!" He came back from Italy, a highly successful lawyer, just a short while ago. He still considers this incident changed his whole life. I would not advocate following what I did; I simply illustrate how a single incident can affect a lifetime—for good or evil.

I have always been aware that I cannot be much help, except incidentally, unless I know the person I am being asked to help. I don't like "one-off" situations. But getting to know means creating an atmosphere of welcome, listening, opportunity for opening up. The atmosphere can only grow round you or me, exude from us. Hence the need for the deep interior. This may be helped by technique, but it is deeper than that, and different. The atmosphere must be genuine and so must have the feeling of genuine interest in the person. I know to my cost that it is all too easy to sum a person up on entering a room . . . she's neurotic . . . he's on the make . . . he's a lay-about . . . this family is inadequate.

Clearly, there are different levels of counselling, and for this reason we need to learn about the family or the individual gradually, so that we can assess them. I used to be very impressed by the brothers of the St Vincent de Paul Society with whom I worked for years. Some of them, old men now themselves, were doing a weekly visit to a whole range of families, whom they had known in some cases for more than twenty years. They would tell tales of incompetence, of ill fortune, of families who lived from one accident to another . . . for twenty years, and were still in need. Surely, we sometimes said, we cannot go on helping out. They will never learn to stand on their own feet! Perhaps they won't! There may be cases and situations where helping out, especially financially, seems to be utterly ineffectual. Reason and psychological advice and social service may well go completely against what the brothers may be doing. Jesus said: "The poor you have with you always." (Matt. 26.11) In one sense this is horribly true. England saw and was to some extent horrified by a story on TV called "Cathy come home", which showed the gradual sinking to degradation of a couple who started off with love and high hopes and ended up separated, lowered and despised, with nowhere to go. There are times when the counsellor has to go against social worker, against the common sense of society, and face the inequalities and inadequacies of human beings. We do not know how much God expects from any individual . . . what his or her capacity is. At this level, we may manage to keep afloat a person or a family which the State may through its servants feel does not "deserve" to stay afloat, because it does not make the effort. There may be many arguments to and fro about best approaches and methods; to keep that family afloat may "obstruct" policy at a local government level or appear to prolong an "unnecessary" situation. This may sound over harsh on social services and local government. I hope it is not; I have lived with these problems, have been through the same sense of frustration and hopelessness, have failed people. But sometimes, not always, the priest has more time than the social services, if he is prepared to give it; he is also freer if he so wishes; perhaps he is also more gullible. He may be a fool, or a fool for Christ's sake! Who knows?

But I come back to this very deep and insoluble fact that we none of us know just how much is possible for another person. No matter how far science goes, how good diagnosis is, how understanding our psychology—we are faced every time by an individual creation of God who comes into a common category as *homo sapiens,* but defies rules by being unique. Sadly, it is all too easy for us to classify "cases", to pull out from memory experience in the past, saying to ourselves: "This person is just like Mrs so-and-so." Well, maybe she is *like*—but she *isn't* Mrs so-and-so! The difficulty is to have the time, the patience, the courage, the hope—(and even the cash!)—to persevere where others may leave off.

It is very extraordinary for me to encounter on different occasions over a period of years the kind of relationship which is possible for two individuals, and yet would be unbearable for others. Some of us lay ourselves open to victimisation or domination; some couples can only continue to exist in a state of what would be to me intolerable tension. I have come across marriages where every psychiatrist and social worker has said that only separation or divorce will solve the situation, yet where, with many trials and traumas, the marriage is still intact, the children have grown through it all and the couple are now more mellow, have fewer rows and are no longer a menace to the community but good neighbours.

In other words what I am saying about a certain level of counselling is that it goes beyond sitting and listening. It has to go out to support the person or the couple or the full family. It is not good enough for the priest-counsellor to offer advice in a detached way inside his own house and home. He has also to go out to be present at rows, to sit for long hours in front or back rooms, to stand between and with and even against couples, to help with the children—getting them to bed, getting them up for school in the morning, making sure they have a meal. He may have to go to a mental home with one partner in the middle of the night, or sleep with the children of a family because they have been deserted. There are endless permutations which can be attacked, criticised or commended by official workers or by fellow priests. The criterion is the outcome, as far as it can be traced. And in this I would here put in a plea that the social services, doctors, police and whoever else is involved in helping the general public take seriously the possible assistance of the clergy. (Noting, of course, that they will only do so if we, the clergy, show by our life, openness, interest and willingness to help, that we are of value).

Community building is important and comes in and out of this book. Community can be encouraged to grow especially from the family, and hence originally from the individual. The concentration of this chapter is really on the individual.

The priest can have a part to play in development for the very reason that he is a priest, and being one he is both in and out of the world. It is here that the real test and the real value of his work as counsellor can come. The healing is often something which has to be faced in quite a young person. I can only say that it may be that a priest will come across a family where child-love is clearly missing, where there is emotional starvation. He has to be aware of this and see how he can help to supply for the deficiency both in relating to the parents and in encouraging the child or children in expressing affection . . . and receiving it. This is tricky, dangerous and valuable—all at once.

In some ways the later development is even more tricky. In the teenage period, girls and boys develop at different speeds or even fail to develop depending upon their natural characteristics and the background events and basic situation of their lives. Humanly speaking this is a dicey area in which young people are vulnerable to influence, persuasion for good or evil, hurt and lasting scarring, or good, ordinary development under guidance. Very often, the priest can do most at this time simply by being warm, being smiling, being approachable. He must also be a person who is clearly God-centred and man-orientated. The combination of a prayerful and "worldly" life helps the young person to approach and to open up. But it is often necessary also for the priest to make a judicious probe of friendliness and listening, an invitation to coffee, to a meal, to a drink, to talk . . . possibly about football or girls or boys or work or school or almost anything . . . including the difficult area of "anti-parent" talk. In this it is not easy to maintain integrity and credibility as between priest and young people, and priest and parent/teacher/police.

One of the aspects of counselling which is "dubious" and open to suspicion by any authority including moralists is the need to allow freedom to make mistakes. It is very difficult for any "authority" to be sufficiently open, lenient and wise to sit on the touch-line while the things which are "bad", "unlawful" or "sinful". Yet part of the "magic" of Christ was that he managed to keep this balance, so that his followers were in no doubt of the law, were urged to keep the law, yet were also inspired with the freedom to realise that at certain times, for certain reasons some interpretations of the niceties of the law could be "gone beyond".

With the counsellor trying to do what he can to live a life of prayer, service and love, he knows because of his prayer just how far he can fail and fall. But he is undismayed, in that he also faces God every day in depth and so in an obscure fashion grasps that he is a sinner who is utterly subject to God's loving mercy and forgiveness and demand. So, when he is faced by some other person with an act or habit or attitude which is apparently a denial of relationship with God or man, he can have both a total acceptance of the law of God, and a remarkably patient, understanding, friendly and loving acceptance of the person. That is the idea—though because each of us is imperfect our acceptance, tolerance and ability to bring home the balance of good and evil in the future varies.

However, the more trust is put in God the less anxious the priest is about success or failure. And in this way he is psychologically better able to help the other person forward. His own knowledge of failure is also a help; it is often not only "there but for the grace of God go I", but "there, despite God's grace, I have been, and now by his grace I am moving on and up and out into freedom. Come with me".

It is not an easy process to come to know oneself either in success or failure, though in failure it is harder. But the acceptance of self is vital to truly balanced and liberated growth. By listening and being interested, by growing in intimacy to friendship, and by accepting without condemnation, the counsellor allows a gradual and authentic development to take place. This is not so much an induced development, but a much more natural growth from the present which has suddenly been accepted in perspective . . . to the future which grows from there—liberated. This is a healing process which is dependent upon the life of the priest and the working of the Holy Spirit. Insight and wisdom both need the gift of the Spirit, and the gift *will* be poured out into our hearts—that we must trust. If a person can come to know one other person in depth and in confidence of trust, then the intimacy and friendship and love which can develop in that situation makes other growth throughout the person's character more free. But the counsellor has to live with that trust, to exert and teach discipline, control and patience alongside the openness, freedom and friendship.

All this may seem to be devoted to growth which is only hinting at the spiritual. But much which is directly concerned with prayer and the spiritual life comes in elsewhere in this book. It is important, however, to point out that the balanced development includes all that makes up the human being, and this is why the healing process is integral. The challenge for the priest-counsellor is to remain deep in God and close to living reality in God's people.

5

PRIEST: ALL THINGS TO ALL MEN ALL THE TIME

The inspiration of Vatican II was to open windows, let in fresh air and so, following the same analogy, to raise a certain amount of dust. The object, as with any spring-cleaning, was to get a better look at the treasures in the home, but also to clean up the utensils in daily use and even to discard some of the paraphernalia that any family tends to collect over the years. Again, in the same line, the difficulty with family is to get a common agreement on what is "junk" and should go, and what is really a priceless treasure, an heirloom which is utterly irreplaceable. It is particularly difficult when the doctor has been in and ordered grandad to sit on a newer and better shaped chair because the old one he has always used is making his sciatica worse—once the doctor has gone, grandad is back on the old chair again.

Something of this kind has been happening throughout the church, in the years since Vatican II. It has been exciting and heady for some, definitely gloomy, unnerving and causing insecurity in others. Because it is not just the surface dust that has been cleaned away; some questioning and remodelling and even discarding has gone on in highly sensitive areas. That this should be so was inevitable, given the initial impetus of the council as it set about its work, departing almost immediately from the "safe" agenda put before it to settle its own pattern upon itself. But that development was not liked by all, so that we have to face and live with the situation today of on the one hand those who dismiss Vatican II and all its works as illegitimate, and then a line of variance and acceptance and editing right across the board. Part of the result has been loss of faith in what bishops and priests and theologians are preaching and doing pastorally, a loss of faith in the institutional church;

and for some this has led to loss or rejection of "The Faith" or simply a loss of Faith.

The central issue is this chapter is a much controverted area summed up in the question: What is a priest? And it is this that I want to tackle, though more by a coming together of hints than an intellectual and theological argument. In truth, I could not care less what the answer is to the question if it is in terms of the cerebral and analytical only. Though I do not claim what Paul can claim in I Corinthians 2.1-4, I feel I can take to myself verse 5 (slightly paraphrased): I do this so that your faith will not depend on human philosophy but on the power of God.

The wonderfully fruitful uses of the mind on the knowledge of God and his creation through the study of scripture and through theological development of doctrine stand out as achievements of man's intellectual capability. But like an advertisement there used to be in the London underground for a type of shaving soap, the motto must be "Not too little, and not too much." Where there is no thought, the danger is a slavish adherence to rules and regulations and definitions, without the scope and flexibility and growth which is so fitting to the nature of mankind. Where thought becomes too "rarified" it can isolate itself from the reality of pastoral living, so that an ordinary person coming across pronouncements finds they are "out of this world". Quite generally, then, we need a balance between sophistication and simplicity. Here I am concerned to emphasise one particular application of this.

I have come across a tendency among some clergy to try to tease out "priesthood" when to do this only on an intellectual plane is like trying to pin down "God" within our thought patterns. This cannot be done, or at least if we succeed—then it is the wrong "God" we have entrapped, because we have ourselves been entrapped into thinking we could define him. As we split and divide and sub-divide names, aspects, qualities, perfections we are elaborating rather than simplifying—yet God is so infinitely simple we cannot grasp his immensity.

With priesthood, the danger is that we go about defining

it rather like someone trying to get to the heart of an onion. Gradually we peel off one layer after another, one function after another. We discard this as inessential and that as something shared also by the wider priesthood of the people of God. I have sat in on discussions where gradually every layer is removed until there is nothing at all to distinguish priest from "lay" person. Now, it is necessary not to be woolly or to make claims for the priesthood which in fact are in no way distinctive. It can be very healthy and liberating to grasp much of the very commonness of priesthood shared with all baptised *men and women* who have never been officially ordained by the church. So long as we have minds and are curious and need some reassurance, we will according to our interest or even anxiety want to get to the bottom of questions if we can. But the very search and the failure to find anything much to hold on to has had a traumatic effect on some priests, who seem to have lost all identity and cannot really make out if they are essentially to be "confectors of the sacraments", social workers or contemplative monks.

While not dismissing the question therefore, I am not convinced that the process of elimination, the attempt to get to the core, centre or essence of priesthood actually gets us very far. I know there are those who with St. Thomas the Apostle *need* to grasp a reality—"Unless I see the holes the nails made, I will not believe". (John 20.25). But even having been through that experience, Thomas afterwards had to live by faith . . . there was no continued reassurance. And indeed, the disciples seemed to be able to live a long time with Jesus, and still not to know him (cf. John 14.8–9). I find it rather the same with priesthood, because I see it so closely linked to the priesthood of Jesus, though so utterly different in kind, that I happily admit it does not seem to me easy to say where Christ's priesthood as it were begins and ends, or mine. I was never very happy about theologies of the Mass which specified too sharply the "moment" and almost reduced necessary attendance at Mass to a limited area surrounding the consecration.

Just as the Mass or Eucharist is a continual movement

from start to finish, an unfolding of thought, word, action and communion which cannot, without doing violence to the whole, be split and subdivided—so a priest ordained is to live always as priest, at every moment of day and night. Some particular action may speak more loudly and clearly of his priesthood, but to me, the whole of my being is inextricably bound up with God calling me to be a priest and sealing the call with anointing. It does not worry me, then, that a lay person can do many of the things I do, and probably do them better. What I do, what I am, is probably in a sense made worse as well as better by the laying on of hands. If the Church limits certain actions and use of power, that is also fine by me. It would be true to say that I have a tremendous "thing" about celebrating Mass. The role at the altar and all that spreads out from there has an impact on me and my living which it is very hard to put into words, or to express in any sensible form. If I was told tomorrow that I was suspended from celebrating Mass and other "priestly functions", I would not only be desperately sad at the personal loss, but I would know that so much else of effectiveness would be gone.

Now, this is interesting. I feel that, if there is any effectiveness in me personally, shown and experienced by others in the way I live and the contacts that grow and the relationships, assistances, counselling situations—then that is through the Catholic Church and priesthood. In this, I know, I am very different from some others who come to a position where they can say . . . all that I am doing as a priest I could be doing as a social worker, as a teacher etc., and with more freedom. I personally am forced to say (and delighted too) that anything I do, anything and anybody I touch constructively is because I am a priest of the Catholic Church. If I were not, what would I have to offer other than just myself?

Some would answer that by saying: you would have to offer exactly what you are offering now, including Christ, not just yourself: and with greater scope. Well, I can appreciate that others may see it that way. I simply have to register the fact that I do not. Oddly enough, the "restrictions" of authority over me have a stimulating effect, in so far as they set me to estimating why they are there, what strength they have, whether they are anachronisms or have real meaning, and so on. In other words, rather than taking the attitudes of supine servility to law or of rebellion and getting out, it has always seemed to me that law is an enabler for the spirit and should not be a blight. I have talked of celibacy in Chapter 3, and do not want to start again. But here is an example. For me, celibacy is challenging . . . it challenges the "world" outlook that is overdominated by sex; we are not always good examples of celibate living, but we can stand over against, we can try to be a sign, albeit of contradiction. But beyond this, celibacy personally releases me to live a life which by its availability, openness, variety, movement and irregularity would make me a nightmare husband for any wife. It is hard; I'm not much good at it, but it is a discipline, and discipline there must be in any "given" way of life.

That is why, for instance, priesthood must be with me as my whole way of life, all the time; and its priorities, such as depending upon close relationship with Jesus Christ, demand a discipline which will enable time for this companionship to grow. But when I take time to be alone with Christ, I do not do this just as myself, for I am a priest. I think I have seen this most beautifully put in Archbishop Michael Ramsay's small book *Christian Priesthood Today*. He refers back to Aaron who bore the sign of the people on his breast as he went into the Holy of Holies to pray. So too the priest. Every time then, I am alone with Christ but with "the care of all the churches" on my heart, especially that corner of the church which has in a lavish way been entrusted to me with a cure of souls, in my appointment whether as assistant or parish priest. Someone like Bernanos gives this another angle in his *Diary of a Country Priest* and other writings. Michel Quoist expresses it in his *Prayers of Life*. It is for me as priest to carry the names of those in joy and sorrow to the Lord, to plead for justice in this unjust society, to cry in anger against evil and violence and prejudice, to feel the love of God in myself, when others cannot feel; or to feel the desolation of misunderstanding, indifference and lack of concern when I sit empty before God and only feel his absence.

But then, I need also to go out from that aloneness with the Lord into his busy world. I still go as a priest: other Christians will go as doctors, politicians, workers, mothers, sharing the general priesthood. I go specifically as priest, and as such the world will judge Christ and his church to some extent by me. This may not be a fair judgment, and it is not exclusively the priest who comes under it, because religious and again lay people can easily have said of them "Well, he/she is a Catholic/Christian and look at the way they live". But clearly, if a priest is in essence or function or whatever else being set up by the Church as a leader or animator, he is put as a light on a lampstand and should not be surprised if particularly stringent comments are aimed at his way of life. If I as a priest, living by priesthood, servant of God, church and people, am only concerned with my privacy, my good name, an easy way of life, a pension on retirement—the atmosphere I make around me will give a funny image of the master I am following who had nowhere to lay his head. If I build my reputation and priestly career on the bricks and mortar of more plant, more expenditure, bigger and better fund raising projects for servicing buildings and debts, I must not be surprised if young radicals and others attack me, and—through the figure I cut—the church, for worldliness or materialism or worse. They may contrast me to their image of Christ—or worse they may dismiss him through me.

There has been quite a reaction among many younger clergy and some lay people against excess of building and all the maintenance costs and cares that go with this kind of living. There should be a very stringent analysis of need before new building is done, greater emphasis upon the possibilities of sharing churches and use of secular buildings. Schools, as everyone knows, are tragically under-used, with many boards of governors, caretakers and local authorities making their use more difficult every year, despite mouthing good resolutions to the contrary. Capital expenditure on plant needs to be set in a national and worldwide perspective of poverty and starvation. But this is where the finger comes back to point at the hierarchy and clergy and religious of the church, asking accusingly what kind of lead we are all giving in economy of living, expectations and conditions, in example of "enough is enough", and in a crusade to get away from the acquisitive drive of our present society. All this has to do with use of money, maintenance and our whole outlook. Where we are so taken up with administration and the energy and time and cash which is expended on upkeep that the practical care of people, body and spirit, is relegated to second, third or fourth place on our priority list—then we are (though we may not realise it) in deep spiritual trouble. I would fully go along with the crying concern of all those who are deeply worried that the church is a part of and also a pawn of today's established and acquisitive society. If this is the inner meaning of maintenance, we should not maintain, we should be seen to stand over against these values.

At the same time, maintenance as it has been used in current church discussion has included not only the upkeep of plant but also the "upkeep" of those who are at present among the people of God as members of the church. I find myself opposed to attacks on maintenance in this sense, because I want to be completely realistic about the world in which we live. It is into this world I have been born, enfleshed, in which I live and am to work. It is a world of old and young and middling age groups. It is a world inheriting the past, living (at least in theory) in the present, and moving towards the future. So am I, but my particular bias may be past, present or future! That is my personal bias. But, I am always a priest. And priest is essentially, with Christ, one who has come not to destroy the law and the prophets but to fulfil them.

This is very necessary to remember in any parochial situation, because of the broad spectrum of people involved, or perhaps not involved. My philosophy has been to try to balance. I can find nothing more beautiful than a ninety-year-old, bedridden woman, who lies there day in and day out, loves to receive Communion when the Lord comes to her, but otherwise has the rosary always twined round her fingers. Yet, I receive a quiet thrill to have a letter from an eighty-five year old who says she has read something I have written, that the Holy Spirit seems to have come to life in her and that at her age everything has changed, and she now prays in a new deep way she cannot describe. Unlike some, I find Benediction, the Stations of the Cross, and the Rosary of very real value for many people, and to myself. Even if I did not, unless I had some inner sense that they were positively harmful, I would feel my priest-character left me wide open to sharing these devotions, if asked to do so. But I would not want to foist anything on anyone; rather I would want to respond to people and their needs.

Within this statement, however, comes the aspect of the priest as prophet. He should have vision and should be leading his entrusted people forward on the way of the Lord. So, he should be aware of developments in liturgy and doctrine and pastoral approach, of national and local government projects, of unfulfilled social needs, etc. This means that at the opposite end of the scale from traditionalism he ought to be prepared to stick his neck out, court some unpopularity by stimulating those who would rather be quiescent, and enter into experiment and new initiative . . . in other words be creative. Here his left ear should be as attuned to young people and their insights and enthusiasms as his right ear is to the old ways, inherent fears and traditional bearing of their parents and grandparents.

On the one hand, he must maintain the older, the sick, the conservative, strengthening the depth of their faith in troubled times, while also gently opening them to new ways and ideas and methods. On the other hand, he must encourage young people, leave them freedom, gain their trust, even at expense of his time, pride and patience, while opening to them some of the wisdom of the elders—elders whose real concern and the efforts and sacrifices they have made in the past must not be ignored. He must interpret the fears of widows and senior citizens whose position makes them feel vulnerable.

Very often, it must be the younger priest who is the link because he should have more flexibility and be less set in his ways. His role as interpreter would then include interpreting to the older clergy the feelings and alienations of younger people, while putting a more mature note into the radicalism of youth. And this can be quite a tough assignment, which almost more than any other may mature the younger priest himself, setting a wise head on young shoulders, giving a sense of purpose and role amid the tensions and frustrations of the average parochial set-up.

Karl Rahner is outspoken and even harsh in his directive on the importance of gaining one new young person for Christ, even if two old Christians are lost (cf. *The Shape of the Church to Come,* p.50). I do not want to take issue with him, because basically I am in agreement. My only query is whether in gaining the new-young the old-old need necessarily be lost. So often it is a question of relationship and understanding, personal trust and respect, which enable a move forward without drowning or losing a few on the way. But, there are bound to be different approaches to such matters.

Should a priest have politics? Is it important that he should be a member of a political party, or openly support a particular group? My answer to that would be that there are many different attitudes, and there has been a great deal of discussion down the ages about church and state and in recent times about relationship to politics. To me, it seems that there is today so much involvement in the world, the world in which God became man, that it would be unrealistic and ostrichlike to make the church and its members a cut-out from society in general. If ever there was a way to make the church irrelevant to the world it would be to attempt to divide spheres of influence. Christianity is a way of life, or should be. The life, except for a very few, is lived in the world. Even those who "withdraw" to monasteries or to be hermits still have some minimum of contact at least, and often a wide influence in the locality and beyond. It is not always necessary to be involved in politics to be political. By being and living in a particular fashion there can be a witness, which may itself come into a clash with the ruling party. This has been seen over and over again in the twentieth century, in a whole series of complex issues such as war, religious persecution, apartheid, torture, racial tensions, housing, employment, care of the elderly, anger at the production of arms and their sale and many other areas of concern, which inevitably mean involvement in policy at a local or governmental level.

However, while saying all this, and doing what I can to live in an involved way within the community, I myself remain as far as possible independent, so as to be able to niggle and urge, congratulate and castigate those in power or in opposition. To some this may seem lack of commitment, but I have found it extremely useful to work both with Labour and Tory, to learn from left and right, to assess the current scene without the bias of a party, and then to work in it with vigour. I can quite understand that this is not everyone's method. It is mine, and has led to involvement in local housing disputes, in legal and social service committees and action, and in a working party in the House of Commons, to lay membership of the Press Council, marching in peace demonstrations and so on. I take the independent stand because I am for Christ and for mankind. I realise that in trying to be all things to all men it is possible to end by being nothing to anybody. I accept also that it may be opportune to be aligned with those who are promoting good, justice and peace at a particular time, and that this may lead to finding oneself helping and being helped by all shades and colours of the political spectrum. Risky, foolhardy, plain stupid . . . all those epithets have been thrown at me. So, I can only conclude by saying that in a limited way my stance seems to work. For others there are other ways. But I have always been a kind of jack of all trades, specialist in none, so "independent" suits my style. I can well understand that others are specialists and can concentrate. For them a more active party commitment may be necessary for their work. When thinking not of "the priest" but of lay catholics, far greater political commitment should be urged because they are all too often absent from the corridors of power in politics, trade unions, local government and so on. Their presence is far more essential than the presence of the priest, and it is possibly here in one instance that the difference of roles in the church becomes clearer.

So has all this something to do with priesthood? Yes, I think it has, because as a private individual it would not be so easy or so effective in terms of strength to be a gadfly. But of course, it has its disadvantages too. People like constant support, a reliable backer, someone to be called upon. Independence of mind can blot the copybook, because there is no real security about what action may be taken on what side. Whether it is Bishop, M.P., local government official or even parish councillor there is liable to be a certain unease! I do not advise the pursuit of such a stand in your life if you are seeking preferment! But if you want to get things done, then gradually you can insert yourself into a position where you can catch the eye at different levels of thought, consultation and action . . . and this is worth while. I may be wrong, but as I read Christ, his attitude was of a similar caste, whether it was in regard to church or state, priest, teacher or ruler . . . and I think it is deeply sensitive to the extent and character of priesthood—though I would be hard put to it to specify rigidly, for instance, that a priestly characteristic is clearly political independence.

I suggest that this too can take one from the area of maintenance to mission, supporting the former, but breaking through to the future in the latter. Because it is the cultivation of attitudes, the growth of outlook, the deepening of religious and worldly experience, which will carry each of us beyond the confines of our particular church or chapel into the big, wide spaces of secularisation and alienation from the churches. I am a person who believes strongly in the power of prayer and also of suffering in this arid and suffering world. Those who are "within" need encouragement and stimulation to deepen in whatever way they can their commitment and their closeness to the mind and heart of Christ. They may not be available for stimulation to new action, political or civil awareness. But their spiritual power, together with that of prayerful monks and nuns, backs up the thrust out into the secular. The same is powerfully true of the sick, who are not encouraged sufficiently often or strongly to be a part in action by sharing their suffering and spirit for special issues in which the priests and parish members need as much prayer-power as they can muster.

In many of the issues which are "about" if we are aware, there is no specifically "Christian content". But Christ's breadth of interest is all mankind, all sufferings and deprivations, as well as all joys. It is not only the problems of Christians which come within our possible interest, it is everything from the birth of a Sikh child to the lonely death of an indifferent atheist, from the homelessness of a woman twice married and with a brood of children, no faith, little hope, and insoluble inadequacy to the gentle couple down the road, who are Hindus, but want a blessing on their wedding. And so on, for it is much more in this area, in the ordinary streets and pubs and homes and shops, to say nothing of the factories and buses and magistrates courts that the daily round of maintenance overspills into the casual meeting—which as with Christ at the well in Samaria becomes a seedbed for the gospel.

The world was and is Christ's parish, so it is or should be the priest's—not exclusively his, for there are all the teeming numbers of ordinary people with no pretension to ordination who also do Christ's priestly work. But, under the care of the Church of Christ, I have been commissioned to a lifework following Christ, preaching, caring, living, loving. So, within that width, does it mean much to say cerebrally—this is priestly; that is not? To me the answer is no; it is a waste of time, and could seriously limit the work God could do through me, if I was too pernickety about what is fitting.

Take a particular small but to me significant thing which impinged on my own life for some four years. I was at

Westminster Cathedral. Every Sunday, at 10.30, there was a very beautiful High Mass. Apart from a priest who was on duty in the confessional there was a three line whip on all other clergy to take part in the Office and High Mass in choir dress, and in choir. The same happened at Vespers in the afternoon . . . only rather more sleepily. It got under my skin (literally making me sweat with discomfort!), but I mean in the sense that I felt utterly confined in the priestly function of Eucharist. However, I realised early on that before that Mass there were several others, and others again after it. Thousands came to Mass each Sunday. Both on Sunday and weekdays it was basically true to say the nearest human contact with a priest for the member of the congregation was through the microphone (which frequently failed to work) or at the giving of Communion. The thousands poured in and out. They passed the be-cassocked sacristans who held large dishes for donations. Practically speaking no priest ever came to the back of the Cathedral. From contact and observation I would think that, good and nice as we were in the clergy house, more positive priestly work was done by the patient service of the Josephs and Bills and Teds and Georges of the Cathedral sacristy than was done by us. Very soon, I took to easing my way to the Cathedral door at every opportunity. The "pickings" of the "fish" floating in through those great doors were fantastic in number, in interest, in need. The sacristans did their best, but often they could only smile, be interested and point to the forbidding prospect of ringing the bell at Cathedral clergy house. When I and one or two others began to be about, they began to refer questioners to us. I think that more than anything else, the door of the Cathedral and the side aisles were for me the grace which got me through a very sticky patch of four years . . . and taught me the great value of being about at the back of any church after or before a service, and at other times as well . . . that is, if you want to be priestly in picking up work with shy, lost, inquisitive and often lonely souls. But, I ask you, is that specifically priestly work? You know what my answer would be . . . what is yours?

Out of this to me priestly work, there arise contacts which proliferate, and how are these maintained? They become very time consuming, but what should time be used on? Often interest, excitement and enjoyment, and deep friendship are part of the "reward" for being open to giving time. I instance one person, whom I hope would agree that we are today close friends, close enough to disagree with each other, to work with each other, and to enjoy a meal, a drink or a time on holiday together. This friendship grew out of ten years of instruction during which he was deciding whether or not to become a Catholic. And since then, apart from the joy of friendship and the joy of his sharing in the life of the Church, there has been the immense amount he has done for many people. Or there is the girl who, early in my priestly life, asked if she could share a taxi from a place where I had been giving a talk, and as we bowled along the streets of London flung her arms round my neck and declared her undying love. For the past twenty-five years we have continued in contact, at a rather different level of friendship, and I hope we shall continue through to heaven.

One of the main possibilities of contact is almost inevitably the card or letter, though the phone is also a constant companion. Now, by and large, clergy are a bit notorious for their bad letter writing, some seeming to cultivate a non-answering service. I fancy there is an immediate and lasting value in a very opposite policy of *reply*, often in only a few lines—an encouragement, an assurance of prayer, an asking for prayer, or just a general chat. There are some letters which answer themselves, there are some which come in just too regularly, and there are some which really take a long time to answer. But it is surprising over the years how a policy of answering letters, if possible fairly quickly, pays off in terms of opening up all kinds of different avenues. Here, once again, there is an overlap of maintenance and mission, but I have the sense that the maintenance must be done, the contact with this person who is slightly neurotic, the regular letter to a nun in difficulties, the swift reply to a scrupulous character who only needs a line of assurance to enable him to be a daily communicant. Perhaps even more importantly the card to the lonely, the request for prayers to the sick, the confiding of need, the accepting of need . . . and these things to and from regulars within the "fold". All this is to me a necessary background to a growth of wider contact with all races, colours, creeds and persuasions which, especially overseas, can only be answered spasmodically and infrequently, and yet may prove a kind of life-saver to the person at the other end. Counselling, instruction, friendship, love, opening up of new paths of thought and ways of life . . . all these can happen . . . if that letter is written today, not put off till tomorrow when there is more time. But of course, to answer quickly is to lay oneself open to a quick reply! Here is just another risk. Perhaps it does not matter so much if an ordinary person without commitment except in personal friendship fails to answer; but for a priest to fail is a failure in priesthood, not just in human response.

Of course, there is no getting away from loss of time, considerable cost, and quite a burden (which sometimes seems self-imposed). I have no doubt though as to the general value, and it is worth mentioning also a particular instance at this point. In the priestly work of guiding souls, it seems inevitable that some people within the parish where you live will find it almost impossible to communicate with you, yet can find an outlet and a guiding hand at letter-distance with someone seldom seen, yet trusted. This is just another of the endless flexibilities in peoples' approach to God, and to each other. It is for priests to "enable" others: if we wait till we have time to answer letters, we will probably never have time. What is more, we will probably never have the inclination. Here is a discipline as heavy as a cross, yet light in the light it gives, and the courage, strength and love which God seems to make possible through the most simple and even banal of notes . . . What an odd little point . . . long ago I gave up sending Christmas cards; the load was too heavy. But each year now, I renew often very valuable contacts by keeping "important cards" which carry addresses till after

Christmas, when there is a marathon session of catching up on replies to genuinely interested and caring or needy people.

I said I was really setting out to get at the question of the nature of priesthood. You will now realise that I have given not a definition but a series of thoughts on one aspect after another.

In my understanding this goes some way to answering the question . . . in other words, it is in a sense only possible to come to the core-meaning of priesthood by being nebulous and diffuse, grasping at hints, going off at tangents, rather than coming to centre points. There is only one centre point—Christ. For Christ whom we are following, the one high priest, emptied himself to assume the condition of a slave (Phil. 2.7). So that the object lesson for the priest is that if he tries to seek fulfilment, he will very probably end up feeling pretty desolate and frustrated, shallow and unused. But if he is prepared to be emptied, to become everybody's slave, fulfilment and joy will creep up upon him unawares, and he will live the reality of priesthood, without really knowing what it is, except in knowing the priesthood of Christ Jesus.

6

NEIGHBOURLINESS UNLIMITED

Down the ages, there seem to have been swings of attitude and even theology towards the dimensions of "the Church", the limits which can be tolerated in regard to diversity, the methods of pinpointing "heretics" and dealing with them, and so on. For one such as myself, brought up in the strict regime of not even entering a church building of another Christian denomination, let alone praying with them the Lord's Prayer, events of the past ten years have been dramatic and speedy. It is not hard to understand, therefore, how there are today different voices in the churches—some crying: on, faster, faster, the sky is the limit! others shouting: stop, back, beware, we are betrayed!

It is under a general heading of neighbourliness that I want to consider the priest and his relationships on a wide scale with other people whose own relationship with God, the Church, church teachings, and the Roman Catholic Church in particular, to the law of the land and any moral code, and even to other human beings, may differ hugely from his own.

As a basis and background, I would take the account of Jesus produced by his followers at various degrees of remove from the Man and his times. Fairly continuous scriptural research makes it difficult for the amateur like myself to make statements at all dogmatically about what Christ did or did not say, who wrote what, and so on. Therefore, I merely suggest here that his followers seem often to have been startled by his reaction to the establishment, the law, the approach to other people of other faiths, and indeed to the interpretation of much of life, attitude and relationship between God and man. The sons of thunder, for instance, were not beyond demanding a strong vengeance against those who seemed to take

Christ's name without authority—or so it is reported.

I want then to begin at what I would call the outside and work in. And the outside I would class as the outcast, the person who has for one reason or another become a pariah to society. He is not just of the "wrong caste" as the Samaritans were. He is rather someone who appears socially unacceptable: and indeed he may well be, and may admit the fact . . . but who will come to his rescue? There are limits to social services, limits to unemployment pay and social security benefit, rules made by authority which have been broken and so the person breaking has put himself beyond the benefit pale. Where does the priest stand in day-to-day relationship with men and women, young, middle and old, who are in the "category" of misfits or who drop through the welfare net of society, in or out of the local neighbourhood?

Unless the priest is quite exceptional, I suggest that relationship is costly in time, money, patience, degree of success but also in his good name. Jesus himself is said to have been criticised because he ate with publicans and sinners; his wisdom and goodness were questioned because they said in relation to the woman who washed his feet that if he was any good, he would know who she was. They failed, as we so often fail, to realise that it was *because* he recognised who she was and accepted her service that he proved his goodness, not the other way round.

If I have an outstanding criticism of the Roman Catholic Church, in general and especially in the British Isles, it is this: that the Church, its image and its members are far too respectable. It is not that the members must all be way-out, disreputable, thieves and vagabonds, but it is the admission that some of us are!—that we are a mixed flock, from which the sheep will only finally be sorted from the goats at the end of time. We are not, if we are to be the people of God, those who are always and all the time righteous. Jesus came to call sinners, was numbered among sinners, made his friends and his followers from a wide range of people. It is very nice to talk of a universal church, but the image presented can make a person like Somerset Maugham write of a character who becomes a Roman Catholic—"thereby joining the most exclusive club in the world".

The average student for the priesthood in England is not drawn from very low down in the social strata; though some could certainly be said to be working class in origin, the seminary training and the approach to students by their families once they are in training tends to put them into a middle class bracket, with middle class pretensions and habits of living. Further, the attitude of the people of God to the priest has been, and to some extent still is, to put them into a "class apart". This has not in the past been so completely true of those originating from and trained in Ireland. Their background can be much more of the people, but the censure I raise against the effect of training, especially in instilling a sense of "apartness" from lay people would stand. Sorry, I can imagine many hackles rising. I am not saying by these strictures that all effectiveness is lost—simply that we cripple ourselves.

From there I would have to go on to say that the ordinary presbytery living, "proper dress" of priests, feeling that they are "special" and so on makes an atmosphere which extends through clergy residences, through housekeepers, through the church itself in liturgy and accessibility to a feeling of "properness", an aura of respectability . . . be sure you wipe your feet before you cross the threshold of the presbytery, and don't expect to penetrate beyond the waiting room, unless you are part of an "in" group. Oh yes, this is judgmental, biassed and provocative! I accept that, but I throw it out because we must be honest enough to face criticism of "respectability". We may wish to justify it. We would be foolish to deny it.

I have no desire to make any big issue of clerical dress because the whole thing is so petty; it is very much fiddling while Rome burns. If and when I am criticised within the parish where I live and work because I normally wear anything convenient, I simply say I would rather be known by my nose than by my collar. But oddly enough, I see every reason to wear a collar outside my own particular patch, where I might be known, because contrary to some present-day thinking, I would rather be known in an unknown situation by my collar, if strangers would not recognise my nose! Let us get on with twenty-four-hour-a-day priesthood, and let us have the freedom to relate as best we can.

Though this has nothing immediately to do with the outcasts of society, I think it illustrates the point I am immediately covering if I refer to Lourdes and work there. Every year from 1950, often by God's loving action rather than my planning, I have been to Lourdes on pilgrimage. Normally I have been there simply to work with the sick, though additionally I have been leader of university people, who have also gone there to help. Way back in the early 1960's, when all clerics in Lourdes wore cassocks and collars everywhere, I was close to a wonderfully good Frenchman, who has for years done outstanding work among the sick, especially in loading and unloading at the station and airport. He told me how much he and others wanted me to work with them on their "équipe" or team at the station and airport . . . but, he said, only if you wear ordinary lay clothes like us. From that time on, year in and year out, I have worked alongside them, sweated with them, spent nights tending the sick when stranded at the airport and so on. But this caused marked hostility from bishops who met me there, because I was not dressed in clericals; I really believe they thought I would have done more good dressed in clericals and not so close to the helpers or the sick. Some lay people were scandalised. I recall being hot and sweaty at the airport one day as a pilgrimage from a well-known Catholic public school unloaded. Presently a delightful and aristocratic lady came up to me, and said: "Excuse me, it is Father Hollings isn't it?" I agreed it was, to which she responded: "Has something terrible happened?" (I found being dressed as I was, meant for her I had left the priesthood!) This digression is simply to stress the sadness of a narrow respectability which can creep in unconsciously to colour all our way of living, and so stifle and exclude peripheral people, the poor, misfits and so on.

Back then to the limits of neighbourliness. There is the perennial existence of men of the road, cadgers, inadequate people who week after week "cannot make ends meet". I have no solution for them, except that they are as human as I am, as much children of God as I am, as much and more in need of some kind of support which will bring them through into love and service of God and neighbour. Though some would say that it is hard to find love and response, especially if there is continuous cadging and even direct stealing for instance, I cannot in my heart of hearts ever come to a complete write-off. Admittedly, I get angry, throw people out, threaten never to help again and all kinds of things which individually may seem un-Christlike and hard. But I could also be accused of being soft, because I have been "done" time and again! No doubt this will continue. There must be some balance, and the only balance I have found possible is to try to do more than give some pence at the door. It is the bringing in of a person, the attempt to listen and to understand, and then to do whatever seems most helpful, even though it may not be what is asked for—this has been a deliberate course of action. Undoubtedly, it leads to more or less endless trouble, but over the course of years there are certainly some who gain something. I am not suggesting that they become "reformed characters" or that they suddenly begin to be daily communicants. No, they don't. But they do gain something. Provided they are not diminished by constantly receiving and expecting charity, there is hope that they will gain from kindness, acceptance, and a certain growth of intimacy and friendship. I sometimes wonder whether I do not know more people who might be called "criminal" than those who are known (or thought) to be solid citizens!

There can be no doubt of the personal benefit to a priest in being involved with individuals who know the "seamy side" of life. Whether it has been prostitutes in Soho, vagrants round Westminster, drug addicts and suicide-attempters at Oxford, down-and-outs all the way through, Borstal boys over the years, the man penniless on the Friday with-a-job-to-go-to-on-Monday, or the mother whose bills come all too regularly to my pocket . . . they all have something to give me in human nature. And often, I find, they have all the emergent traits in my own character, making me see myself in them—and because I deeply believe in the relationship I have with Christ, so also though I cannot particularly see Christ in them, I accept that if he relates to me, so too he relates to them. It is also true all the time that the feelings, reactions, passions which rise inside and all too easily burst out, are potentially destructive. They make me want to stop the fools mucking me about, to show them up, to strike them, to shut the door, and never open it again, to despise them and reject them as outcasts, to tell myself not even Christ would tolerate them, so why should I?

I am sure that this way of living can be infuriating to sound, sensible, hard-working people. They not only see no good in such a reaction to the "no-good", they see positive harm. It is a scandal that "the priest" is involved in this way, when he could be doing the proper things like visiting the school, visiting homes, chatting up people, taking communion to the sick. Well, I admit the validity of ALL that; and I maintain that both "demands" need to be met by the priest, if only he can find some way of doing this. And he must always remember moneywise that he is supported by people who often are giving more than they economically should, out of faith and generosity and a desire to help God's poor. Their hard-won earnings are not to be squandered by a priest to help his own righteousness . . . though it may be apparently wasted on certain individuals. The measure of squander or waste is the measure of the priest's closeness to God, and his commitment to the immediate "good" people of God who support him while at the same time not forgetting the forgotten, and allowing them a part of his interest and care. Time and again, he needs to sit before God, and let all the claims fight themselves out in his troubled mind and heart. This is often the essence of prayer—a wrestling with the Lord. There can be deep suffering in making the balance. It is perhaps easier to forget the forgotten and get on with the decent, honest and upright; or for some it may be easier to forget the decent, honest and upright who support financially so well, and to go out after the "fallen".

It may well be that there is in each of us a particular "flair" for one type of work, or ability to get on with one type of person. But for many of us who are pedestrian people, we have to make-do-and-mend on our ability, because there is not enough specialisation, so each of us rather stupidly becomes a jack of all trades. However, there are these areas of need, these people and whole families who fall between various stools of assistance. It is often not enough just to be jack, it is necessary to know the ins and outs of particular situations, collapses etc. The alcoholic and the drug addict may have something in common in addiction, and they can be got together in an addiction unit, but they need a great deal of long-term, independent back-up, and their needs, in my limited experience, are not identical. We can read about addiction, but unless we are taught or pick up from first hand experience the reality of the affliction and possible methods of cure, we can be worse than useless to the individuals who are certainly about in the area of any parish and who need help. They are human, they are sick, their sickness often makes them difficult and not very nice to know. Would not any person committed to love of neighbour, and especially a priest feel called to try to do something? Yet, both these problems in recent years are on the increase, and it might well be that to get in at the curing stage is just too late really and the only effective means is to so contribute to such things as family and community development that the problems have less room to shoot up and spread.

Often, the person afflicted with drink or drugs, or for that matter gambling, is so caught that some form of debt or theft inevitably follows. In this way, the effects of the addiction spread through families and beyond. Looking around, it seems that it has been left to individual initiative to begin many good works for those in distressful captivity, because church and establishment bodies are really too busy building or developing for the comparatively good and comparatively problem-free. It would become a mere catalogue (which is not the object of this exercise) if I were to go into all the areas of deprivation, addiction and need which rear up in most urban areas and are widespread also in more country districts. The list is so long, because I believe strongly in the extensive nature of the work which falls to the priest in his role as priest, even though there may also be other agencies who by statute cover the same fields.

The principle I am wanting to write in here is that there are all levels of work, many of them associated with individuals or groups who apparently have little or no relation to the "visible church" in the locality. They do not darken doors of presbyteries or of churches for religious and worshipping reasons, and they may well be considered lapsed or "married outside" or something. But here there is very great need, while maintaining firm moral principles, to have what I would term a broad and interested and compassionate approach. The language of some Roman documents would seem to miss this point.

For instance, "The Faith" to be accepted "on faith" by the ordinary Roman Catholic is a great gollop of matter. It is not easy to see how the very uneducated or simple receive the message, except by saying that they have "simple faith". The wording, the nuance of meaning, the terms worked upon by the Fathers and the Councils have importance and purpose when you have been trained a little in philosophy and theology, and know a bit more about the history of controversy down the ages. In one way, the whole may be more easily accepted when the philosophical theological explanation is too deep for the state of development of the person concerned. It is not unlike the authoritative voice of the parent speaking firmly and surely to the little child, so that the message is accepted "on trust" or "in faith"; the church has that authority and has always been called "holy mother Church"—and, as with children of human parents, authority is less questioned before maturity, or at least adolescence. The danger is that the leaders of the church like to keep control over children rather than encouraging "too much" discussion, controversy and intellectual freedom.

But the truth is that growth in education, especially at a tertiary level, has opened the doors of many minds. Not through disloyalty or antagonism or evil influence, but through genuine intellectual development leading to questioning, there are those whose deep interest and penetrating search for truth leads them to great problems as it were between reason and faith. Sadly, priests can become dogmatic, defensive or dismissive regarding people with such difficulties. Yet these are often potentially the cream of minds, and where that is not true, they are normally at least using their minds or living through the experience of doubt. One side of the matter is difficulty with doctrine; the other is difficulty with moral teaching, sexual ethics, the legalism of marriage rules and so on. The latter is frequently the area of greatest distress, where it is enormously important that the priest takes the individual as he or she is with all the complications, doubts, disbeliefs, hang-ups, antagonism and sense of lostness. Anyone who has been a priest or counsellor or even just a friend knows the agonising that some people go through on moral questions which immediately impinge on their daily lives. People must not be classed as "cases"; they are real, and individually important to and loved by God.

Once again, an open-shut attitude may well be true and correct in terms of Canon Law. Its acceptance may also be easier to apply in black and white terms, could one say impersonally? But when the pastoral concern is uppermost, when it is understood and lived out that "the sabbath is made for man, not man for the sabbath", or "the letter kills but the spirit quickens"—then a great deal of time, patience, sensitivity, generosity and love have to be called out in each personal problem. In some ways, recovery of belief, re-establishment of a moral position, sorting out of the person in relation to self, God, society and so on are as slow as the movement of a glacier, and not always so steadily in the one direction.

Over and over again, it seems there is just not enough time for all the help and counselling which is demanded. It is easy to understand the temptation to say: That is what the Church lays down, and there is nothing I can do about it. Yet, in marriage cases, as an example, not only is there the immense work now undertaken by advisory councils, but also the care and time given by diocesan tribunals. And still, there is much that is to be lived and worked out on the ground in the parish, where real, personal understanding and friendship and interest between the clergy and those living in the area can build up a community of faith and love in the local church which becomes a reality, though it might set some Canon Lawyers' teeth on edge!

If we take the example of *Humanae Vitae* which has more than any other single Roman Document of recent times caused pain and distress, we know also that it has heartened and strengthened others. But it is unlikely that the general effect has been quite what was intended by its publication. The immediate and violent reaction in some quarters, as we know to our cost in this country, led directly or over a period of time to a real loss in terms of priests who could not in conscience apply the strict ruling, or see any strength in the document's argument or its interpretation. Now some years have passed; some feel *Humanae Vitae* is a dead duck. It is in fact alive and continuing to speak . . . but the message it gives is interpreted and re-interpreted, as well as being accepted, rejected, or ignored. My personal hope is that this will lead to a deeper and newer understanding through intensive study, as the dust of battle clears away. Perhaps one of the side effects has been that its very strictness has led to a new understanding of freedom of thought and the rights of conscience. I make this as a factual observation after some years of pastoral experience. It seems likely too that the 1976 document on *Sexual Ethics* may have the same effect though probably in a less dramatic way. Both have underlined the greater awareness of the distinction between this kind of document and the pastoral approach.

Human beings are human beings are human beings. We are made by God as individuals, with the same basic nature, but with the subtle difference of uniqueness. We can generalise about *homo sapiens*, but we do not really slot neatly into categories. If attempts are made to slot us in, something normally gives. We are faced with principles—and their application. Each year we reach new psychological insights into this fragile yet hardy being who is man. It is to be hoped we are progressing not only in such humanly achieved insights, but also in deeper knowledge of the spiritual so that the whole man can be built up. Man's opening up to a life of deeper knowledge of God should run alongside general education and be strengthened as a living reality in seminary life and priestly training by the practice of prayer. Prayer should come more strongly into child and adult education, through parochial instruction and worship, so that we may live lives which are at the same time more godly and more human. The great danger of what has been happening lately lies in the increase of split thinking, dual living and the sense of a loss of integrity. This is destructive and dehumanising. It must be remedied by the closeness of principle and practice made possible by the Holy Spirit through a deep living in prayer and in the immediate world. For the real world needs truth to live by, shot through with realism, love, unselfishness and self-sacrifice which will take all our powers up in love of God and our fellow men.

The whole area of marriage is central to our human way of life, and in particular to community building. We have only to look round at statistics for separation, divorce, and one-parent families to get some idea of the size of the problem. In a sense the situation needs tackling in at least two directions. The entry into marriage as a lasting, lifetime commitment is much more difficult today in the atmosphere of our society. We are not managing to encourage those about to enter marriage to "train" for the full-time work and life and love as a new and lasting family. Instead there is quite an amount of "release" from the marriage vow because of "lack of due discretion". I quite understand the difficulty when a priest meets a young couple who are fully decided on marriage. However doubtful the priest may be it is hard to convince them that "it won't work". The very high percentage of teenage marriages which today fail is a sad reflection on the preparation and entry to the Sacrament especially when annulment follows through "lack of due discretion". There is very big personality and character growth in the later teens and early twenties—that we know. How does the concept of total and permanent commitment fit in here? How should we today tackle teenage marriage? I don't know the answers. I do know we should be so seriously concerned that we spend more time and energy on training and encouragement to train, as well as discussing continually canonical and moral aspects of the marriage contract. The other direction is what happens when there has been a marriage breakdown, which is totally irreparable, especially when this happens in the mid-twenties with one or more young children involved. The pastoral situation, of course, comes not only in the support of the separated or divorced, in attempted reconciliation and in long counselling sessions, but it also comes in the situation of the divorced and remarried and their relationship with the church, the sacraments, the education of their children and everything which is involved with their "new" life. There are very serious and prickly and deep matters to be explored further at the combined levels of theological, moral, psychological and pastoral. I am not rejecting or belittling what has already been done, but squarely facing the living crisis of the following of Christ today in the married life in the church. This is too serious, too central, too delicate to be dismissed or put off. It must be tackled at all levels. It is not good enough to say that all has been decided, because we are living for the future and there will always be possibilities of development and new insights so long as the world continues in God's plan to develop towards the completion of his kingdom.

Inevitably, discussion and feeling inward and forward in the mind and purpose of Christ takes time, patience and trust. Meanwhile, there is the day to day meeting with tragedy—physical, mental, moral, spiritual. This is the battle-field for the priest, because he has to sit and be available for the attacks of those who are embittered, the tears of those who are estranged and the pleadings of those whose one desire is to serve God, but who find themselves excluded because of a situation which seems to have no right exit. Here, the priest-counsellor needs time and space for prayer and silence and aloneness, if he is to be able to have the balance, depth and compassion which he can only fully learn from God in prayer through the gift of the Spirit.

This need is especially emphasised when the counsellor is himself under considerable pressure. His life may be made difficult and come under pressure, if surroundings and associates are restrictive and unsupportive. He may well also be torn in his mind and conscience when faced by documents like *Humanae Vitae*, or the 1976 one on *Sexual Ethics*, which at first reading look as though they are heading back in thinking, or even by local episcopal attitudes. It would be irresponsible to overstress the pressures, but it is my personal experience that some very good and dedicated men and women feel themselves to be edged towards an unacceptable position in the church. When their hearts and full powers are centred on serving God and their fellow human beings, a certain insensitivity, legalism and distance from reality by those in authority sets up tensions which are not easily reduced. This is the more true if authority is not really approachable at a level of a dialogue which has meaning, warmth, trust and a breadth of intimacy and friendship, which allows room for fluctuations and some flexibility. In this, I have no desire just to carp at those in authority. To some extent, we are all of us bad in our lack of communication. Without laying blame anywhere specifically, we are in urgent need of supportive action, openness in discussing pastoral problems. Within parishes and areas, there is not enough sharing of caring or sharing of attitudes and methods of approach to common problems. If a priest feels himself isolated, using pastoral methods which raise eyebrows, living in a style which is openly criticised, touching people and feeling the effect on them of God's grace, himself deepening in prayer and wonder at the Lord—then the strain of the dichotomy can seem to grow unendurable, especially if there is no one except God to share with. If running through this there is a heavy load of suffering in people, conscience-twisters, insoluble personal marriage problems, and a call for long hours of counselling-listening, then again both in young priesthood and in middle life particularly the strain makes itself felt. One part is crying out to be a good priest, to be loyal and obedient and zealous in carrying out the policy and will of the church as it seems to be expressed. The other part is crying inwardly at the plight of the outcast, the seeming impossibility of living and being Christlike in today's situation and the impersonal quality displayed by the very people (including oneself) who are publicly proclaiming the Good News of Jesus Christ.

The folk hymn asks: When I needed a neighbour were you there? The often quoted passage in St. Matthew 25 gives us one possible question—"When did I see you needy?" . . . but the answer of Jesus Christ really tests our attitude and openness of mind as to where we find him . . . in the hungry, thirsty, the stranger, the naked, in prison. When we walk along the straight and narrow path of righteousness, it is very easy to forget that there are ditches and drains and wrong turnings where real people are . . . good people . . . people of God . . . children of God . . . of whom it could be said: "There but for the grace of God go I" . . . But, if walking that straight and narrow path of righteousness, we become aware of the drains and ditches and wrong turnings, is it not our mission to go out to our neighbour who has "fallen", not necessarily among thieves . . . but "fallen"? And if we do, may we not have to face the odd looks from the "saved" as Jesus did when he ate with publicans and sinners, when he sat with the Samaritan woman at the well? This is the cost of discipleship, which demands neighbourliness. The priest of Jesus Christ must face criticism, ill-repute and antagonism, even (or especially?) from the household of the faith . . . if he is going to follow Christ!

7

COMMUNITY RELATIONS

The Good News of Jesus Christ is to be spread through the people of the world in which we live. His news is of unity and peace. Our reality is disunity in faith or religious expression, and much antagonism between people of different classes and races. If we are asserting that we take seriously the message we are supposed to be spreading, let us look at it and then at present and future possibilities.

All men of good will should be working for unity and peace, no matter whether they are politically or religiously affiliated, or not. But specifically the Christian is given a firm guideline if he follows the prayer of Christ to his Father:

May they all be one.
Father, may they be one in us,
as you are in me, and I am in you,
so that the world may believe
it was you who sent me. (Jn.17.21)

As Christ said elsewhere, there is no good in salt if it loses its savour. He calls us the salt of the earth. He asks for unity so that the world may believe. Unity and peace are hardly the identikit by which to recognise Christianity today. Has the salt lost its savour? Yes, in many areas it has—areas of credibility about desire for unity, peace, justice, loving one another, sharing the goods of the world. Once it was said of his early followers: "See how these Christians love one another." Today we need to go back to the prayer of Christ, and to his statements about love and what love means. These we must take to ourselves, if the preaching of the Good News is to be in any way effective. Christ taught by living, preaching, doing and loving. So must we.

But we will not carry much weight in what we say and do about unity unless we are convinced ourselves that Christ really wanted unity and peace. Looking at ourselves and around, we know it is quite possible for us to say we are following Christ, and at the same time to be at loggerheads with others and even at loggerheads within ourselves. It was indeed time for the Roman Catholic Church, in Vatican II, to recall Christ's prayer and then to re-set the sights of all her members on the definite path of work towards unity. New insights suggested new openness; sharing of ideas, of prayer and even of buildings with other Christians began to be encouraged where previously these had been thought dangerous. But a statement of policy from the Council did not change the ingrained habits of thought and action in a very large portion of all ranks in the Church. Though much has been done, progress has been patchy because not all priests, people or even bishops are equally convinced of the urgency of working actively forward to unity. Too often there is not even hostility—just indifference!

The situation resulting is a patchwork. It is natural, but not encouraging, that individual bishops and priests have led at varying paces. Some have scarcely moved in ten years. Others have taken every opportunity to advance. These latter have sometimes been led by clergy, but where clergy have dragged their feet, the laity have often gone ahead on their own, as encouraged by the document on Ecumenism from Vatican II. This has meant that in some areas, prayer, study and sharing of experience have gradually pulled down long-established and seemingly impregnable barriers. All that has been permitted so far has been achieved; worries have disappeared, and the general feeling is that of frustration: "What are we waiting for?", people in this situation ask, and the temptation for them is to go beyond the churches, because they feel the Institutional Church is marking time needlessly.

Personally speaking, the experience of sharing has been vitalising. It is easy to stay inside one's own tradition and to grow narrower. The insights and traditions of others have constantly reminded me of the vast range of truth and goodness, which is too big to be grasped equally effectively all the time. I know I am richer from sharing. Far from losing the basic tenets of the Faith these are lit up and appear in sharper relief, because in so many cases they are shared, but sometimes with a different emphasis. I know that I am working at a pastoral level and do not take part in theological debate which produces such documents as the "Agreed Statements". Nevertheless, at this local level, the interest, the broadmindedness and the development which have taken place over the years have been very remarkable. In such a practical arrangement as having one of the Southall parish masses in an Anglican church each Sunday, there were some at the beginning who said they would never come, because it was wrong; some others were more mild, saying it did not "feel" right. After a number of years of worship there by the congregation, most of these fears have evaporated—not least because of the obvious growth of community sense in that part of the parish.

Similarly, at this very ordinary local level of workers, shopkeepers, housewives and old age pensioners, there has grown a community feeling between the local churches, leading to a joy in sharing services without fear, and varied other activities which all build up "the whole man". It is clear too that for a considerable number of such people who have been involved over a period, there is very real frustration over non-participation in the Eucharist, with a certain feeling that the theologians and ecclesiastical authorities are going to be out-flanked by the rank and file of the People of God. It could well be said by those in authority that it is necessary to be patient and to be absolutely clear about doctrinal matters. But while this clarification is going on upstairs many different things are going on downstairs. Attending services including the Eucharist with full participation is becoming more common; the denomination of church in which a child is baptised seems of itself less important to people when we now accept as valid the baptism given in other Christian churches. This is especially true in mixed marriages. The marriage ceremony itself may be celebrated in churches of other denominations—"for a good reason". But it is difficult to arrive at the definition of such a reason other than the wishes of the couple who are to be married . . . and the rigmarole of papers involved sometimes seems out of touch with the reality of the situation.

In regard to marriage, it is to be hoped that the need to obtain a dispensation for a mixed marriage will soon be removed. Already the disappearance of the demand for a promise on the baptism and upbringing of children by the non-Roman Catholic party is a slight advance. The logical ecumenical development will be the future omission of such requirements as a dispensation to marry a non-Catholic or for marriage in another Christian church before a minister other than a Roman Catholic priest.

But there is still the central stumbling block which exists particularly in a "two church" marriage, that is when two Christians who are both zealous in their own denomination become "two in one flesh". With the acceptance of the baptised state of the non-Catholic, with the two entering the sacrament of marriage, and so together making the sacrament (albeit at present with a dispensation to do so), there comes the deadlock of the Eucharist. They may, if they wish, exchange their promises during a Nuptial mass—but at present they are not allowed by the ruling of the Roman Catholic authorities to receive the sacrament of Holy Communion together, unless the non-Catholic first submits to reception into the Roman Catholic Church.

At this point I find difficulty in the seeming lack of the reality in the "multiple voices" of theology, dogmatic, moral and pastoral. My concern is that in the attempt to be verbally precise and in every way theologically correct, with a view to ensuring the unadulterated handing down of the Church's teaching, we may become pharisaical, because we bind insupportable burdens. These burdens may well seem theologically logical, but at another level, that of two sincerely and deeply Christian people, they can be very destructive. Such a couple are earnestly seeking God, loving and cherishing each other and their family, striving against the erosions of modern society. In many cases I know, they simply by-pass the provisions of the Church, believing after full thought and discussion and the joy and struggle of living as man and wife that the Lord understands. I remember an illustration of this which in expression underlined both the sadness of the problem itself and the attitude which can rise from it. At question time after I'd given a talk on Ecumenism late in 1975 near the south coast of England one man stood up to speak on the experience of "two church" marriage in his own case. He told of his happy married life, with the great sadness that his wife and he were not able to go to Holy Communion together in their local church. But he said, they were more fortunate than some: living on the south coast, they periodically slipped across the Channel to France, and had a "dirty weekend" there—going to mass and sharing Holy Communion!

This practice of inter-communion is growing, as anyone will know who listens and observes—and not only in a situation like the "two church" marriage. For instance, a bishop of the Church of England talking about these matters, told me how he regularly goes to France and stays in a certain abbey, and is ordinarily asked to concelebrate Mass there. That this kind of action and reaction to the rule of the Church is taking place must be well known. It could be easy to dismiss it as a few "way out" people being disobedient and thereby upsetting the whole ecumenical growth by trying to move too quickly. On the other hand, I have heard more and more people from such situations and others of equal immediacy suggest that it may now be the rules which are insupportable and retarding growth in the one life that they are given by God to live.

The danger of double-living and double-thinking can both jeopardise people and bring the Church itself into disrepute as being irrelevant, out of touch with reality, and even lacking in integrity. These are hard accusations, but they are being made more widely all the time, so that there is growing up a "parallel church" made up of those who maintain strong allegiance and practice within the body of their own denominational church, while at the same time they by-pass certain official rules. They are not wanting to give up "practising" their religion. Indeed they break the rules *because* they want to practice, and often they are doing so in the context of the local community, their own family unity and the development of their children in the knowledge, love and service of God.

This situation puts the priest in an invidious position because he has the close contact with the "care of souls" entrusted to him by the Church, and yet he can come to feel the tension between the letter of the law and the spirit. It is fairly easy to hide behind the law in complete orthodoxy, and the further one is removed from the day to day contact with a real couple who are immediately involved in agonising decisions, the easier it is to carry through the law. But the priest of Jesus Christ, if he has a real function to be on the streets and in the homes as Jesus was, cannot escape entering situations where pastorally he may be far more liberal and encouraging than the letter of the law could possibly indicate.

From this kind of living, I have learnt to meet situations of crisis with as much love and individual care as possible, praying for guidance from the Spirit, where the law is "insupportable" and so understanding as crude reality the phrase of St Paul: "He is the one who has given us the qualifications to be administrators of this new covenant, which is not a covenant of written letters, but of the Spirit: the written letters bring death, but the Spirit gives life." (2.Cor.3.6). It is a lonely area to move in, because doing what is pastorally right on one's own judgment is liable to bring condemnation from those who are more "correct" in their approach. One is seen as not being totally trustworthy or orthodox. If the whole desire of one's life is to serve God and his people within the body of the Church, the strain of living precariously, frowned upon, "unorthodox" can be very wearing.

I am writing this not to cause aggravation but to stress the position in which many priests and lay people find themselves. The situation is real and immediate. The reaction to it is ambivalent, both from the lower end . . . priest and people . . . and from the higher end . . . priest, bishop and the central legislature. The one thing we must not do is to ignore the tensions, hoping they will go away. It is more likely that some priests and many people will go away, if ignoring or loftily "passing off" the problem is the accepted attitude "upstairs".

This tension problem is also much more widespread and is not confined to ecumenical matters. But it is especially important in ecumenism, because here the Church, and her local leaders, seem to be saying one thing . . . let's all work towards unity . . . and doing another . . . either by doing nothing sufficiently brave to remove irritations, such as dispensations, or by seeming to re-iterate in fear much of the unnecessary narrowness of the past, constantly looking back in case they upset "the faithful". The Church's declared goal is full unity—not tinkering about. Many of the faithful pray often for a stronger, more spirit-filled lead, because they sense the vision of the future of unity together and in some places they are experiencing almost all of what this feels like.

Though we are living today in a very centralised society, both in church and state there are rumblings against this bureaucratic and depersonalised system. To build a local community is highly desirable. It is not easy. To build it in terms of God and Christ demands common understanding, worship and work in the locality, for common ends, not denominational church membership. In the small compass of a local community, differences are underlined by the very smallness of numbers. Yet this situation can also be the ideal seedbed for growing together, because the local community has deep ties, a knowledge of each other and, apart from the occasional feud, the day-by-day friendly living in close proximity.

This discussion of internal Christian divisions and efforts to come together in unity highlights the greater difficulty there may be in reaching common understanding and friendship with those who belong to other faiths. Being neighbours physically is not enough to make neighbourly relationship. We choose our friends; our neighbours come upon us, or we upon them, normally because of work or the decision to live in a particular place. From there onwards, much depends upon the attitude of mind and openness to others. A personal illustration is my own relationship with Jewish people. In young days, I was uninterested and cannot remember having any attitude towards Jews. War service took me to live among Jews and Arabs and was also responsible for increasing my general interest in other people. Here I reflect directly on the way in which living among, reading about and getting to know Jews and Judaism began a rich vein of development in my life. This has led on to work for better relationship between Christians and Jews especially through membership of the Executive of the Council of Christians and Jews in England.

As Christians we have a wonderful advantage in discussion and prayer with members of the Jewish Faith, because we are sprung from the same roots, worshipping the God of Abraham, Isaac and Jacob. Jesus himself was naturally steeped in Judaism, worshipping in the synagogue and temple, quoting constantly from the Law and the Prophets. We tend to forget or ignore the fact that the same Law and Prophets have been in assiduous and continual use among the Jews ever since then, while we often read or sing the Psalms and listen to lessons from the "Old Testament", as we call those parts of scripture. To me it is a moving and thrilling spiritual experience of unity in prayer and belief—as far as this is possible—when I am in an assembly of Jews. I can never forget Jesus's life and prayer; I can never forget the early Christians in Jerusalem and elsewhere still going to the synagogue as well as worshipping in their homes. Sadly, history tells us of antagonism, killings, wars and hatred between Christians and Jews. Some of us may have felt the antagonism at times in our own country; very many of us have lived through the Hitler persecution. As Christians we should play a special part in working to dispel hatred and to build understanding and love between ourselves and Jewish people.

The Council of Christians and Jews is the main "religious" body working at a local and international level to aid this understanding. Unfortunately, only a small number of Roman Catholics are committed to work with the Council. I hope more and more will become involved, and so benefit themselves spiritually and culturally, while sharing our own insights, and together working for justice and peace in the world.

Jews and Christians are at variance over the person and nature of Jesus Christ. Therefore, some Christians find it logically easier, some emotionally more difficult to develop a relationship with the Jews than with those faiths which do not have a Judaic background. It is easier, because of our common religious inheritance, more difficult because of traditional blame for the death of Christ and a sense that the Jewish people should have recognised Christ. But today both of these last points should be dismissed as not valid or relevant to our situation and understanding. We ourselves know only too well that we cannot on many occasions even persuade members of our own "flock" to continue to believe in Jesus, let alone preach his Good News in such a way that all who do not yet believe in him come crowding to recognise him. We must encourage ourselves to greater interest in Judaism and share more with Jewish people. If we feel their faith and witness their practice, we shall grow gradually to change our often inbred attitude of condemnation, and even of despising, to admiration and love.

When we turn to look at relationship beyond the Judaeo-Christian, we enter an experience many have never encountered personally, though with mass media and immigration combined there is sometimes a kind of vicarious experience which seems slanted to antagonism. Though many may not have lived among those from countries other than England, Scotland, Wales and Ireland, today's cities are almost all multi-cultural. The cultures are very varied; I am not now only talking about "coloured" immigrants, as we have tended in England to call those who do not belong to the "pink and white" types such as I am. Particularly with the Common Market and with the new mobility of world populations, by no means every immigrant is recognisable because of a darker skin. Such is the great variety of peoples classified under the general but somewhat misleading title of "immigrant", I must here limit what I say to those who are basically of ethnic origin from Asia, Africa and the West Indies. Most are distinguishable in "white" England as "black", "brown", "yellow" and so on. Many Africans and West Indians are basically Christian, whereas the vast majority of Asians are not. These are generalisations but to me useful ones, because anyone beginning to live in a multi-cultural society needs the sensitivity to realise ethnic differences among people, especially those originating from vast continents. For instance, there is a horrid way of classifying all who come from the Indian sub-continent and Sri Lanka as "Paki", which of course they are not! This is a derogatory term itself for those from Pakistan—and also a slighting ignorance for those of other countries. Each race meeting another has a tendency to feel "they all look the same", not realising that each race experiences the same difficulty to begin with; it is as hard for a black African or West Indian to see difference between white people as it is the other way round. Only by getting to know each other can it be possible for us to begin to recognise and appreciate each other.

It is natural in man to have fear of the unknown. The degree varies, but the fear of the unknown is not just of things and situations but of people. I can only write as an Englishman, but a reader of another country should translate to local experience. We should not deceive ourselves.

In most if not all human beings, whether from biological make-up, environmental background or any other reason, there exists a deep down fear of the unknown and prejudice against the "foreigner"! Writing in England, I know that for centuries, despite continuous immigration, there has developed a broadly "national" or insular mind within these islands, which can be pilloried by citing such extreme expressions as "Wogs start at Calais". For many of us even Europe is foreign, a place "abroad" to go to for a holiday; anti-Common Market feeling is partly a sign of this attitude. The attitude lies not far below the surface and it can go very deep. Terms like "Frogs", "Eyties", "Wops", "Krauts" and "Dagos" are not just nicknames, but often express heartfelt contempt and dislike. Interestingly those who become established, especially Scots and Irish, become defensive of England as their homeland against other "foreigners" who come there, as defensive as the Englishman born and bred. Deep down, as a legacy of colonialism and empire, many in the islands have lived with an almost unconscious sense of superiority over black, brown and yellow. Somehow no one was quite equal to us and we came to consider "coloured" people as "un-civilised" or even as more animal than human. Where worse elements have not existed, there has often been, even among missionaries, a kind of paternalism and class distinction which has maintained a different standard of living between the missionary and the native, and some-times hindered the development of an indigenous clergy and sisterhood because of the difficulties of shared living. If there is any attitude which cuts across the Christ-given command: "love one another as I have loved you", then we need to tackle it, whether it is fear, antagonism, desire to despise or anything else. Whatever a man, woman or child looks like they are all part of the family. (If we move out into other worlds and we discover other "human beings" who have our spiritual and intellectual make-up, but do not look like us, then we will have the task of accommodating our thoughts and feeling to them. It may surely be even more difficult to come to like an intelligent lizard or insect-like being as equal—yet so we should, if we realise them to be also "children of God").

At what point in Christ's own living and teaching, or at what point of historical development, the basic under-standing of the equality of man emerged I am not scholar enough to posit. Suffice it to say that the Old Testament teaching was narrow and nationalistic, tribal is perhaps one description, despite an innate sense of the universality of God's love. It could be said of Christ that his attitude was frequently exclusive—preaching to Israel rather than beyond. But in both Old and New Testaments there are bright flashes of breadth and depth—Ruth, some Isaiah, Jesus and the Samaritan woman, the centurion, and the charge Jesus gave of preaching the Good News to every creature. Most of all there is the command to love one another, which seems limitless—without distinction of colour or class. Early in the history of the young Church, there was Peter's vision of the basket of strange creatures let down from heaven and his subsequent sense that "anybody of any nationality who fears God and does what is right is acceptable to him" (Acts 10.35). There was also Paul's openness to those who "have been called, whether Jews or Greeks" (I Cor.1.25). If these lines and others are correct interpretations of the "mind which is in Christ Jesus" (cf.Phil. 2), then the basic and essential Christian attitude is and must always be that all men, women and children are God's creation, that they are all equal in his sight and in his love; hence they should also be equal in ours. Whatever our likes and dislikes, inhibitions, subconscious motivations and so on, our following of Christ demands that we accept all human beings as our brothers and sisters in Christ. Further there is the demand that we go out of our way to welcome them in the name of the Lord, especially if they are strangers or downtrodden or poor.

Maybe this is a counsel of perfection. It is no worse for that. The problem and difficulty lies in our response. We know that we edit this response and sometimes even pretend not to hear the call. It is all very well to lay down the counsel and say that each and every Christian should love all mankind, but in fact we do not. Therefore, while underlining heavily the call of Christ to his followers, we must recognise the response in ourselves for what it is, good, bad or indifferent, and hope to move forward in our lives towards perfection, starting from where we are now. At the same time each of us must beware that we do not claim to be Christian and to portray the attitude of Christ, when we are still far removed from such an ideal.

From some of the roots of prejudice and paternalism there has grown a kind of historical memory in which we can see ourselves as always on the giving end of religion, education, civilising influence, culture—and the native inhabitants of less developed lands to which we have gone, as receivers of our bounty, know-how and service. Of course we have actually gained a great deal from them, but in our perspective as colonisers we think "they" always remain indebted to "us", so that we expect gratitude from them and recognition of what we have done for the more "backward" areas of the world. Now the collective memories of those who have lived under our colonial rule can be very different, because of the varied histories of conquest and development in lands inhabited by black, brown and yellow peoples. All the same there is the general basic historical memory that the white man came as an invader, a conqueror, a master ruler and exploiter. In intelligent and educated minds there rests the knowledge that we have taken out more than we put in, that what we have done has fundamentally been for self-interest and not for the country concerned, despite the incidental benefits of development and education. None of these benefits has ever outweighed exploitation—and exploitation continues as I write. Far from the black or brown member of a new nation feeling much in our debt, the more aware among them feel the debt to be heavily on our side. It is possible to overstress this aspect of the matter, but at the same time we should accept that there are totally different interpretations of the same historical facts, and we should attempt to understand—or all dialogue will fail before it begins. A very powerful re-education will be necessary to bring the average white man, woman or child of whatever class, trade, profession or political affiliation to what for many will be a radical re-orientation of thought: that we are currently maintaining our high standard of living through a world-wide economic system which assumes the continued exploitation of the less developed countries. The gap between "them" and "us" grows all the time.

On a world scale, we need to study and become aware of the immense problems in the developing areas, problems often inherited from our colonial rule, and now continued by the very way in which we "in the West" expect to live.

This will come home to us in a very hard way, if we begin to understand and through understanding begin to accept our responsibility in Christian terms for loving all mankind. The hardness will be in realising that there cannot be any solution sufficiently radical and large scale which will not involve in its process the relative lowering of our own standard of living. All Christians urgently need to face the widening gap of riches and poverty, which is not always very far from our front door, but is especially destructive in the developing countries. For priests who are expected to be preachers of equality, justice and care for the poor, the world picture should require of us a re-dedication to a life of sufficiency without indulgence, and openness to local need. With this should go concern and growing knowledge of the size and immediacy of the problem, so that we can become active in every way possible, and at the same time activate others.

From the world viewpoint in terms of Christianity's influence, we should realise the growing numerical strength of Asia, Africa, the Caribbean and Latin America. Peoples of these countries and continents are projected statistically as comprising well over fifty per cent of all Christians by the year 2000. Already the presence of the "third church" has been felt in the recent Synod of Bishops in Rome . . . Europe seeming to some to be growing smaller, older and more tired in terms of ideas, vitality and influence. When we live to some degree "parochially", we are not immediately aware of "the signs of the times". But it is our duty to read these signs, and they point directly to the continued spread of people travelling across the world, forming groups within the society of countries other than the one where they were born. The test for Christians is their ability, willingness and understanding to work strenuously for the development of friendliness, warmth and sharing in the multi-cultural societies which are already forming. It is for Christians to set the example by sharing, by listening, by teaching and by learning. We must not simply do nothing, hoping everything will "remain the same". Vatican II re-discovered the Church as the pilgrim

People of God. Our pilgrimage includes mixing, sharing, going forward in unity.

But going forward in unity does not mean absorption of one culture by another. There is a beauty in our variety of colour and culture, there is an awful soul-less gloom in the attempt to level everyone to a common uniformity with no difference between sexes, no variety in religious expression, no multi-cultural contribution. If we talk about integration, we must be sure we do not mean absorption. As Christians, we have the wonderful example of the work of God, indeed not only of his work but of his very being. The Trinity is somehow one and three. I don't understand this, but I can appreciate that love is somehow expressed to us as one, and yet in Father, Son and Holy Spirit there is a different aspect of the same love. As human beings, our common humanity is one, but there are wonderful (and sometimes awful) expressions of this humanity. Common humanity is not made better or more beautiful by being uniform. Indeed it is necessary for our individual development to fullness that we should be stretched to grow in appreciation of ideas and cultures different from our own. Unfortunately, in the security and laziness of our nature, it is easier to live without being expanded, which inevitably makes us inward-looking and unappreciative of others.

As regards relationship between those of different colours and creeds in this country, most urban areas are already living multi-culturally, whether they acknowledge this or not. Country districts are less likely to have more than the occasional "immigrant". The fact is however that every forecast of new arrivals or births among those already here projects greater numbers and therefore greater spread of this multi-cultural situation in the future. We would be unprofitable servants if we did not open ourselves to live and grow in such a future. Therefore, I hope no one will think what I am saying here is irrelevant to themselves because there is no immediate problem. We *must* work towards the future, training ourselves for the times and situations which lie ahead.

Whole books have been and will be written about the

area of community relations which covers people of different races and religions. I have only two additional things I want to underline here. I do this because I have been fortunate enough to be inter-racially involved for a number of years.

The first heading is common to all indigenous people when strangers to their country come among them. Though there are deep threads of fear and distrust in us, mankind is really very loving, welcoming and caring. All of us should cultivate the attitudes which go out to greet the newcomer, to make life pleasant and friendly for them . . . and to involve them in the community round about. But we will not be able to do this, unless we ourselves are really a part of the community. Quite a lot of difficulty in mixing and developing friendliness is there because we ourselves have not mixed or become friendly even with those next door. If we do not ourselves have community, we cannot welcome others to our community. But if we are part, then having them to mingle with us teaches all concerned, and the experience is rich and rewarding. However, it is really for the indigenous people to open themselves and their homes and community to the "stranger". The strangers may feel shy and may well be slow to come forward. There are language barriers, apparent colour barriers and so on. The initiative is with us . . . and that is the rub, when we do not feel especially open or welcoming! A little willpower and some positive action like inviting a family in to have a cup of tea begins a breakthrough in knowledge and acceptance. It is important that in this there is no patronising attitude. We have as much to learn and receive from them as they have from us.

Secondly, there is the whole religious dimension. Not invariably but very often in my experience, people from other countries, especially the developing ones, are far more religiously minded than we are in our ultra-materialistic and comparatively rich society. This is a great challenge to us, since we are meant to preach Christ and Him crucified, to live lives of prayer and dedication, to be examples of love and care. It seems true that on the whole, the established Christian churches are not inspiring for newcomers. Frequently we lack warmth and welcome, our services are uninspired, our message is flat and without bite or enthusiasm. Yet we really believe we have the words of eternal life . . . don't we? So we must by our life-style, our prayer and example make available the light of Christ which is never put out, but can be hidden under the bed!

Having lived now for six years in Southall, where the majority of Asians are Sikhs, with a smattering of Hindus and Muslims, I have come into frequent and valuable relationship. That does not mean it is easy to bridge the gap of reserve, shyness and language. But there is time, if we can make ourselves available to be about, to listen, to pray with people of different faiths, to be appreciative of them and what they have to offer. Often, we can be of service in social welfare matters, in education, in family troubles, in housing. But most of all I have found the wonderful response to a life of prayer. There is no substitute for the Christ whom we carry with us. If he becomes luminous through us, we are doing our job and spreading his love. And if others of different colours and creeds catch on to this, then they will be more with us and it will not be so much a "we" and "they" situation . . . WE will gradually all come to be one as and how He wills it . . . but this will take time and conscious effort, perseverance and hope.

8

DEVELOPING PARISH COMMUNITY

I lived in Soho as the third junior priest in the parish, learning my way round priestly and parochial life in the very centre of London. The move to Westminster made me number seventeen in the batting order, still in central London, but also at the centre of the Catholic Church in England. Moving to university life was coming away from the centre to the "fringe" in the minds of many bishops and priests. Coming to Southall was coming back to parochial life, but with this difference that now I was parish priest and in a position to do what I thought should be done.

Much of the thinking and development which became crystalised in Vatican II was by this time available to parishes. Part of this could change the idea of parish priest radically, leaving him no longer as autocrat running his parish according to his mind, but rather trying to work as part of a team, giving equality to more junior clergy, welcoming religious and lay participation. The balance as I saw it was between the old use of power to help to get things moving when people reacted against anything new, and stimulating others to realise the part they should be playing alongside myself in the whole work of the parish.

The background from which I came was more open than Southall. By that I mean that in liturgy we had gone ahead with the reforms and innovations, even to the extent of such minor though apparently "crisis" customs of receiving Holy Communion in the hand. I was fully committed to the voice of Vatican II, there had been experience of freedom in the Oxford chaplaincy set-up, but in the parish I needed to learn about parochial living. Undergraduates and graduates had done a lot of planning and suggesting. By and large, there had been informality, knowing each other on christian name terms, people dropping in casually. My first experience of Southall was not unlike the arrival at

Soho twenty years earlier. The front door was locked, I ate my first visiting meal alone with the parish priest in a large dining room. No parishioner seemed to penetrate beyond the small waiting-rooms on either side of the front door.

To some extent I began to change this immediately, simply by living a different life-style. But at the same time, because there was both a priest already in St. Anselm's doing very good work indeed and a parish council with a lay chairman already in existence, there was an immediate opportunity to try to restrain myself and wait around in a looking and listening attitude. We decided that we would do just that for a month while we got to know each other, and while I tried to get to know what was already going on. Prior to coming, from what I had heard or read, I had a picture of the presence of immigrants in the local community, of various factories, British Rail and London Airport, of most people being on shift work. From discussion while visiting, it became clear that if it were possible, it would be a very good thing to have some religious sisters in the parish, with a specific mission among other general calls—to form groups to teach the children not in Catholic schools of whom there seemed to be many, to work for and with the older people and the poorer or more in need. There was the whole area of community relations, not only among people of varying ethnic origins but also among the churches and with the civic authorities. Not knowing quite what to do about finding Sisters, I had one of those strange and immediate interventions of God. I was at an end of term college party in Oxford when I met a nun I had known before. I asked her what she was doing, and she said—setting up a small community to work in a parish. So I asked her where and she said in Acton, to which I replied by asking—"Why not Southall?" She said it was too late as the house in Acton was arranged. I went on my way sad at missing such a chance and rather mingling a telling-off to God with a request for help. The next day another sister rang from London, asked if I had really meant what I said about Southall, and told me that the Acton house had fallen through so what would they be wanted to do if they came? It was out of this conversation that we pre-viewed the needs of the parish, and also out of this that we were able in September to begin with four sisters as part of our attempt to start work as a team. (More detail on this is given in Appendix 1.)

There was no doubt in my mind, that we should try some sort of team work. The Sisters all came for that purpose and for the parish of St. Anselm's, Southall, whatever that might mean in terms of actual work. They had to look round with us two priests and see what seemed to be necessary. The Chairman of the Parish Council, though good, was too priest-centred to be able to take much part in the original discussion. Probably I was largely to blame for this failure in co-responsibility. Previously I had had little experience of how to bring this sort of person into active sharing of ideas.

We decided after a month to open up the situation by issuing a questionnaire listing possible kinds of involvement in sharing parish life—what areas of work were there or could be there. All were given forms to be filled in and handed back during Mass one Sunday; the point of departure for filling the forms was name, address, age, sex. After that, everything connected with liturgy—serving, singing, reading, collecting, altar-linen-laundry, church cleaning, offertory promises. Then questions about house masses, family and discussion groups, visiting sick and helping them and the elderly. Youth featured strongly with formation of a choir, guitar playing, club activities. There were questions about helping in the community with general welfare, community and race relations, social activities, housing, ecumenical activities.

This was our first attempt to use the liturgy for any kind of community work. There was some unease but remarkably little. Almost all listened to our talk after the Gospel about service and most filled in their forms. A few of course spoiled their papers. Carrying the completed forms to the altar with the offerings for the Mass seemed to make real sense.

The piles of forms which resulted were treated in a very

thorough and competent way, almost entirely by lay
people. A large team was organised for collating. It took a
long while to do. When we were ready we opened the
rectory doors and had the place flooded with parishioners
for a fortnight, as we asked volunteers from each section to
report to an organiser, discuss day, time and place for a
possible future meeting. Naturally, there was neither a full
turn-out for filling-in the questionnaire nor was there a
hundred per cent success in the follow-up which came after
the initial response. But for many it was the first time they
had been asked to do something of this kind by their priests.
It was certainly the first time they had been inside the
rectory in an informal way. Many found themselves sitting
beside the woman they had been next to often in Church
without even saying "hello!"; or talking to the man they
passed each morning on the way to work, neither realising
the other was a Catholic. Once they had got thoroughly
sorted out, they began to meet in groups, in their own
homes, the rectory or across the road with the sisters.

The next move was to develop house-masses. These
were not unknown in the parish already, but they were by
no means widespread. The initial decision we made was to
try to make sure that they would be neighbourhood masses
rather than a few friends of the host-family being collected
from all round London. To help with this, the parish was
roughly divided into small street or neighbourhood
groupings and an invitation was made to a particular family
in each neighbourhood to be the first host. The difficulties
were immediate though by no means universally the same.
The hosts were chosen because it was thought they would
not have hang-ups about other families coming into their
homes. This is a very real problem for some. The home is
very private. It is different asking your relations or friends
in, but strangers! There is an awful sense of being
threatened . . . we haven't decorated the room, the settee is
getting old, there will not be room enough, we wouldn't
know what to do—and so on. It was possible very largely to
overcome these teething worries by beginning where we
knew we could. After that some of the more scared came

along and found it was not too intimidating, and with a little persuasion also came in on the circuit. However, there have always remained those who not only cannot be persuaded to have Mass in their home but will not even go to Mass in someone else's because it is seen as disrespectful. In addition, and this is not being racialist but being practical, I have known some who simply find the natural smell of another ethnic group in a confined space is impossible to bear without feeling ill. It may seem stupid, but it is a fact. It may be possible to overcome it, but as a fact at a particular time, it may just be there as a stumbling block. (And as another present fact within the Catholic church there are those who are racist even at the Eucharist!)

However, the house masses settled down and prospered with a pattern emerging for covering the whole area of the parish with some regularity. At the end of each Mass those gathered would be asked who was ready to take the next Mass, and a host would be found together with a date. Where possible, the same readings were taken for a period (say three months), covering all house Masses in that period, and a discussion started among the congregation, either just after the Gospel or after Mass. There are ups and downs; some are less keen than others, but overall parishioners have taken on the idea and there is no trouble in continuing house Masses to the limits of priestpower. The balance lies between spending an evening with a smallish group or going out parish visiting.

The development of family or house groups, which are for discussions rather than worship, has not been so successful. It is partly the shift-work nature of the community, partly a sense of inability among people who have been unused to anything like formal discussion, though the discussions themselves are often helped enormously by their uninhibited and clear simplicity and directness. Probably we have not worked as hard on them as we should, and have allowed the house Masses to take their place because these are less terrifying than a straight discussion. But we all need to think in terms of their usefulness and their possibility. From my own experience with the Young Christian Workers I knew well that discussions can be very good indeed among people who would class themselves as "not educated enough" or "not good at discussing things". Certain parishes, in more middle class areas, in the university campus or in some city centres where business people like to gather during the lunch hour or in the early evening, have more familiarity with the medium of meeting and discussing . . . therefore the sense is that in these situations things go better. But when there is perseverance with other groupings, which seem less immediately able or willing, real value emerges and proves a great aid to further community development and also to parish council membership.

One of the difficulties in group work seems to be becoming too much of a group. When a number of husbands and wives have come through the teething period of getting to know each other, dropping their inhibitions and really beginning to get down to deeper discussion, everything is good and worth while. However, given that the group stays together, it becomes difficult for them to break up and go on to form new groups. This was certainly something I found with the Young Christian Workers. The groups were excellently close, but had to be very high-minded and strong-willed to hive off to form new groups. In reverse, it also becomes more and more difficult to graft new single people or couples into a too-well-established group. I have never personally been very successful in breaking through this problem. The groups we have in Southall are excellent. Unfortunately they are limited in number, and there is always the danger of running out of steam if they continue together for too long, if people move away, or if there is no real programme for development and discussion which moves into action. Once more, as with the house Mass, this form of parochial activity is very time-consuming and may militate against parochial visiting. We soon found that one way of aiding the growth of independent discussion as well as freeing the priest was to make clear that the priest might not always be able to come and that this was no barrier to the group, who must learn to stand on their own feet; further we made it clear that in any case the priest would not turn up for the meeting till an hour or so after it had begun. This would normally mean that the host and hostess for the evening took on leadership, so spreading the load.

As for topics, it has been astonishing as time goes on to find the wide range of interest and possibility in discussion. There is a real diversity because of the diverse make-up of the group membership. Some groups have never really come away from week-to-week or month-to-month discussion on a one-off basis. Others have ranged through current work in the church, such as a one time Laity Commission questionnaire on priesthood and people, qualities needed for a bishop and the whole of Church 2000. Rather more difficult and intense study and discussion has been focussed on the agreed statements on Eucharist and Ministry from the Anglican/Roman Catholic commission. Some of these have developed happily into ecumenical discussions.

Much of the work which began to emerge had behind it the parish council and so will be discussed later. But one of the focal points in so many parishes is the need for more new work in the field of young people, of their desires, needs and possibilities. It is easy to say that the great difficulty which emerges is the non-appearance of leaders. Ideally it would be lovely to have great facilities, great trained leadership and great crowds of young people benefitting from the first two. I have never yet been in a situation where this was in fact so. It may well be my own fault. In Soho we only really had a football team which regularly went out to Hackney Marshes to the only ground they could get. In Southall, we had a very grotty little hut, we soon ran out of trained youth leaders and the football club came to a point of being very in-group, getting older and not being able to open themselves to new blood. Most of them anyhow had long ago given up coming near the church. So there has been a series of attempts with management teams, doing up of the small grotty hut and branching out into activities. I would not say they had been a success.

Perhaps the only substantial growth was from the beginnings of one or two children gathered round one of the sisters. She started to play the guitar at the evening Mass on Sunday and gradually from this developed a youth choir, with the young people themselves taking over the leadership. Much of what they have done really comes under liturgy, because they began as a choir and have continued as a choir. But they have from there also developed out into different things at different times, depending upon the strength of the leadership. At one period they had a strong team working a "good news" project for helping elderly people with their gardens, house decorating and shopping. They have constantly maintained an interest in and help for pensioners and those in homes for the elderly—visiting them, singing for them and going out collecting money through carols.

In more recent times, there has been a new branching out into discussion which now seems to be going better and gathering some momentum. Otherwise there is a great deal of coming and going of young people, a biggish boy's holiday in the summer, and catechetical work which will be mentioned elsewhere. Undoubtedly in popularity nothing could rival the discos put on under the strong-arm guidance of the men of the parish. These Saturday night riots of noise and coloured lights attracted crowds of youngsters not only from the immediate area but from outside They lasted well and with great attraction, but as so inevitably seems to happen in due course there was a more and more concerted effort to break them up. Sadly eventually there were bricks being thrown and stewards injured and the whole lot had to close. It is to be hoped that sometime something like it will come to life again, for although it is difficult to see quite what the value was, it was a focus, it kept a couple of hundred young people occupied on a Saturday night. It also helped some of the excellent men and women of the parish to know that they were doing something, at considerable cost to themselves, to cope with the inadequate facilities for youth in the locality.

I suppose everywhere there is a similar challenge. It is saddening when this is seen as "the problem of young people". The natural reaction from them is to see "the problem of old people" . . . and given such a view, it is extraordinary how young some "old people" are in years! We can all of us become crusty at any age, shutting ourselves off in selfishness. When Jesus told his disciples they should not prevent children coming to him because the kingdom of heaven is made up of them, it would seem he was asking each of us to stay young in heart. This seems to be one of the secrets of Jesus Christ, and one of the secrets of some of his followers like Pope John XXIII. It is possible to attract and lead young people if you can yourself retain the openness, joy and enthusiasm of youth. I do not mean that you are perpetually leaping about, playing silly jokes on people or telling rather funny stories, trying to be young. I mean much more the flexibility of mind and the breadth and depth of heart which welcomes younger people, allows them to be real, at home and adult and respected because the older person is a good listener. This costs patience and has no monopoly on vision or truth and may lead to a broken heart. It is not likely to lead to a heart attack! I am not personally very persuaded about the value of much of the "youth work" which is done. I am not sure about the coverage achieved or the depth of change or growth in youth club devotees. What is the purpose of a Youth Club? I do know that individual leaders have a great effect on individual boys and girls because of something they have which may defy analysis. It has to do with goodness, with sincerity and integrity which is luminous, with a warmth and givenness which can be trusted. The building of the character of the leader is more important than expertise in youth-club management. That is easy to say! It is not so easy to pick out and lead the leaders. I merely want to register that priests and others given to God and his people have a real opportunity if they can grow close to Christ in their prayer and givenness and concentrate on training leaders. These must learn to rely upon him and their own fulness rather than the completeness of their equipment or the purpose-built efficiency of their youth centre. The latter can be aids only; something much less material and superficial is really central. It is well summed up in loving God and loving your neighbour—really doing so, like Christ.

At the other end of the parochial scene and high on the priority list at the beginning and throughout the time I have spent at Southall is the welfare of the elderly and the sick. We have been and are very blessed in Southall not only in our own church organisation established long before I arrived, but also in the voluntary work of the local Old People's Welfare. Our own group of women from the Catholic Women's League has been running an Over 60s Club with great success and for a long time. With weekly meetings, outings and holidays, and Christmas and birthday parties, they keep such life and fun among the elderly that it is a joy to be with them and to feel the happiness they generate among themselves and their members. They accept men and women to the club, black or white, only they must be over sixty. One of the joys for me of this is that the leaders have direct contact with the home situation and know what is happening healthwise, look after the members if they fall ill, tend them through death and even through burial when death occurs. Without being involved personally with the elderly it is not easy to realise just how much can be done to help them to stay within the community and enjoy the evening of life with others, fully alive till death. Probably old people suffer more than anything else from plain neglect. This neglect is not necessarily malicious. *We* just do not think, or, sadly, some of us think twice before taking on a work which may be costly in time. We find it hard to persuade ourselves that it is worth while in terms of God and also in terms of our common humanity. Moreover, because of the complexity of life, it is often very hard for elderly people to know how to go about collecting their pension, getting rate rebate or even paying their rent. Someone from the social services is really responsible and we could feel that we are interfering. Well, we may be. But all too often I have found there is no one else who will *actually* get on with doing anything!

The burden of what I have been writing in this chapter from the beginning of my arrival in Southall is the building up of community. Ideally, parish is community. Often it is too vast, too sprawling. People from one end do not know people from the other. Those who go to 8 a.m. Sunday Mass do not know the 11 a.m. congregation. Often it is as simple as that. To some extent, then, the need in building community is to get more and more people to make contact with more and more people in that kind of lasting way which will spread like the pond ripples—out and out in larger circles. I have no doubt myself that the general manner of living of priests and people will have a lot to do with that: a way of living directed to opening up relationship with the neighbours. You can see that some of the things we have been doing are likely to have the effect of building community. I am glad to say they have. Though there are gaps and failed attempts and some disillusion, the general effect over the years has been one murmured over and over again by visitors . . . the parish is a caring community, people are willing to help each other, there is a sense of joy and love about the place. Of course, that is all right to hear, but God and the community normally see that such a glow of euphoria does not last long . . . one is soon thrown back into some terrible domestic squabble, a hurt pride, a let-down by someone trusted. But, over all, the family feeling is there. The failures should make us try all the harder to fill in the gaps and improve the atmosphere in reality.

After house masses and groups and the other individual efforts to cope with particular areas of need, the evident problem was how could the load be spread even further. It might seem that the priest was trying to get out of his duties. To my mind the basic fact is that the multiplication of clergy is no answer to passing on the good news, or to the increase of caring in a community. If we are sadly lamenting lack of vocations to the priesthood and religious life we are moaning up a cul-de-sac: I mean quite simply that the future of evangelisation and community building is in the hands of the ordinary man, woman and child, the generality of the people of God . . . or it *should* be. This is one reason why I hold that the time spent on training and helping the development of all ages of lay people is of far greater value than many other things which occupy the priest's time. The theory is simple . . . one priest trains twelve men and women, who can then go out to spread the good news to twelve times twelve. This lesson is better learnt and practised in some of the more evangelical and splinter churches or sects. Given the potential number of apostles in the Catholic Church our spread of mission is lamentable.

One of the further lines of development that I have longed to get started is the sub-division of the parish into streets or zones, on a more permanent and effective basis than house mass groups. This we have tried. Very largely the effort has failed. I am still convinced it is crucial. How the pattern works best will depend upon areas and density of population. But it is clear in my mind that both the parochial structure, in some form or other, and smaller groupings have value. If the parish is too large, then leaders and smaller groupings have to be encouraged within the parish. In our attempts we have called them zones and had zone wardens. We found that almost everything then depends upon the zone warden having a clear idea of what is wanted from him or her, the zest to get on with it, and the personality to unite rather than divide or alienate the locality. Our beginnings were good; we suffered intensely from movement of leaders out of the parish, and also from the over busy way of life that seems to have become habitual in this age. Ideally, the zones can look after the comings and goings, the sick and housebound, the crisis within families. They can assist in spreading news of the parish, bringing the clergy in to new arrivals, furthering community through localised gatherings, and so many other things. All of this has a multiform purpose and pay-off. The leaders grow in confidence and usefulness as community workers, people know each other better, breaking down barriers, and those who come together in the bigger parish gatherings and Sunday Eucharist bring with them a spirit which communicates itself and catches on to the spirit of the other groups. Despite my gloom at the comparative failure we have had, I remain very optimistic about the way smaller groupings within the large can work.

One way, which seems to go against what I have already said, has been for us the ordination of a married man as deacon. There are various theories about what the function of a married deacon should be. Some say he is to be a Bishop's man on some specialised work in the diocese. In this particular instance with his wife he is a definite extension of the clerical life of the parish, a direct member of the team. As a deacon he assists at the Eucharist and other occasional functions in liturgy and thé sacraments in the Parish Church. Before and since diaconate he established relationship with the local Anglican church in his far end of the parish, which has led to weekly use of that church by us for Sunday Mass. He has the responsibility for all the organisation and maintenance of this sharing. He has also helped to develop much of what I have been suggesting as the role of the zone leader in the building up of a zone in that particular area. So here I am caught in a dilemma. On the one hand I can see that he has developed in a way that does not seem to have been quite possible with the other zones. Is this because of him, the area or the additional help of the diaconate? I think in his case the diaconate has definitely helped. I am, however, still of the firm opinion that such a clericalisation would not be necessary in each zone. For there is very little except the title that the deacon can do which cannot be done by the ordinary lay person, man or woman, provided there is training, good will and a desire to work for the Lord in the vicinity.

I would personally see quite a lot of sense and benefit to the local community if the church saw fit to admit the married deacon to priesthood, or to have a place for married clergy. I am not tremendously moved to enthusiasm simply by the diaconate, except where a person feels called only that far. I can see real advantage in having more individuals, not necessarily on a full-time basis, who could gather people in smaller groupings for the Eucharist; or in this particular case could share leading the Eucharist on Sundays with the full-time priests of the area. If we are clear, as I am clear, that the Eucharist is central to community, then that conviction should lead to the possibility of provision of the Eucharist. This needs wider discussion than is possible here. At this point, the importance is to stress community building, to see the way a married deacon has helped in this, to question whether a layman can really do the same without orders, and to underline the sense that fully working laymen are the key, with the leaders of the Eucharist more readily accessible, but not only in terms as at present conceived of parochial full-time and celibate clergy.

In this line of thinking, it has been interesting to hear the reaction of parishioners. Many of them are not at all convinced that one of their own number is a proper substitute for a priest whether as a lay visitor or a deacon. There is still a residue feeling in some quarters that if they have not been visited by the priest in their home, the church does not care about them. Personally, I think this is at one level a beautiful idea; at another level it is very constricting and demanding upon a priest, and he has to face the fact that he cannot effectively visit his parishioners in their homes sufficiently frequently to help their development. He can get to know them a bit, but frequent visiting demands more time than is available. A visit every six months or once a year cannot achieve depth-relationship. But the acceptance that relationship can be very real and fruitful with a sister, a deacon or a leader in the area is a way forward with much more potential. I have found it very valuable to sit back and watch some lay people grow and develop into leadership in this way, becoming focal points for those who are in trouble, have a query or want more knowledge and growth in prayer. A brother helping a brother is like a strong fortress, says the psalm. But this understanding is one we would have to work on, after initially, as clergy, believing it ourselves.

Moreover, a brother helping a brother is a biblical

quotation, but it does not go far enough if we limit it to strictly male contribution. Down the centuries the part played by women in the church has been of an immense order, but is has happened always with the "authority" of the male church, more than in its own right. Today we are still far from a general acceptance of the equality of men and women, not only in what is "open" to women in the church, but also in attitude. I sincerely hope that the development which has taken place in more recent years will be continued not just in the working out of theory, but in practical living. At the present time the number of women dedicated to God in religious orders and secular institutes and other modes of "total" service, is very large indeed. There are very few fields of work or professional career in the secular world where women are not either fully accepted or at least working their way to parity. But within the church there is at all levels a very considerable conservatism or antagonism. For instance, despite the fact that the church has provision for women to give communion, large numbers of priests and parishes ignore or refuse the commissioning. As a practical matter, we have found it quite invaluable to use this particular function, because the whole congregation benefits so much from the ending of over-long-drawn-out communion queues. And I use this not to continue an attitude of "making use of women", but because when we began, some, not least women, disliked the idea and said it should not happen. But the objection very soon wilted away and the acceptance is almost total today.

Naturally, the subject is beyond this minor expression, because in justice the church should be foremost in advancing and safeguarding equality. It is now much more likely that women will be automatically expected to form part of church commissions and so on; in university circles they have been working as co-chaplains for some time. And the interesting thing which we have found through discussion groups has been that there is really no objection when thought has been given to the matter to married clergy, to women ministers of communion or women preachers. If only as a whole we made determined efforts, woman power in the church could be released for God's service far more than at the present time. Certainly the clergy and sisters of this parish have found the value of sharing, with fields of action according to ability, with joint discussion of policy, with much sharing of prayer, responsibility and communal living. And this is not to exclude the laity, because here the women play an even more leading role in much of what goes on at all levels. It has been very lovely to watch the growth and development of confidence and leadership as the opportunity has been offered to them.

Discussion has further made it plain that with thought there is soon no objection among the ordinary parishioners to the general idea of women being ordained to the priesthood. Clergy are often more cagey! Of course, at the present time, not only has there been a very strong and considered statement from Pope Paul turning down the idea of ordaining women, but there has also been publicity for the problems which would arise when the church of England goes ahead, problems with the Orthodox churches as well as Rome. However, the last word has not been spoken in this matter; there has been considerable exploration of scripture and many theologians and scripture scholars maintain that there is nothing fundamentally against the ordination of women. There is a strong climate of opinion over all, especially in ecclesiastical circles, which may well be more psychological than theological. The best possible way forward would seem to be continued work by scholars at their level, while the rest of us do everything we can at all times and in every situation to make sure that women in our society are encouraged and free to be fully themselves. It is not sufficient to have theories; the practical living of equality and patient persuasion. In so many areas of life and thought a real breakthrough into the future becomes a breakdown into opposition from fear which quickly crystallises when there is too little thought or knowledge and undue haste or bad tactics by the organisers of the would-be breakthrough.

Much of this has been evident in Southall and it is amazing to me how far we have moved together in six years. It is sad that not all have moved and that some can even be bitter at developments. Here however, I see no way ahead which does not provide the opportunity for someone to be scandalised or alienated. This is distressing. It is also, I'm afraid true. It is once more a reason for going to God in prayer, facing the fact of the possible damage and the possible growth. Only with him in depth and then openly in team consultation can there be a forward development which is not marred by fear or forced as a one-man concept. To grow in community we must grow together in all directions. But growth is often painful and means giving up and dying as well as new development. We do not all move at the same speed. In going to God, we can afford neither to go at the speed of the fastest nor to wait for the slowest, though both should have freedom. This means that there will be tension, both frustration at slowness and irritation at too much speed. The priest as shepherd or leader is responsible for all God's people; the flock is too big for him alone; he must inspire and animate others who also can provide a lead and a trust. In the community of the Lord we all have our gifts to contribute, and it is one of the main functions of the priest to assist in creating such an atmosphere of trust, love and inspiration through holiness that all sections of the community are prepared to unite in God, though not all can or should be expected to agree with everything that is proposed or happens.

9

LITURGY: EUCHARIST

When I was asked by the chaplain of the Guards' battalion with which I was serving at the time why I wanted to be a priest, I said I wanted to help people, and he asked me whether I had any desire to say Mass. My reply was negative and caused him to take a step backwards! Now I am twenty-six years on in priesthood. It may be merely by indoctrination that I have absorbed the priestly language and mentality. I don't know how it would strike an outsider looking at me. Anyhow I now set the Eucharist and presiding at the Eucharist, including preaching God's word, as the central way I have been given of helping people to know, love and serve God in community.

There could be a situation where God or St. Peter or whoever was chosen interviewed a number of parish priests and asked them what was the most important thing they had done in the parish during their tenure of office. One might say, I built a church; another I built a school; another I built a parish social centre, another I paid off the parish debt, another I got a really good youth club going, another I sorted out the housing problem in my area. St. Peter would commend each one of them for the use to which they had put their individual talent, but might still have a far away look in his eye. Then quite a mousy sort of a priest might speak up and say the most important thing he had done in the parish was to try always to present, preside and pray at the Eucharist as deeply and sincerely as he could, drawing the people to worship God by hearing his word and receiving the Body and Blood of Jesus Christ. And St. Peter's face would be transformed and radiant with love.

Without discounting any of the marvellous works undertaken so selflessly by priests, the further I continue in trying myself to be a priest the more I find myself centred on the Eucharist. I do not want to cut out works, charities, studies, building, visiting and all the multifarious things a priest does in his daily round. What I want is to be quite clear as to the source and wellspring of all that is effective: God—and God especially through Eucharist. It is from the priest or person who is centred here that the other things flow most effectively. And so I have come round full circle in my thinking and living. Now I try to leave open the help I can give to people by committing myself first to God and expecting the flow of power from Him. This does not exclude effort and struggle and use of all that God has given in the way of talent. But the weight primarily and continually is thrown back on God. He is responsible.

The priest has been given a special or presidential role at the Eucharist. Though the Eucharist in itself is a gathering together for the memorial of the Lord's supper, the Church as guardian of the sacraments has limited the re-enactment to ordained ministers. It is therefore of very real importance how those ministers or priests are in themselves and how they celebrate, not only because they can intentionally invalidate what they are doing, but also because the people for and with whom they are celebrating can be attracted, drawn and deepened in understanding and love—or they can be repelled, baffled and caused to consider irrelevant the whole sacred mystery.

Therefore, in speaking of the priest and liturgy I am not immediately concerned with discussing the theology of liturgy or the exact situation of the priest as minister, but rather wanting to look at the attitude of the priest and the whole surrounding of liturgy which do not touch the validity or invalidity of Eucharist or again of Baptism, Confirmation and other sacraments, but seem to make the difference (in a given church at a given time among a given congregation) between a "living" and a "dead" liturgy.

One aspect which comes out directly or indirectly in all that I have written in this book is the building up of community, of people—you and I as people of God. Eucharist is central to this because it is the method and instrument for our coming together to make the most important demonstration of the greatest commandment. It should be the source of strength and love for each of us to achieve the living of the second great commandment. We come to it, priest and people, individually and in families or groups. Some are literally "alone"—walking or driving as a solitary person, finding a seat by a pillar, near the back away from others if possible . . . perhaps wanting to be part and yet held back by shyness or fear . . . not really seeing that it makes any difference to coming to Mass anyhow. Others pile in as families, with children falling over benches and each other. They may know other families or be caught up simply in their own little unit. We are a people, yet like quicksilver we come and go, adhere to each other and then are quickly broken away. For each the Mass is the Mass, but how differently we view it—as joy or a bore, a deep spiritual experience, an event not to be missed and to be shared utterly, or a dead, empty duty to be got through, impersonal, a drag, irrelevant.

Once I was trying to help a girl. Part of the helping was to have a party when she was twenty-one. Afterwards she said: "It was good news! I've never had a celebration before of my own; I've never never had a birthday party!" She was an orphan, she had grown up always in community, and she had pretty certainly had a birthday party of some sort each year. But somehow it had never been personal to her, it had always been an institutional thing, it passed her by. Now it was hers, she was real in the midst of community. She had come into her being and was able to take a new and more real part in community.

The teaching which we live out and realise in Eucharist is the coming together of individuals as community . . . to celebrate the individual and universal salvation which comes by Jesus Christ. It is the very combination of these two elements which makes what I might call the strength and weakness of Eucharistic celebration. When we are too individual, we miss the vital aspect of community worship and almost resent the presence of others who are shuffling or coughing, disturbing the still serenity of *my mass*. The priest too, in a funny way, can come to long for a "quiet mass" in peace, almost without congregation. But at the other end of the scale, we can insist overwhelmingly on the community aspect, and be so busy singing together, standing together, answering responses together that we get caught up in a whole movement, taking more or less part according to our mood. This does not allow silence for a long enough time during the Mass for it to sink in that I am one, myself, alone before God; and because I am one I can will to be part of this Eucharistic community. Balance is essential and not easy to maintain when we are grounded in one way, moving to another way, and have strands of every kind of attitude in the one congregation at the one time.

But the priest is the servant of God first, then the servant of the Church and as servant of the Church servant of her members, the People of God. He is therefore in a tough position, because though in theory all three should be as one it is fairly usual that this is not so. Liturgical vision, liturgical policy, liturgical implementation of policy, and public acceptance, rejection or indifference (both by priest and people) are widely diverse. As servant of God first, the priest must always be a man of prayer. Given that he is, this may make things clearer but not necessarily easier. His very clarity of vision of God may highlight the discrepancy between the liturgical documents, the spelling out of them in "rubrics" and the sterility with which they can be applied to life in the church building. The first stress therefore should be upon the personal holiness of the priest-president, with him so regulating his life that he gets an abundant time to be alone with the Father, as Jesus did, while at the same time allowing all the flow of life around him to permeate and radiate him. Because he is a man of God and a man of the people, he needs to be close both to God and to the people.

The illustration of what I mean is Jesus Christ himself. He was a Jew, born of a Jewish mother, living in the midst of ordinary people. He learnt to be not only a man, but a Jewish man, with all that that meant in temperament, background, history, exclusiveness, chosenness and so on.

He lived and absorbed the political, moral, religious and racial feelings of his time. He used them all for his preaching, when he had spent sufficient time getting to know God, himself and those around him. The illustration we have of him as a boy is sitting in the temple with the elders, listening to them and discussing with them; and afterwards going back with his parents for further years of listening and growing. There is a great deal for us to listen to in the hidden years of Christ. This listening combined with our direct living experience of our immediate situation helps to get across his message. So in trying to follow him into a share of his unique priesthood, it seemed to me in training that I needed to know the people with whom I was going to try to live, work and preach. For England, I already had a knowledge of "the English" Church—a mixture of English, Irish, Scots, Welsh and Italian—because that was fundamentally my own background upbringing in home-school-university-army life. Though one of the priests under whom I had grown up and who taught me many things before and after my army period was a Cork man—deeply and simply holy, very human—I felt I did not know the Irish. So I was happy to go to Ireland and to attempt to steep myself in the religious background. Whether I was sensible or scientific I don't really know. I lived among them, and as particular highlights, I did the pilgrimage to Croagh Patrick on the day of the Reek, and also the penitential stay at Lough Derg. Later, when I came to Southall, thanks to the inspiration of one of the sisters working in the team, she and I went twice to spend the summer in the Caribbean, attending the Antilles Pastoral Institute and so mixing with bishops, priests, sisters and lay people from all the islands. In addition we visited the islands from which most of our people in Southall came, namely Grenada and Dominica, with other periods in Trinidad, Jamaica, Barbados, Antigua, and for me the Bahamas. Only recently have I been able to go to India by the generosity of an Indian friend who dreamt he should give me a ticket!

The reason for putting in this discursion is that the feel of the different parts of the world has considerably opened my own mind and eyes and heart to the possibilities of the deep and true contribution that comes from each different ethnic and cultural background. For some this may seem a long way from liturgy. For me it is very close indeed, because I cannot conceive of God in Jesus Christ wanting some kind of aseptic worship offered in a neutral atmosphere. With the older rites of the church, there was liberty for considerable local influence. But sadly the western influence coloured the liturgy which the Europeans took to different "pagan" parts of the world. While tending to condemn local expression, the Europeans invested religious worship with local Europeanism, which was made synonymous with "Catholic". The arrival of the "third church" is now changing the outlook, but this comes hard to many Europeans. Where there is already an existent third church in a European setting as with Asian, West Indian and African presence in England, the way forward is probably through accommodation to the inspiration of different ethnic groups in a non-exclusive way so that we may share the goodness we each have to contribute.

The holiness of the president which helps to focus the Eucharistic celebration is not a matter of his simply being understanding, broad-minded and tolerant. He has to live out incarnation in which God and man are united in love and service. It is God's will—his love—that we know him, love him, and serve him and others. Accepting the central givenness of himself in Eucharist, our part is for each to be channels of his Word. Our effort and desire is to open the channels by every possible means, so that the meaning and knowledge of the Word of God permeates, widens and deepens in mankind.

There are very many different elements to learning, hearing, feeling, sensing, absorbing. The working and playing out of the liturgy demands our personal sensitivity and technique, our personal holiness and our hard work. The Eucharist is not just a haphazard coming together of odds and ends from the highways and byways. It is the gathering of God's people for the specific and primary purpose of giving him honour and glory. We cannot afford in God's service to be slipshod. That does not mean that we have to be rigid and formalistic. We have to order ourselves according to the rite and to the situation, blending the two, rather than letting one dominate the other. Here also it is clear that it is a coming together, and so primarily this is a community worship to which the individual brings his individuality as his or her contribution to the general hymn of praise. But, in respect for the community, it is important that the individuality does not obscure, obliterate or bias the message, nor must the individuality alienate or distract the community as a whole.

By the division of the Eucharist into "sections" we can hope to clarify and simplify what we are about at each section. We can also destroy the single beauty of the seamless garment. Really, Eucharist is fullest when we are all there from start to finish making our common praise echo through our sorrow and knowledge of forgiveness, our hearing of God's word, and the receiving and sharing of the memorial meal, a meal which makes the whole of Christ's sacrifice present to us, and so helps us to realise our own offering in response to his love when we go out into his world in service. In the Eucharist we share his passion, death and resurrection. I think we have failed to teach the people of God effectively the full wonder of this. We must work at it, so that they do not miss out on the beauty and fullness by simply coming late or leaving early, feeling there is not much to miss, or failing to grasp the treasure of actually sharing in the Body and Blood of the Lord because it has never been their custom.

At the same time, there is every reason, because of the teaching which is necessary, that we should *realise*—that is make real—the teaching potential of the liturgy of the Mass. If we are able, as a family, to put in and take out something which is deep and full of meaning in the penitential rite, then we can go through our whole day in the kind of prayer which, if we repeat it and absorb it, fertilises all we are and all we do . . . Lord Jesus Christ, Son of God, have mercy on me a sinner. Our united prayer at

Mass is only one expression. Our unity should continue through the day and night and week. As each one of us goes from the Eucharist we are to make God present in the ordinary life of the world in a tangible way, through our constant prayer.

The word of God which comes through the readings and the homily has the same possibility and the same danger. There can be a detached, aseptic reading and preaching which reaches and touches very few indeed. There can also be the living of the word, because the preacher has himself been living the word through the week, so that when he preaches, he speaks to God's people what he himself has learnt. In order to make a reality of these rather pious words, we set off in Southall to try to practise what we hoped to preach. The first step was to agree that there would be a meeting over a working lunch each Monday. This was specifically to discuss and argue out the theme for the liturgy in church the following Sunday. It seemed to us that in a general way, without being too inflexible, it might be possible to consider the theme ourselves and then to leave the development of the thought which might emerge to each individual priest or preacher. But that did not seem wide enough. We also involved in the working lunch the sister who was mainspring of catechetical work for children in non-catholic schools, and the headmaster and one or two of the teachers from the catholic primary school. In this way, it became possible for us to give them the opportunity of trying to get across the message for *next* Sunday during *this* week. It also helped in that, if there was any work by writing or drawing which emerged from the classes and groups, it could be brought to the church and displayed in the baptistry or round the walls as might be appropriate. From this, the clergy could tell a little, if they looked, how the minds of the children had been working. The parents could be involved through their children's work. The whole congregation had a better chance of growing together and growing in depth from the readings and the homily, which now was a projection of the reading, prayer and thought not simply of the individual priest, but of a much wider community.

This led on to a more complicated or sophisticated development. Taking a serious and prolonged look at the readings of the lectionary, we came to the conclusion that very seldom, for our congregation, was it valuable in terms of receiving and absorbing to have more than two readings and a psalm at the Sunday liturgy. Indeed, it sometimes seemed necessary to cut the length of one or both of the readings chosen. There were times when simply a small piece of one reading taught the lesson of the day better than all that was proposed by the lectionary. To come to this conclusion, we had to ask ourselves about the purpose of the readings. If it was to cover (in a given period) the New and Old Testaments, then we could only do so by reading all that was proposed, whether it was grasped, understood and absorbed, or not. But if we were in the responsible position of having been delegated and trusted by Christ and his Church *to teach*, then we had the added responsibility of looking at our friends and neighbours, listening to them, estimating what would be useful for them, and then doing all that we could to bring them to deeper understanding and love of God's good news.

This was a trying decision in that some of us had been brought up in the thought that the Church through the bishops had laid down the strict form of the liturgy and not one jot or title must be altered. But in looking at it and realising our responsibility for a people whom in a true sense the hierarchy of the church did not know, we came through to a teaching sense of the weekly liturgy. This has proved itself over and over again in the living liturgy of our weeks and years here in St. Anselm's. Do not think that we have set out to overthrow what the Church is trying to do. We have set out to fulfil it. If we have three readings which bear, for instance, on the great commandment, if we look at them, look at our people, ask what lesson do we think the Church and we are trying to get across, then it may be better that the simple statement of the great commandment, stated and if necessary re-stated, is taken as the single reading, with a few words of explanation from the priest or preacher.

The only time when those people of Southall who are Roman Catholics ever really meet together in great numbers to listen to and to grasp the message of God is on Sunday at Mass. In the week it is possible to gather some through the school, through house masses, through groups, through special courses . . . but always only a few. The main burden of teaching comes on Sunday or not at all. But this means that some of the wonders which are being taught cannot be covered by a one-off homily for ten minutes at Mass. No one, surely, would for a moment agree that even the most brilliant could sum-up the duties of married life in five or ten minutes cold. Or what about all that is connected with the Eucharist itself, or the sacrament of Penance, or prayer? So it became necessary to widen and prolong the teaching of particular subjects . . . six weeks on Baptism, the whole of Lent on Penance one year, Eucharist another, and so on.

We adopted a multiple plan in attempting to widen and deepen knowledge. We stuck to the Monday lunches, the general discussions. The parish council encouraged the development of a liturgy group. But additionally as a team we planned for four, five or six weeks at a time, taking what we could from the lectionary, but deciding, for example, that Lent would be best employed, as there was a new rite of Penance, in discussing and probing into Penance in general and this rite in particular. On another occasion, it was the turn of re-vamping the whole grasp of the Eucharist over a period of all the Sundays in Lent, with a concluding celebration of first Holy Communions on Maundy Thursday at the evening liturgy. When this kind of course on a sacrament or special subject is put on we further boost the spread by having a Monday evening session for an hour and a half on the same theme as the Sunday, consisting of a half-hour talk, a half-hour in small discussion groups, and a final fifteen minutes of plenary session. Finally, for the build-up during Lent to first Holy Communion, the parents and children concerned were invited to a series of special afternoon masses on the

Eucharist, with the parents and children working together at home-work between Sundays.

"Wall illustrations" are one of the techniques which we have developed under the inspiration of a creative and imaginative sister who is a member of our team. To explain this a little. Our church has a vast expanse of apse-wall behind the high altar. We discussed the church, calling in an artist from another area who has spiritually and artistically explored the problems and possibilities of liturgical development within, and making use of, church buildings. (There are many talented people about who can help not only priests but the whole Church in proclaiming God's message. Sadly, the parish priest has often in the past been designer and decorator and liturgical expert in "his" Church to be. Part of poverty is to accept the riches of others. We must open our eyes to talent, expertise and vision wherever it may be found . . . and then allow it to be used for God's glory. If we ourselves feel knowledgeable and responsible, this demands humility). His artistic vision saw that the vast empty whiteness of the apse would be warmed and made more familiar by hanging curtains from about a third of the way from the ground. So we decided to have these in three sets of liturgical colours, white, green and purple. They immediately made a real and happy difference. But more than this, they also, (and I do not think this was his intention!) provide a back cloth for pinning up painted, montage or cut out illustrations of the theme of the Sunday or the season.

I suppose an immediate reaction to that last idea might be caution, doubt or even horror. All I can do here is to enlarge a little on the method and reason behind it—and then say you'd really have to come and "feel" it and perhaps see some of the slides of past "lessons from the sanctuary". The reason for using these illustrations is simple. We are at the Eucharist involved in "hearing God's word" . . . and hearing can be helped powerfully, as can prayer and meditation, by seeing as well. For almost all the known life of the Church, starting in the catacombs of Rome, there has been a history of the decoration of the walls and later windows . . . decoration which was at once a thing of beauty and a teaching aid. Basically we in Southall have been seeking to project God's word more powerfully, we have been using the walls as teaching aids. This is brought about in a threefold way. Firstly, teachers, catechists, clergy and sisters discuss the message. Then secondly, in their class-or-group-teaching they try to put across the word, helping to illustrate it in a planned way by making a montage or cutting out for a build-up picture. Thirdly, the children learn and the expression of what they have learnt is taken in illustration to the church where it is displayed publicly, so that all the parish benefit from their work; they can share it even more intimately with their families as they recognise and point out their particular piece. At this stage too, the clergy can use the work as direct illustration of the word they are preaching.

Briefly on the build-up: the latest at the time of writing was Lent, and a course on Eucharist. The Old Testament readings illustrated stages of the Covenant—Noah and the bow in the sky, the sacrifice of Abraham, the law given to Moses, the Passover. These scenes were built as tableaux, two on each side of the sanctuary. (There was not as much young peoples' involvement in this as we would have wished, owing to sickness and lack of preparation leading to a last minute hitch.) As the tableaux began to grow on the sides, so we built up the Last Supper scene in the centre, as the New Covenant—the bare table was for Abraham's sacrifice; the cloth over it, the rainbow; then Christ himself in figure at the table personifying the New Law of love; and finally (out of chronological order) the Passover with bread and wine placed on the table, and the apostles gathered in Eucharist.

Taken over all the Sundays of Lent, with all the other methods of teaching, it strengthened the link between church-school-home-Eucharist. It rightly occupied the minds of people before the Sunday worship and held them during the homily . . . and perhaps left a residue which aided prayer and thought during the week. At the end, though the individual scenes were not "works of art", they were in another sense truly that, and the whole was expressive, teaching and attracting. Though I do not think this was intended, the Last Supper was in fact much more beautiful and "together", than the picturing of the Old Testament Covenant history.

Naturally, for the major part of the year, the curtain is plain. Only periodically does it become a modern "stained glass window". It is worth noting though, that when recently I had a visit from a man who was working on the use of Christian art in Church, I mentioned how we worked with temporary and discardable illustrations. He was not happy at my analogy of stained glass or at any suggestion that this was "art". Later, he saw slides of the previous Lent. I think he had modified his views a little by the time he went away!

It is interesting that the outcome of Vatican II in liturgy was the *missa normativa* . . . the norm which was thought and set out with the intention that there should be the possibility of "alternatives" to the norm. Now, most of us at that time had not been used to much change, except in the Preface or at a Mass for the dead. Perhaps because of this past experience the "norm" has become for many clergy as rigid as was the old rite between rule and rubric. I remember being sub-deacon once in the late 1950s when at London University. The Master of Ceremonies had not turned up, but the preacher was an eminent priest who had often been MC in his own congregation. He gladly stood in as well as preaching. But the deacon was a visiting Dutch student priest who had ideas of his own. In the silence soon after the Consecration, I heard the MC say in a loud voice: "Really!. If the deacon doesn't do what he's told, the Mass simply can't go on!" We can exaggerate in many different ways. I am not urging exaggeration. I am suggesting that the liberty given for variation should not be withdrawn or neglected. It is essential that the full heart of our re-enactment of the Lord's Supper as a memorial of him in his death and resurrection is and remains always authoritatively guarantees and blessed by the Church. But at this time perhaps more than at any other we need the dual strength of valid continuity with Jesus Christ as it has persisted in the Mass down the ages, plus a flexibility of setting which will both preach the word and deepen the spiritual union of the whole person, young or old, with the Lord. In this it is easy to fail to distinguish essential from circumstantial. If the solemnity and beauty of the organ seems to me a fitting setting for the Mass this does not mean that the Mass is dishonoured when young people or others prefer the guitar. The Eucharist was instituted by Christ for people, because Christ did not disdain to become man and dwell among us. But in dwelling among us he showed the combination of simple centring on the will of his father and human, approachable realism in face of the needs of the people.

Because of this wisdom of his it is most necessary for us to realise that worship will vary in expression though the centre core is still and universal. Even within the one parish, there can each Sunday be a wonderful variety in celebrations from traditional through to some form of folk Mass. And there can be variety week by week too, as the Church has so long shown us by her contrasting seasons of the year. If this is accepted and the extra care and work which is involved is undertaken, then every Mass will be a celebration of the Lord's Supper celebrated particularly for birth or death, marriage or healing, or the realisation of our prayer: "give us this day our daily bread". But throughout the differences there should be central and almost tangible the intangible mystery. It is often complained today that the mystery has been lost. This can be true, but it is not necessary, if the priest and all those gathered in the Eucharist are themselves steeped in the mystery of God through prayer before they reach the gathering. To come cold is not to add to the sum which is of the very mixture of Eucharist. It is for this reason among others that home liturgies are so important. They can help us in our development as a smaller part of the big community so that, when we come together in the big community on a Sunday, we bring the spirit of our personal prayer and of the home liturgy shared with our family and immediate neighbours. Again, the home liturgy takes extra time and preparation, on the part both of the president and the congregation, but it is especially valuable for the president because it gives him a different feeling for Eucharist and a greater power to preside at the big gathering.

Our priestly ability to listen to and work in with the mind and heart of young people is in need of constant encouragement. For some there seems to be an immediate rapport, for others it is a hard slog. To all of us this large and important part of "the parish" calls out for consideration and a say in everything to do with Church. But it is especially in liturgy that there is scope for flexibility, already to some extent catered for in new masses for children and so on. The possibility of young people engaging themselves in liturgy and so drawing in their companions is considerable. They are not by any means all "way out" in their ideas, but even if they were there should still be time for us to listen so that we can be part with them in the infinitely difficult work of articulation and presentation of God's word—and of our response in glory, praise and honour.

The result of letting undergraduates and subsequently the young people in the Southall area into preparation of liturgy has been both dynamic and enlivening to my understanding. There have been times when what was proposed seemed more gimmick than anything else, but other times when the simplicity, directness and spiritual insight have taken me deeper than I have ever been before. The president must often then sense the reality of his position as the leader of a group which is pulsing with its own life, wants it realised, guided and helped to mature, but is also very conscious of its own genius. It is easy to understand how many a priest has not wanted to be shaken from routine or exposed to dialogue or taken out of solemnity with clapping and dancing to the Lord. But once you have been through the experience of this kind of liturgy and what it means and does to the young people, then if you are in any way open, you will know something of conversion. I know that. I know too my personal joy at sharing in growth as I can feel and see the individuals and the group emerging. They are not a long way through life, they are not beyond failure and loss of direction, but they come further, grow more fully into God and man if they are encouraged to grow in the Spirit, with flexibility, patience, listening and love. The demands of youth should throw the leader into the arms of God in prayer and into the ascetic of humility laced with an abundant sense of humour, affection and joy.

What I am saying of young people goes all the more for children, if they in turn are to grow into young people and still be coming to worship when they reach the teens. At an earlier stage, they need more simplicity, more colour, more editing of the rite. They also respond to a mixture of mystery and tangibility, to some discipline, but a fair measure of informality. The latter scares some priests and parents who take it to be irreverence, when in fact it is being real in the Father's house. All this cannot be expounded in a few words, but the underlying principle is that open affection, love and welcome for children, so evident in Christ, are needed by us if we are to win them to his love. But all that does not mean a rowdy-rushing all over the place. Once again it is the balance which achieves warmth, with childlike dignity, with prayer.

In Southall we spend quite an amount of time trying to see where we are going and what we are trying to do in bringing children to share fully in the Eucharist. For instance, there is much flexibility in the approach to preparation for first Holy Communion. We have multiple possibilities, because basically we would prefer the parents to be responsible for leading and instructing their children towards this sacrament. But there is a deeply inbuilt resistance to this on the part of many parents, which highlights how in the past we taught them to rely totally on the work of priests, nuns and school teachers. In this way, we have undermined their confidence to such a degree that they firmly believe they are incapable of teaching their children.

Some parents are now coming to accept the challenge and the possibility. They have facilities for helping them to tackle in their own homes, just with their own children or with neighbours' children coming in, a simple but effective course. Then, when they feel the child or children are ready to receive Communion, the priest examines them, and they come individually or as a group to make a simple "family" Communion. Where children are in a Catholic school, some parents prefer them to be taught in a "school-class" situation. These parents often still prefer a "white" First Communion, so why should they not have one? But the very variety and spread of the first Holy Communions has made us have an annual solemnisation one summer Sunday. This we make a Eucharistic day—for the whole parish, especially urging those who have made their first Communion during the year to come, but also underlining the community aspect of the Eucharist for everyone. This seems an appropriate day also for a procession of the Blessed Sacrament and Benediction.

Liturgy is living, moving and beautiful. It is at once the same in essence and endlessly different in detail, according to the development of the structure of community, the make up of children, adults, families, the handicapped or other groupings. Liturgy must be *alive*. We must not be afraid. The beauty and power the Lord uses through us at the Eucharist demands every effort of mind and heart to make it available for God's people. As in our own lives we live through the pains and joys of the life of Jesus Christ, we need to find the expression of his saving work in the Eucharist. Then by sharing fully in Passion, Death and Resurrection, we shall feel the forgiveness of God and the union of Holy Communion, which will strengthen us to go out and preach the Good News.

10

LITURGY II: SACRAMENTS

The Incarnation is the most startling and "unbelievable" revelation of the Transcendent God. The untouchable, unknowable is suddenly among us in a new way—"The Word became flesh and dwelt among us". The Johannine writer hammers home the point by saying:

We have seen with our own eyes:
we have watched
and touched with our hands:
the Word, who is life . . . (1 John 1.1)

Before Jesus Christ is born, God is God, he speaks through the Prophets, he gives manna in the desert, but he is invisible. Out of his wisdom God sends His Son, and the whole response of man to God takes a new dimension through Jesus Christ. Clearly this does not change God's transcendence but gives man the way through to his transcendence. Earthy, fleshly man comes to the divinity of God through the humanity of Christ. Since then, it has been possible to "picture" Jesus—that is "enflesh" him in our mind's eye through images. A painting or photograph of someone we love is not a substitute for the person—but humanly it can be not only a reminder but an aid to concentration, through which we are carried beyond the lifeless image to the living reality. A painting or photograph is not essential. Indeed some would say of the loved one: "I'd rather not have a picture. Nothing could do him her justice. I'd rather just use my head and heart." But the image can be useful if it leads the viewer to the reality.

The new "visibility" of God remained on by Christ's gift in the Church. As the one mediator, the one priest, Christ left effective signs of himself. The Church—the whole body of believers—was to be his most visible sign, his witness, his sacrament as a priestly people. Within the church his fullest presence was to be the gift of himself in word and sacrament in the Eucharist. There were other signs most of them involving touch and all continuing the Incarnation by presenting to the human being something external and graspable which leads through to the transcendent.

My line of thought in trying to live out the Sacraments as a priest is that within the whole priestly people (the Church Sacrament) there are those specially commissioned or ordained to be sacramental through the Sacrament of Orders. The Church though promised that she would never lose her priestly character can be *more* or *less* effective depending upon the members' Christlike living. It is true of the sacraments that they are in themselves effective, but because they are incarnational they are both to be revealed being dispensed, and to be lived out afterwards. Within the whole priestly people, the ordained minister is responsible for specialising in being so attuned by his training, his life of prayer and his living caringly among people that he can lead them, animate them and witness to them. His follow-up of the Sacrament of Orders effectively covers his whole presentation of the word and the sacraments through his life and work.

This all means that he can be held responsible especially when the sacramental life of the Church seems moribund. And it is with this in mind that I write this chapter, not as a complete rundown on the sacraments but as a stimulant to the stimulators about the part the ordained play in stimulating the people of God in their priestly role.

An old Latin tag which sticks in my mind from seminary days is: *sacramenta sunt propter homines*—sacraments are for people. And this is the attitude of mind and heart with which any minister of the sacraments should go about his daily round of life and work with people.

As with so many parts of religious expression, the attitude to the sacraments can become rigid, protected and so less available and less effective. There is good in the Church laying down the how, when and where—the order—of giving the sacraments. But in my young days, there was little or no questioning of the order; it was as it was; it had been that way for a long time; there was no question of changing it. I well remember the horror of my parish priest in Soho when evening mass was suggested; and the very real difficulty with some people at the change of the pre-communion fasting regulations, as they firmly refused to take any form of food or liquid after midnight, and so having ordinary meals throughout the day would not receive communion at an afternoon or evening mass.

These are only small examples, but they open the way to looking at the possibilities. If for instance we take development in the use of anointing the sick, we can see how dramatic a change there has been for the better. An old Irish doctor who had himself had a stroke and was back at work, but likely to have another, was talking to me one day about the great desire he had. He said he longed to be anointed, and I immediately asked why he shouldn't be? His reply was he did not think he was sick enough, as he had had the experience in the past of calling in a priest to anoint someone who was really ill, and the priest had refused, saying she was not actually dying. When I explained the new rite, he was overwhelmed with joy and gratitude, and we had a happy and holy anointing during a Mass at his home. A couple of months later, he collapsed and died quite suddenly.

It has long been my habit to have the holy oils with me all the time, and over and over again this has been most opportune. I have written about spiritual healing in Chapter 4. In anointing the spiritual combines with the physical on many occasions. There is also something "indefinable" present—the effect of the sacrament— which brings a calm and peace to the sick. To my mind, greater familiarity with the use of anointing, and the assurance among people of its healing nature as well as its value as a preparation for death brings about a far better reception of the sacrament. There is now a real joy and welcome rather than a sense of the death-sentence when I suggest anointing. Families are more ready to call us in in sickness, fewer and fewer people die without the sacrament, more receive it several times or periodically. The effect is a spread of faith, a new warmth for the sick, and a strong instrument of God in the hand of the priest as he visits homes and hospitals, accidents and disasters. Moreover, the linking of anointing with a Mass for the sick helps both those who are brought to the celebration and those who care for them, who do the fetching and carrying, provide the hospitality and so on. I realise these things could seem to be peripheral to the sacrament, but in a serious way they are central, because they are increasing the circle of healing and making whole, not only in the one who is in immediate need, but also in the minds and attitudes of onlookers, unbelieving neighbours or relatives, or members of the family who have lapsed.

This sacrament is, of course, only one aspect of care of the sick. The other which is so important is Mass and Communion. Here, the extension of the sacrament can best be seen in the permission for holy communion to be taken to the sick by religious or lay people commissioned to do so. The beauty of this is that it provides far more opportunity for frequent communion. There is also the possible extension of prayer and reading of scripture, and a little home service, which are all necessarily curtailed through shortage of time if the priest is the only one who can administer the sacrament. Personally, with care and respect for the sacrament safeguarded by instruction and community spirit, I would like to see wider use of the permission so that more and more people can be involved closely with the Lord, with the housebound in a spiritual role, and as messengers whose contact will increase their personal commitment to the Gospel. There may be dangers and fears. Let us overcome them by living in hope and trust and courage, taking the Lord in extension of the church-Eucharist to those for whom he so specifically came . . . the lame, the blind, the sick, the housebound, the poor. When it is more difficult today to get people to the church building, let us try to take the Lord more positively where he would have been in his own lifetime, with publicans and sinners, visiting the sick, out in the streets. Let us multiply the opportunities for meeting Christ in Eucharist where two or three can gather in his name.

It is interesting that some priests and people feel "lost" without daily Mass and Communion. At the same time, others are saying, feeling and practising the very reverse of this. I mean that some priests do not say Mass daily, some students for the priesthood will only go to a Mass if they "feel community" with the group with whom it is being offered. I have met the second attitude in regard to "community" also among lay people, especially university and college students. I have three suggestions. Firstly, I would not limit the effect of the Eucharist to sharing only when I felt a part. Ideally, I would want every Eucharist to welcome the stranger, so that I would never feel excluded from any group which has gathered in Eucharist. Indeed, I would want to be admitted to a group of strangers knowing I could share the Lord with them, gain from their community, and perhaps add a small dimension by my presence . . . ideally, if I was welcomed! But secondly, I would in no way feel bound to say Mass daily. I do not mind if ocasionally I do not say Mass—I mean it does not necessarily make a gap. Do not think the Mass means nothing to me! In other parts of this book you will get a different and correct impression of its importance in my life and its centrality to priesthood. But for instance I have had periods when no one called on my services, wanted a Mass, when I was not "part of community". Then I have sometimes simply prayed to the Lord, who is present in different ways at different times, or I have gone to a Mass which was not really a "community Mass" as a member of the congregation. (Apart from other considerations, it is important for a priest to experience now and then what it is like to be at the "receiving end"!) My third point goes the other way. There are almost limitless possibilities for groups to gather in Eucharist, often more "effectively" away from a church building (I mean as community, as gaining from the reading and discussion, as sharing prayer, as deeply committed to the passion, death and resurrection). When this is the case, and I am called upon, I would gladly offer the Eucharist as I might be required to do throughout the day, or throughout the evening. On a Sunday, a priest has often to celebrate two, three, four or even more times, because of the "Sunday obligation". Why not on a weekday a Mass for a class in school in the morning, a Mass for a sick person at her home in the afternoon, a Mass for a neighbourhood group in the evening? We must be flexible! But there must be some Christ-reason for what we do, what attitudes we take.

In a way, the most puzzling and difficult of the sacraments in my experience is Baptism. I say this because it is so important in its totality—bringing us to the Body of Christ, the enrolled people of God, to the other sacraments, to a limitless development of service, love and union, only to be realised to our capacity in heaven. Yet, it can be "given" to a small child, at the insistence of parents who never go near church, who do not instruct the child themselves, and do not send him or her to a church school. So it is possible for this baptised child to grow up totally ignorant of the wonder of his her "life in Christ". What then does the latter mean? On the other hand, I have known cases where a child has been refused baptism, though the mother is regularly at Mass, because the mother and father have only a common law marriage. As far as I can see, though no way is perfect, we need to build the community nature of baptism, bringing children to a living community, of which their parents are part; we need to try to prepare for the sacrament with the parents, distinguishing from one family to another, not by "favouritism" or "discrimination", but according to their ability, their background, their ethnic tradition and how they are themselves. Surely, Baptism is a *very personal* thing. It is not an innoculation or a charm against the evil eye, it is a welcoming to brotherhood on condition that the child agrees to be a brother. It is quite some offer—and quite some pledge. If the child is too young to enter into a personal pledge, the least we can do is to try to make very certain of the parental pledge, never allowing "in-discriminate" baptism without preparation.

There should be a lot more discussion and study of

Baptism . . . meaning, rite, follow-up, preparation, age, flexibility. One or two things can be said apart from this. The link between Baptism and the rest of Christian living needs to be emphasised. We live out our baptism daily, fulfilling it in the Eucharist and in our general witness within the church as a priestly people. The visible link occasionally can be helped through the liturgy, especially in the full use of the Holy Saturday ceremonies and the baptism of a child at Mass on a Sunday. There is also the encouragement to people other than the family to attend Baptisms, and to the family to continue the celebration at home. The West Indian families are particularly good at this and we have much to learn from their custom of real celebration at Baptism, and at other sacraments. Baptism is to be lived out in the family, so it is very right, very fitting, that there should be renewed emphasis at the baptismal party . . . given by the family as part of the priestly people . . . that this child is now a child of God, a member of God's consecrated nation and must be helped to grow in the community of love and service.

There should be no surprise at the baptism of a teenager or an adult. This should be accepted as part and parcel of every-day living. Who is to know why something has happened or not happened? . . . The less we gossip in Church and the more we say "alleluia" to the mercy of God, the fuller will be the glory of God.

I have written of Liturgy in Chapter 9, so I now only briefly mention some aspects of Holy Communion. We become very stereotyped in our celebration of first Holy Communion. Properly thought out and prepared there can be a great variety. For instance, different times of year may be chosen, different ages involved and different kinds of celebration arranged. I would myself be particularly emphatic on the pastoral good of bringing to Holy Communion, if it is at all feasible, all those who are in any way retarded, mentally handicapped or otherwise too easily classified as "unable to receive Communion". The dividends are incalculable. There is a wonder, joy and apostolic possibility among these children of God. In the more ordinary way, some find added meaning in their children receiving Holy Communion for the first time very quietly, without fuss, at a Sunday Mass with the family. There have been times when children have made their first Holy Communion at a house Mass. I am not convinced about this as a general rule, unless the next communion is a meeting in Eucharist with the wider community, because I am clear that at present anyhow the bigger community as well as the small is vital to pastoral coverage of the country. But for instance one occasion stands out in my memory. There was a very sudden and sad death. We had a house Mass in the home with all the relations, and neighbours gathered. One of the young ones of the family was to make her first Communion in a few weeks' time, but, they asked, could she not anticipate the day and receive on that bitter-sweet evening? She did receive Holy Communion that evening; I rather think the occasion will remain with her always.

In many ways, I personally am in a dilemma over Confirmation similar to the one involved with Baptism. The habit has varied in the Christian Church. I was confirmed about the age of eleven, which was late in my day! I was missed by the bishop's visit at seven. Most of my peers had "been done", so I felt a gawky fool of eleven among seven- and-eight-year olds, but my mother made sure I went through. There was not at that time a lasting "mark" which was thereafter continuously visible in life, because later, as I noted in Chapter 1, I gave up both practice and belief. This is the dilemma. Many parents want their children "done" at an age when they can still be made to go forward by parental will. But should this be so? What does it mean? What effect should there be from receiving the Sacrament, and what attitude of mind, heart and soul should there be? Is this a matter for parental decision, hoping for a personal acceptance later on by the "victim"? Or is it a free act to be entered upon knowingly, willingly and with some sign of perseverance to make it reasonable to admit a young person to a truly adult commitment to Christ? In the old wording, we were called "soldiers of Jesus Christ". A soldier is prepared to die in service of commitment. I know in history we have examples of young men and women who have pledged themselves, and some have died for Christ even before the teens. But somehow, it seems we have not yet tackled the meaning of the Sacrament . . . or am I simply being too rigid? Should it be possible to be confirmed either at baptism or aged seven or eight, or in the teens or before marriage?

At Southall, we have been consciously pushing the age upward, on the line of asking for a firm and independant commitment from the boy or girl. We now work on the basis of an annual visit of the bishop to confirm new candidates—which keeps numbers down, satisfies the fears of parents who feel it is "time he was done", and raises the development of response and responsibility a little. If the young person concerned is obviously not interested, does not attend instruction or is "only doing it for mum", we try to discuss at least postponement for a year. We are not yet really satisfied or happy. Perhaps there is no reason why we should be, but perhaps too we should at least be asking what we are at, what we are hoping for, what the young people can be expected to "gain". Perhaps we are asking the wrong questions, should go back and begin again! Anyhow—what we have done is gradually to develop a course which is testing and hopefully educative. The pattern of the last course was to begin in October for a May Confirmation. Each candidate enrolled personally and then one condition for being admitted to the sacrament was regular attendance once a month on a Sunday for a course. This consisted of the ordinary parochial Sunday Mass at ten-thirty, followed by a move, with prepared sandwiches, over to the local school. A team of clerical, religious and layhelpers was there gathered, under the leadership/ planning/guidance of a lay woman. From then until about three or four in the afternoon, in small groups or large, they entered into Confirmation as a living Sacrament with talk, discussion, film, slides, art work, writing, and music. This course lasted every third Sunday of the month between October and April. Then there was a whole day away, in the

Easter Holidays, and a return for practice and finally for
Confirmation at the end of May. For us, the numbers were
over-large. Last year we enrolled one hundred and twenty-
five in October and with drop-outs we eventually had one
hundred and six to receive the sacrament . . . not too bad a
perseverance! A good outcome of the large number was
that the bishop asked me as parish priest to share the giving
of the sacrament, as he had done on a previous occasion . . .
an excellent idea which both draws in the parochial clergy
and makes the time spent on each person that much more
elastic, as there need be no sense of overpowering numbers
in the queue.

"Queue" in my memory means confession! I disliked
and feared confession from an early age, especially in
regard to the waiting and shuffling up a bench outside the
box, and the often "unknown quantity" inside—the
reaction of the priest behind the screen. But it was all part
of the routine practice in the Church, and only recently has
it become widely apparent to me that many people of all
ages prefer a face-to-face confession situation. It has long
been my personal practice to hear confession anywhere at
any time, if a person wants to pour forth troubles, doubts,
entanglements and selfishnesses. Taking hold of the
moment of repentance rather than waiting for a confessional queue on a Saturday is spiritually important. This
is one reason for having an open door in the home of the
priest. But it goes further than that to the down-and-out on
Paddington Station, the scrupulous man at the church door
just as Mass is beginning, the person on the opposite seat of
the inter-city service to Birmingham.

The history of the sacrament of Penance has been such a
varied one—from the early days of once a life-time to the
introduction by missionaries from Ireland of the different
kind of repetitive confession-graduated-penance-rite.
There was a definite shift from the grave, rather public
community aspect to the individual, private and frequent
practice. This itself led in two directions . . . towards the
individual spiritual direction approach which really affected only a select minority . . . and the increasingly routine,

in-out confession of the large majority. The present-day renewal of outlook from Vatican II has very rapidly involved a decline in frequent confession. The emphasis of the new rite is much more upon the quality rather than the frequency of confession and must be very welcome to pastorally involved priests. The great hope is that it will also quickly be seen by all members of the Church to be a sound development in spiritual growth to maturity and not something to be deplored because the numbers at the confessional box have dropped.

I was much encouraged several years ago when an Irishman in his sixties came to me after a talk I had given urging face-to-face consultation and confession. He said how he had dreaded confessional queues since his youth in Dublin and this possibility of confession out of "the box" face-to-face was a wonderful liberation. Though I have found some older people are wedded to the confessional as such and to their pattern of regularity and frequency, I have experienced as many who are delighted with the new rite, when it is properly explained. But it is important pastorally that those who wish to continue as in the past, and are not subject to weening, should be allowed the same facilities as they have been used to before. Though "dependence" on frequent confession can be less than ideal, some people because of their make-up will probably always remain in need of that kind of support. The priest's work is to help them to grow in the Lord, but before growth, it is necessary to survive. Some take all their time and energy, and a lot of other people's, in struggling to keep going.

However, the newer attitude is much more in keeping with growth to maturity. The member of God's people should grow in wisdom and learn to be adult. The work of the priest should be in enabling this to happen. It is therefore appropriate for the priest to be a man who is himself deeply and constantly given to prayer and learning of the love of God in his own life, while he also listens to the world and lives in it. Doing so, he will himself know temptation, will be aware of the sexual, psychological, society and family pulls on individuals. He will be open to counselling and healing as I have already suggested in Chapter 4. It is right to train consciences, but it would be wrong and destructive to build up in people the sense of constantly teetering on the edge of mortal sin, when they are in fact living day by day and week by week in a prayerful human way, subject to the petty frustrations, selfishnesses and ordinary minor temptations. There is every reason for encouragement to grow, for personal teaching about prayer, for consultation towards the building up of a full life in Christ. All this should be positive and forward looking, with prayer, Eucharist, and full commitment to life and service as the key notes of direction. The actual occasion of full sacramental confession with absolution may be infrequent. The advantage of the priest and penitent facing and knowing each other is that there can be a much better understanding of the particular need. So it may be for one person that joining the penitential rite at Mass, following it with Holy Communion, and then living as well as possible may be his regular recourse to the forgiveness and love of God. For one reason or another, a different individual may need absolution more frequently. We are very varied as human beings in our development of relationship.

In saying all this, I do not want to lose sight of the fact that there is a great deal of evil about in the world as well as good. We must not fall into the trap suggested in C. S. Lewis' *Screwtape Letters,* where the Devil suggests his greatest tactical ploy with humans is to make them think he does not exist. In practice, it is very easy for us to come to acquiesce in situations and attitudes of the environment in which we live. This has been particularly apparent with the emergence of a greater social conscience—concern for the neglected, the starving, issues of justice and peace near at home and abroad . . . the whole area of "sins against the community". So often, we take for granted a way of life, an accepted practice which is basically dishonest, an attitude to this or that person which is destructive of persons, families or even countries. To take time to sit down and look at ourselves, to look at the teaching of Jesus Christ, to look at the world round about—this is a necessary part of Christian living. Christ has called us to perfection. We must be aware that this call will take us well beyond the ordinary, if we listen to it. For this, we need all the help we can get, because at present we are not sufficiently standing against the materialism of the world, we are not sufficiently given to generosity in loving and serving others. The author of *The Cloud of Unknowing* in entering further and further the depth of prayer discovered the sense of being "a lump of sin". While not wanting anyone to be "sin-ridden" and so filled with anxiety and even prevented from freedom to grow, it is more likely today that we border on the superficial in our prayer life, and so become less sensitive to our failure in relationship to God and man.

The creation of opportunities for pauses in life to make a survey is essential. This can be done publicly at each Mass, where silence needs to be introduced more purposefully. There are also opportunities in the encouragement of penitential services, the careful thinking out of the approach to instructing children on sin and confession. The new permission for occasional use of general absolution is excellent, and already in practice has been pastorally fruitful. Thought should be given to allowing it more freedom, for the discretion of the ordinary priest, because a number of occasions present themselves in our daily pastoral work. I mean by this that especially at funerals, or Baptisms during Mass, or at Nuptial Masses, as well as at the great feasts of the Church's year we can be moved to want to return both to God and to the family and community. This feeling should not remain an emotional surge, but can become the true beginning of a new way of life. It is good to be able to present the opportunity at such times for the welcome of God's love as seen in the readiness of the Prodigal Son's father.

Counselling has a part to play in the Sacrament of Marriage, as it has in the Sacrament of Penance. But in the former, it is of very great importance to begin before two people get to the stage of exchanging promises. Too often

there is little or no guided preparation for this way of life—
which is a real test of generosity, unselfishness and patience
in the true sense of love, beyond the simply romantic
picture. Especially in today's world, with all the tensions
and acquisitiveness and widespread acceptance of divorce
and remarriage, to set out upon the Christian ideal of
taking each other "for better for worse, for richer for
poorer, in sickness and in health, to love and to cherish, till
death do us part"—is quite a task. I know I have been guilty
myself of not making full use of the Catholic Marriage
Advisory Council, in their efforts of pushing instruction for
engaged couples. But I am sure in the present climate we
must create a new attitude towards marriage preparation. It
is so important to begin rightly before marriage as well as to
assist in the follow-up of marriage—especially through the
caring of the local community and by helping to make
parents accept responsibility for bringing their own
children to God—rather than beginning the mending
processes when cracks in a marriage appear, or looking for
broader reasons for nullity.

There are so many questionings of marriage, particularly
in regard to its lasting nature, that it is to be hoped the
"experts" will bring all their strength to bear in further
developing our understanding of God's will in our human
relationships. It is evident that the strains of married life
today are not being taken up in the power of the Sacrament
of Marriage, but that rather the tensions of Roman Catholic
marital sexual ethics, combined with the current state of
society, are probably binding insupportable burdens on
many married couples, and leading to frequent breakdown
in relationship. If such a statement is challenged critically,
then care should be taken to go into the evidence at hand. If
there is truth in the statement we should not try to cover up
the evidence, but be brave enough to face it, and with
prayer, openness to professional advice and great concern
for God's will for human beings explore the future.

Immediately, let us encourage the combination of giving
and receiving in married love and life, the balance between
the two partners, the need to prepare beforehand and to

learn generosity—by family living in childhood, education in service at home and in the community, and a real, continual commitment to prayer. Marriage will be throughout life a combination of hard work and human effort alongside spontaneous and joyful self-expression. We are a mixture and the best which is in us becomes fully involved and activated by our engagement at the various different levels of our being. If the priest or single person has to strive hard at being celibate and humanly fulfilled at the same time, then the married person too has to know that discipline, tolerance, generosity, patience and many other things make up the fine threads of the web of married life. Never having been married, I lack some qualification from experience, but as an outside and critically loving observer, I am day after day in admiration at the beauty of a good married life, and saddened immeasurably by the break-downs. Time and again in a listening capacity, I have heard the depth of sharing, commitment to each other and the children, total giving in time, energy, and the whole self. I have wondered at the relative dedication in marriage and celibate priesthood, and often found us celibates wanting in comparison.

One angle that may sound gloomy but needs stressing is the community support which is necessary for marriage. Of course families are "units", but they do not really live in isolation. Some of the value of community building is the way we can help each other. There will in the course of married life be times of joy to be shared and sorrow to be borne. Especially when husband or wife is hit by illness, outside support is deeply valuable. There are crises and even prolonged situations within marriage when it might seem that the whole web is going to be torn apart, but when "support at the edges" keeps the fabric there, and gradually bonds are strengthened again. Perhaps in this area too we do not find it possible to anticipate at the beginning of marriage experience that there may at periods seem to be only the rather arid and thin thread of "fidelity" keeping the web together. There may be times when love seems to have died, or at least the "feeling" has gone. When this is so and perhaps tempting outside relationships appear, the sheer continuance in being married seems senseless, because other prospects are so much more attractive. It is at these times that the testing of love and proving of love takes place most fully, rather in the way that belief in God can grow most strongly in his apparent absence—if we are faithful in empty darkness.

The priest has his part to play in listening and being available and supporting faith and hope in the darkness of day-by-day existence. And it is at such times that he needs the gentleness and strength of Jesus Christ to support the fabric of married life without interference and without merely trite and fatuous remarks: prayer together, listening, a cup of tea with a distressed wife, or a glass of beer with a seemingly abandoned husband . . . the combination of real, down-to-earth human relationship blending with strength and trust coming from God.

It is this same combination which is essential in the situations which arise through the labyrinth of moral law in regard to various aspects of marriage. Here, at the centre of the expression of human love, if we are really convinced also of our relationship with God there should be a total union of love, which has no place for selfishness. Certainly each remains self, individual, but the union is very close, very personal, and should be completely shared physically, mentally and spiritually. There is a height and depth of ideal love and union which we should be always striving for, always growing towards. Yet we are still imperfect human beings, and though we can and should have clear ideas about what constitutes selfishness and abuse of each other, part of growing in love is these very failures and our continued striving. We are also set in the world of today, not yesterday or tomorrow, and Christ has given us the task of working out our salvation here and now. In this, a husband and wife are not always alone, because their very love and union create new responsibilities and new extensions of love in children. It is here that it is so difficult to lay down other than in "ideal" principle the code of conduct of two human beings, pledged to each other to the fullness of their weakness, supporting each other in mutual love, sharing life and love with children—themselves voluntarily taken up in living this life of love, not in theory, but in practice. Here it is that the combination of strength and gentleness, love of the Law and love of the imperfect human being, His child and brother, comes to its peak in Jesus Christ. It seems to me that each one of us who as priests have responsibility for sharing our knowledge of the love of God have a tremendous task to witness to this love which is both demanding and sensitive, not breaking the bruised reed or quenching the smoking flax.

Lived out, in the whole life of the people of God, the Church's sacraments are a gentle, strong and wonderful ingredient of all that is planned by God to support the economy of his creation. If we neglect to use what he has given us through Jesus Christ, we neglect the true following of the One who has made us "a chosen race, a royal priesthood, a consecrated nation, a people set apart to sing the praises of God who called you out of the darkness into his own wonderful light" (1 Peter 2.9). As priests, it is part of our particular function that we so study and make available these sacraments that they are for the rest of the "royal priesthood" a living, speaking reality in our day-by-day witness to the eternal High Priest, Jesus Christ.

11

OPEN LIVING

One day, not long before writing this chapter, a man arrived at St. Anselm's rectory by the front door. He rang the bell and I went out to him to see if I could do anything for him. I was dressed in an open neck shirt and he immediately asked for the parish priest. I admitted I was he. He then said he had heard a lot about Southall and the kind of way we lived at St. Anselm's. He said he was himself a priest and he was horrified at what he had heard—and so he had come to see for himself, because he thought it was awful and he could not see how anyone could live that way; certainly he couldn't.

I use this event to begin this chapter because it voices something which is said over and over again. It is said to me, to my fellow clergy, to the parishioners, to the sisters. And what is more, people write to us and come to see us. Whatever is being spread about concerning our way of life, it has attracted attention. The reactions are varied, but without bias I can say that there seem to be more who are intrigued and want to know more than there are who are horrified and want to condemn.

The priest with whom I opened this chapter agreed to stay over with us and we simply let him live and eat and talk and look. At the end he went away happy, reassured and rather surprised at his own reaction. He had joined with us in the liturgy and he had met the various people who dropped in on us at the rectory. I do not know how he reported back to his friends and associates in the area from which he came. His letter of thanks seemed genuine and moved.

What follows is an attempt to put into words what we mean when we talk about having an "open house" presbytery.

The openness is relative. Normally the front door is

unlocked. In summer it generally stands wide open too. There is encouragement for those who are of the parish or whom we know to walk in without ringing the bell. The door is locked at night when we go to bed. The church also remains open all day, despite vandalism which includes breaking open the bookstall regularly, setting fire to curtains and destroying or removing all money boxes. People know they can come into the kitchen. Groups gather there for tea or coffee, people come to meals, ask to use the telephone, pop in and out to type, clean, print the newsletter, count the collection, without having to bother anyone or needing attention. Most of the time the atmosphere is relaxed, easy-come-easy-go, friendly and in this sense open too.

The main thing which makes a house "open" or "closed" is really the mental attitude of those who live there. We have to begin by asking ourselves and each other who is welcome, who or what are we protecting by shutting and locking the front door? Though there may be good reasons put up for protection, there is no doubt we are protecting our property and ourselves. We protect our property against damage and theft; we protect ourselves against invasion of privacy, unwanted persons and general interruption or irritation. But the fairly continual "irritant" element is the very element that is both most in need and most awkward in deed! I mean the ex-Borstal or prison lads, the drug addicts, the apparently permanent lay-abouts, the persistent arriver-at-meal-times. To me this is an essential element in the following of Christ to whom we must be open. What are we to do with no-goods, junkies, lads on probation, alcoholics, thieves, depressed neurotics, would-be suicides? Send them away? Say we are sorry, they are not 'our line"? Their presence gives a real sense of insecurity, not least to one's property which can tend to disappear! I am sure at times we all resent them. At times the pressure becomes too great to bear when they are all "about" in various states of disruption. And this is when we all grumble and grouch and burst in different directions.

It is only fair to say that some of the notions set up by this phrase "open house" are to our knowledge wildly far from the reality of our living; but on the other hand there are some aspects which would probably fulfil the worst fears anyone can imagine or have thought possible . . . and I say this because they have really got us down ourselves. But despite that those of us who are at it at the moment have no doubt at all about its value as a way of living, though when there is a change of personnel we suggest to the powers that be that anyone given the choice of coming to join our team should first of all come and see for himself what it may mean. And we fully realise that not everyone will want or feel able to live this kind of life.

It is important to stress that what is written here, or written up elsewhere, is rather like some of the lives of the saints . . . all highlights and strange happenings. Unfortunately, like the mass media, Church gossip thrives on the extraordinary. The wonderful, basic and ordinary does not generally make headlines. So, when writing of the open house and the atmosphere, it should be pointed out fairly early that there are long periods of silence and emptiness, when nothing is happening, when it is possible to think to oneself . . . well all this is a lot of boloney. There are other places I know which are twice as busy, twice as noisy and twice as effective! If that is so . . . especially the effectiveness—we would be only too glad. We are not giving a blueprint for all parishes or parish situations. This is an example of a way of tackling life in a parish today. Therefore, if you come here you must not be surprised if for instance you have your breakfast and after Mass at nine, nothing happens in the house or in the parish, unless you go out to find it. You could well spend three hours before a midday meal studying Aristotle, Marx, Kung or even Jesus Christ without interruption. The same could be true of the time between midday food and supper at six or evening Mass at seven. There might not be a doorbell; sitting in your own room no one might come to see you. After the evening Mass, it could happen that you could sit from say eight until your bedtime and be totally undisturbed. Should you care to go to bed at such a time as would allow you to get up at five, six or seven in the morning ninety-eight per cent of the days of the year, you could guarantee to be able to give yourself totally to God in prayer . . . IF you got up!

What I am saying is this. As we have lived it, the open house can be a great strain and noise and nuisance. But also in itself it is not necessarily oppressive and overwhelming, because the actual "open house" existence is "inside" the building. A twenty-four hour non-stop bustle is simply not what we have experienced. There is space, there is time, there is silence, if you want to use it. But, it is also true that there are all the other dimensions of the demanding-parish which need to be faced. Ought I to take communion to old Mrs so-and-so who is bedridden and would love it but would say to me if I did not go: "I know you are so busy, Father. It is wonderful you have time for me at all. When you didn't come last week, I knew you must be busy, and I said an extra prayer for you" (And, God forgive me, I had a bit of rheumatism, it was raining and I said to myself, as I decided to stay indoors: "I know Mrs So-and-so will understand, and anyhow, I'll go next week. Now I'll read that booklet on Communion of the Sick which I haven't read yet!")

So, even in an open house, choice enters in. It is probably one of the most maturing but most painful aspects of such living that the choice has to be made frequently and seems so devastatingly opposite to the end which is proposed as good. I write this from inside. I write on a Sunday afternoon. Should I be writing? Our co-working deacon is doing baptisms, the others have just sent midday guests off in various directions, our lady-producer-of-food has been persuaded to take the weight off her legs; the lodgers are out painting what is supposed to be a new law centre; in half an hour, a girl who is having a breakdown is coming in with her husband to talk. Should I sleep? Or pray? Or read the Sunday paper? Or just be quiet? Or watch the TV? Or try to write this book? Soon there will be the evening service and then Mass, with the youth choir coming in to practice beforehand. Should I shut the door and have a siesta or

read the Sunday paper? . . . that seems to keep coming up
. . . In an open house, anything almost may be right or
wrong, but it is a feast of Our Lady, and all morning I have
been preaching that she managed to say "yes", to live
"yes" and not to introduce the destructive word "but",
which so often is a cover-up for "no". So . . . what about
me?

I have always believed that I should do whatever I can to
forward the work of God, so I am not particularly bothered
if one moment I am preaching, next washing up, then on to
clearing a drain and from there taking communion to a sick
person. I also believe that there is no reason why I should
not play my part in helping to finance the parish where I
live and work, just as I expect every other parishioner to
support not only his pastors but the parish, which includes
the buildings, the heating, the bread and wine for
Eucharist, and the odd pound for those of us who cannot
make ends meet. In some unknown fashion, God has given
me a facility with the pen . . . or the typewriter in this case. I
don't think it wrong to write and talk about God on His
Day! Whether or not I should be having a siesta,
meditating or reading the Sunday paper is anyone's guess.
If I am really bad tempered later, I'll think I should have
had that siesta rather than hitting these keys.

This is only a stupid example. Each of us has to make his
own choice, his own mistakes, and hit upon his own way,
for himself and within the community. My choice has been
to try to combine depth of prayer life, love of God, service
and love of people and paying my way in the community in
which I am living. The particular way in which this has
been possible in Southall has been within the open
community, where as a team we enjoy working together
and each putting in our small part to the whole. It may raise
eyebrows or seem out of this world. So be it. However,
there are other parishes we have come across in this country
and also in different parts of the world where the same kind
of openness is practised and with similar happy results,
which gives us encouragement that this is not just a mad
flash in the pan, but a valid way. The other point which is

worth stressing is that quite a few clergy, younger especially but not all of them so young, have found that the very closed and regimented way of life in some parishes is more than they can take and have gone so far as to leave the priesthood as a result. If the saying is true that it takes all types to make a world, then clerical living in the parochial setting has been too stereotyped in the past.

What is the theory behind the "open house"? Basically it is attempting to put into modern expression and in the present kind of parochial situation a sense of the closeness and availability of Jesus Christ. We do not go so far as to say with him that we have nowhere to lay our heads, but we try to look at him, to see how the people crowded round him and left him little time for himself. We find him living in poverty and know that we are far from poor as a clerical class. But poverty is not merely financial poverty. We try to be poor in that we are open, in that we can be invaded and our privacy disturbed; sometimes we can feel very poor indeed when the house is crowded, the noise great, the demands rough and loud, the thanks nil. Does this have any effectiveness in the Christ-sense? From inside it is hard to say. It certainly seems that people in general, and perhaps more particularly young people feel more free and are more ready to come to us. There is always a problem of distance and closeness between priest and people. We think this is considerably broken down by the open door. People do come in and out, young people and old "feel at home" in the rectory where we live. I'm not sure that there are many clergy houses where the parishioners feel at home.

From the openness there comes also the use of the house as a centre from which the parish does things, not just the clergy. The openness fosters the possibility of people of different levels meeting informally on common ground, the various elements of the parish mingling and being less cliquey, while those who are in trouble can be absorbed and find acceptance again in ordinary society, say after a prison sentence has been completed. If the openness is one which considers the whole area as parish and every single person living in Southall as a child of God, there grows a wider contact in and out of the house with members of other churches and other faiths. The front door is not a barrier to be breached by the courageous but a way into friendship. Living in a multi-cultural area, white, brown and black come in, christian and non-christian.

Quite unconsciously we, both clergy and others, tend to find it easier and warmer to mix with "our own sort" religiously, racially, socially. I say unconsciously because some of us would immediately react to deny this. It means taking a look at one's life, one's friends and how and where one relaxes. Our freedom of choice we use every day choosing what pub to go to, what shop to patronise, whom to invite home and whom not. Some are better at mixing than others, young often more so than the middle and old, but we all have our limits. Yet the scriptural and Godly basis to the community of God's people is that all men are brothers. Our interpretation can follow Orwell's—some are more brothers than others! For it is not easy even with the guidance and help of the Holy Spirit to accept again and again with a smile the scrupulous, neurotic woman; to hear patiently the man needing money for the weekend who "has a job to go to on Monday"; to stand and be insulted by a drunkard, who has a way of kicking in the front door; to allow a lad sent by Probation to stay in the house though he has pinched a lot before and everyone has to lock their doors; to accept a homeless family at midnight and to find they expect to cook food for the babies. These all equally brothers? Or is there not bound to be difference in attitude and affection?

Once you have said "come in" to one, they all tend to come. It is no good getting a reputation that there is one law for the rich and one for the poor when you come to the rectory. And so to some extent there has to be a policy and the first essential is that the clergy and housekeeper if there is one—the basic make-up of inhabitants—have to have knowledge and acceptance of what is happening. I do not think I personally am always good at consultation, but perhaps we have improved as we have gone along. Much of what is possible and what is intolerable can only be worked out as it is lived out. Keep the door open is fine, let people come in is fine! But does that mean that they can come into the kitchen just any time, make a cup of tea for themselves and take a biscuit? This has to be worked out with the housekeeper, and even when it is, there may then be those living in the house or coming in who so abuse the facility that the policy has to be rethought. People can come in . . . who are people? Again, there is some distinction made between the parishioners who come in for a coffee morning on a Tuesday after the morning Mass, with coffee laid on and a discussion—and the group of "dead-end" kids who invade the main room, switch on the TV and eat fish and chips all over the carpet. Both lots are welcome, but the first tend to clear up for themselves and the second tend to cause considerable irritation to the nose by fishy smell and to the clothes when you sit on the odd bit of fish or the odd chip!

When we began, the effort was to get the parishioners more used to coming in and out, to feeling that this was their house as well as the priests'. So we made considerable efforts to see that there were meetings in the house. The first Christmas, as we had no hall big enough for the bazaar, we had it in a small hall under the church, and then all through and round the rectory. We invited individuals and families in to meals, we tried to give a cup of tea and a biscuit when people had to wait to see a priest. If there was a meal on, and someone arrived they were normally asked to share if it was possible, or to have a cup of tea while we ate. The housekeeper had answered an advertisement which forecast the kind of openness, but even so it was a bit much for her husband who was very elderly and deaf; she herself did magnificently. From the start, we had the policy of all of us doing the washing up, so that when there were "guests" they joined with us round the kitchen sink in a friendly and informal way, which made a very good social occasion, and took the drudge and sting out of vast quantities of dirty dishes.

The young people learnt the way-in largely through the development of the youth choir, because they held their Sunday rehearsals in the main room for an hour or so before the evening Mass. Though not the busy pastor's idea of peace on a hard Sunday, this has been invaluable in contact and in a freedom with them and ourselves which, if at times demanding, is a good augury for the future. One of the important features of this has been that not all the young people are catholics, nor are all of them practising. While some might feel that it could be damaging to let them be, it is perhaps an essential part of an open system that the religious status and the degree of belief or practice are not criteria for anyone's coming in. They come because they are people, because they want to come, or someone has brought them along, because they found their way in, because they were intrigued or lonely or seeking or any other reason—fundamentally because each is a person, a child of God, one of us. That is enough; what happens from contact is up to our acceptance, their growth and the Holy Spirit.

An encouraging side over the time as far as individual young people has been concerned has been quite a good continuance through the teenage-lapsing period; with good personal contact which does allow the kind of communication between the priest and the younger person which is helpful to both. They are not afraid to come in; they are not afraid to ask for help, for advice, for things from the priests and the parish. There can be fruitful incidents like the eighteen-year-old who announced he intended to make a retreat the following weekend. Where? Oh, in the rectory of course; you give me a room and a few chances to talk to you, and I'll read and pray and be quiet. Or the other seventeen-year-old who came in to say he would be having a week's holiday; could he come and live in the rectory and follow me about each day for a week in everything that I did so that he could see what it was like being a priest.

But not all parishioners are equally easy and it does mean inevitably that some problems will recur and that it is not easy to shut the door just because somebody is taking up too much time. The balance of patience and firmness is not always either easy or appreciated! But in a way it can be a great help if the situation is such that a lonely person can be happy to sit watching the TV, or someone overcome with emotion or dead-beat or the worse for wear from drugs can lie on the settee in one of the waiting-rooms to recover. The fact that we expect this kind of thing means that we are not surprised or upset when we go into a room and find that someone is flat-out. Mind you, it can be annoying, because you probably have to find somewhere else to go, but you get used to it and do not really mind provided now and then you let off steam about the whole situation!

The letting off of steam is crucial. If the atmosphere between the clergy and with the housekeeper, and even with the sisters who live very closely by us, is tense and angry, the results are bad; if for one reason or another communication breaks down, the situation really becomes impossible. The principle of communication within the house is of primary importance. I do not think we have necessarily worked out how this is best achieved. So much depends upon the individuals who are forming the team. Perhaps the first point is to attempt some kind of equality so that the clergy anyhow are working together and also independently, not always asking permission from the senior man or feeling unable to take initiatives. The sharing of everything as far as possible is basic, whether it is duties, Masses, washing up, meals, ideas, moans, worries or anything that you can name. Then there is the actual time together. I personally am bad at this . . . watching Match of the Day is not one of my joys, and often there is so much going on there is little time to settle down to chat or watch until late in the evening. So we have made a definite time every Monday evening at ten-thirty when we are just together over a glass of beer to talk about anything and nothing. Of course, there are other times as well like meals, our discussion of liturgy, a period set aside each Saturday to discuss duties for the next week, a monthly morning or evening with the rest of the team, that is the sisters, for prayer and discussion.

An extension of the open house which is more prob-lematical is the possibility of accepting individuals or even a family into the rectory to share the accommodation when they are in serious need. The house, which had been built for two priests and a housekeeper in our case, was fantastic. In addition to his sitting room downstairs, the parish priest had a huge bedroom and private bathroom upstairs, and the assistant priest a bedroom and a large sitting room on the first floor. In addition there were three bedsitting rooms on the first floor and a very large room on the top floor which was a kind of suntrap easily capable of holding three or four beds. I don't know why the house was built in this way, but I personally would find it hard to live in such a house unless it was full, when thousands in the area are homeless. It took very little time to suggest that these rooms be occupied, and the first inhabitants were the sisters who had not yet got occupation of their house. To them was immediately added an Indian priest who was learning English.

But if you declare yourself available, or if you are just moving round the town with a silly sort of smile on your face being friendly, things happen because people come to know. The Social Services, the Probation, the Police and the Courts all in turn began to ring up for the odd night's accommodation, for appearance in court and so on. Our first semi-permanent lodger was a young Sikh who came in late one night because someone had said we would help as he had been thrown out of his home by his father. I instance this person, because he had some problems which involved my appearing for him in court and visiting him for three months in a detention centre; but after staying with us for the best part of a year, he has gone from strength to strength, and having a very good steady job now, I recently helped him to open an account with a Building Society, as he has married and is saving for a house of his own with a clean record for the past five years.

It does not very often happen this way, but when it does it is worth all the other aggro and agony that occurs. We really become very fond of some who are with us, and they help a lot about the house with others who come in, with making people feel at home and with anything that is happening.

Unfortunately, there are "crises". Firstly, picture an evening: tired clergy, tired "inhabitants". Scene: dining/sitting/TV room. Choice on TV: News at Ten or a documentary on recent pop music. Clergy come in from visiting, House Mass or discussion group, hoping to see News at Ten, to find the room full of people, all kinds, "ours" and "others", already switched to the documentary . . . so whatever happens, irritation for one or another. A truly "family" situation known in every home, but not so manifest in clergy houses.

Secondly, two a.m. Doorbell goes. Very drunk ex-prisoner who is living on the top floor hasn't got a key and wants to come in. Rather cross priest lets him in, expresses his irritation and is told: "You're all a lot of Catholic bastards . . . "—a good meditation point for the Sunday sermon, but not easy to live with!

Thirdly: Monday morning, one priest arrives at breakfast grumbling that the bathroom was filthy. Another says the lads upstairs were doing a kind of war dance above his head at one in the morning. The housekeeper puts her head into the dining-room and says it is no good the clergy thinking they will get any clean sheets this week as there are none in the cupboard and the lads must have taken them.

A fairly frequent crisis which sends everyone up the wall is when someone has a bath and lets it overflow, because the water comes through into the kitchen, swamps it and fuses the lights! There are the occasions when they say they are in for meals, the food is cooked and they do not turn up; and when they turn up and there is no food because they said they would be out. There are the late night shouts, the occasional drunkenness and sometimes a fight; there are the meals when no one speaks and the tension is electric. All this as I am sure you can feel raises the "nuisance level" in the house and when it is really bad we all feel wholeheartedly that we would like to throw them all out, shut the door and be thoroughly private. Generally speaking, after a discussion among us and a day to cool off, we all agree that they must stay. But we had one occasion when the three boys who were together in the top room ganged up on us and came to a pitch of aggression which we finally decided was being destructive all round. We had a great deal of loss of money, damage to our parish minibus and then a confrontation in which they demanded all kinds of things from us. We took long and serious consideration of this and gave them all an ultimatum to find alternative accommodation before a certain date. It was pathetic and tough; it left us picking up the bits, which interestingly we are still doing, because leaving us accommodation-wise did not mean they left us care-wise—they still come back to the time of writing . . . and one we hope is on his feet . . . one out of three!

Perhaps the major discomfort which an open house brings is the sense of lack of privacy. We are no longer safe and private behind the front door. We can be safe and private if we go to our own rooms or the little section of the priest's room upstairs which has been cut off for a retreat for the clergy. Even then, you may have to lock the door of your own room! But the way this lack of privacy impinges on us is not necessarily most noticeable at the time of watching TV, with a lot of others, perhaps men and women and non-clerics. Nor is it necessarily in the people popping in and out unannounced. The most trying time for all those who have lived as basic inhabitants is during meals. The meal is something which is central to our existence and our community living. Without meals we are simply "lodgers", we are not family. But I expect that many families who have been able to have friends or relatives for a weekend, and really enjoyed it, have also known the release and sense of freedom when they have gone. Living in St. Anselm's rectory is a little like living a very long weekend where there is no let-up! Nevertheless, if our theory of openness is to work, we must include and make central the eating together as a family with all the tensions and joys which this involves. Many a priest has never really been in mixed company except through family gatherings or the occasional social activities. He has trained and lived with his fellow priests-to-be in some seclusion in a seminary, and consciously or unconsciously expects to live in a priests' house of one sort or another without the intrusion of lay people. Meals all male and clerical, numbers small; conversation a bit inward or lightly on football, the parish bazaar or similar topics.

If there are three priests, a deacon, a visiting priest, a couple of the sisters from across the road, the person who is doing the cooking, a girl who has come in to type, a married couple who are involved in preparing an away-day, and two or three who are recently out of borstal, one on drugs, another a con man . . . and all of these at supper together, and some at breakfast, and some who are not working in for midday and then all of them again for supper . . . and this day in and day out, with the numbers up to twenty or twenty-five at Sunday lunchtime . . . well it can be that a priest grumbles that it is not what he is used to, it's tiring and it's more than he can take. So, it may be that we modify it for a time, we cut down the numbers until a crisis breaks and the house is full again and the table this time feeding hungry kids just arrived from Uganda or Malawi or wherever the present hot-spot is—which may be Northern Ireland or Shepherd's Bush or anywhere in the world of God in which we live.

The question by letter, by phone, by doorbell, by word of mouth in the street is "Can you take?", "Can you take?", "Can you take?" or just—"Can you help?" The big couple of questions we have to ask, remembering that justly or unjustly we stand for Christ in this situation, judged or misjudged does not matter—the big question is: Can we? followed on by: *Will* we?—and if the reply is 'NO!", then all creation is listening for the answer which we may give on phone, by letter or at the door to the question: WHY NOT?

Sure it may not be fair. The people or person may not be "worthy", it may be a try on, it may be a cadger, or a simple thief wanting an easy way in—so what? I wish we knew the answer. It takes quite some time often either to say "yes" or "no". I suppose I personally am more stupid than some, but I cannot help asking myself what kind of a figure I will cut when I ask for a night's rest in heaven! This may be silly or emotive or special pleading . . . but it is what I personally have to face each night before I go to sleep and each morning as I struggle to say to the Lord: "You know all things, You know I love you".

One of the invaded areas of privacy which has been hinted at is more mingling of the sexes. We were favoured by God in that the sisters failed to get possession of their house when we all wanted to begin work together, so it seemed the most natural thing in the world that they should use the vacant rooms in the rectory. This they did for about three months, having a dormitory for three of them at the top of the house, while one who was teaching in the school had her own room. They ate with us and we were able to have long planning sessions and very open discussion. Having lived in university life this form of mixed communal living was nothing new to me, but I think it was especially new for the sisters, and I believe it did a lot to cement our relationship as a team from the start as we came together to know the joys, hopes and problems of Southall, realising that we all had the common goal of preaching Christ to Southall. Indeed, in parenthesis, it has been one of the increasing sorrows of the situation that this religious order, which so openly at the beginning asked for volunteers to come for the particular project of being parish sisters working in and for the area, has subsequently been unable to keep the original vision, moving sisters in and out without managing to keep the needs of the parish primary.

But the interchange at a close level of the two sexes in vision, planning, interpretation, liturgy and catechetics has been invaluable. In this, lay men and women have also been prominent and of excellent and stimulating value. However, it is at this kind of level that a different privacy or privilege can seem to be invaded. The modern church has brought into being liturgical commissions, laity commissions and so on. Those who work with them have grown accustomed to, and come to relish, the different insights which come from clerical and lay minds, from male and female. For some clergy who have not been used to such

cross-fertilising, to have the laity, and I think especially
women, discussing liturgy with them as equals and making
suggestions which enhance the role of the laity at the
expense of the clergy seems to constitute a threat. At least
one of the clergy who worked with us at one time felt very
bitter (and told me so in no mean fashion) because he felt
his authority questioned and his status undermined. We
had a particular Easter when all this showed very starkly.
The liturgy committee made up of the clergy and lay men
and women were discussing the Holy Week and Easter
ceremonies. For a couple of years we had had reading of the
Passion by a mixture of clergy and lay people, with
choruses and so on. Suddenly there erupted a wave of hot
anger at the "usurpation" of the position of the clergy. A
young deacon and one of the then assistant priests made it
quite clear that they would not stand for any lay
participation. The feeling of threat to their position came
out clearly in the very heated discussion. For me it was a
combination of sadness, irritation, and upset for the way
the lay men and women were sat on, together with a
hindsight realisation that it took us further forward in our
living. That year at Easter we were set back considerably.
Since then the question has never even been mooted
again—somehow we have lived on forward. It is no longer
relevant.

For me too it was a good lesson because it became clear
that the degree of openness had simply been too much.
Age, experience, temperament and background mean there
will be a different saturation point of annoyance or
tiredness. This was especially true of the irritation some
felt at having to watch TV with a mixed group of those
living in the house and those who might have dropped in.
And out of it emerged a small clergy-only room on the first
floor. This caused me some heartburn as it seemed
immediately to be a threat to openness. But as it has worked
out I can see the real value in it, because though the room is
not tremendously much used, it is there, and its very
presence to some extent psychologically eases the tension.
Today with change of personnel, mixed groups use the

room for prayer and discussion so it is not only for clergy relaxation. Gradually I am coming to learn the way in which hard reactions can alienate, and how even slight modification can go a long way to clearing controverted issues. After all, we are very different individuals. God who is so magnificent in his breadth and height and length and depth of embrace would surely want us to be fairly open-armed as well. But we should remember in saying this that the symbol we have of the open-armed love of God is Christ stretched on the Cross. We don't like it, but we need a bit of stretching!

Part of that stretching and the openness which flows from it is significant in this particular corner of Greater London where we live in a multi-racial situation. Having looked round and tried to talk and make contact inside and outside the Catholic structure and personnel of the parish, it became clear that the differences of background and religious upbringing in the various parts of the world from which the Catholic parishioners came needed special understanding and adjustment. This is mostly something which is covered in Chapter 7. But in addition, there was the situation, the belief and the relationship of the non-Christian people who are so numerous here. The pre-dominant religion is that of the Sikhs, but there are also a number of Hindus and Muslims. The open house lent itself to trying to encourage some contact especially with the Sikhs. Though they are very friendly and welcoming in the Gurdwara (the Sikh temple), they are self-contained, and the actual contact through conversation and meeting at home had been patchy. There seemed to be one or two things to try. I went myself to pray in the Gurdwara, and made some individual contacts which led to invitations to weddings and once or twice to meals at home. We helped re-house a number of all three faiths when they were in difficulty, and had the young Sikh with us for a long time, followed afterwards by another who is still here and much more settled. Through court appearances, working with the local community relations council, trying to help the Asian women especially, and doing some English classes for individual people, a knowledge of us spread round. We also made sure that we were involved in People to People week and invited members of the Gurdwaras and temples to our big feasts of Christmas, Easter and so on. Gradually, one or two came for a kind of spiritual talk and treated me as a guru.

We were quite clear that we were not proselytising. We ourselves were seeking information and when asked were passing on the good news of Jesus Christ. The major part of the good news however, was that we were trying to live lives in the street, church and home which were Christian in the fullest sense. This meant being people who tried to live a life of prayer, worshipped with sincerity and fullness in the church, and were prepared to open our doors to those who wanted to come and look though without any intention of joining. It was not until sometime early in 1976 after nearly six years of myself and the sisters being in Southall that two Sikh priests and two laymen came to me and asked to talk to me about Jesus Christ. Before, there had been individuals, never priests or a group. Since then another priest and I have been talking. There is more contact and interest in each other, what we each believe and how we worship. But I am not myself convinced that we in the Catholic community are really ready to welcome them with open arms. It is more important that we *are Christians* and are seen and felt to be Christian, than that we actually stand up and preach. In many ways, the central pivot of the Sikh religion, after the *Good Book*, is the individual Holy Man. The holy man they understand and recognise no matter what faith or church he belongs to. By their fruits you will know them. When there was trouble in Southall in the summer of 1976 over the murder of a young Sikh and the racial tensions and demonstrations which followed, the Sikhs turned to us with a trust which was moving. The depth of their religious strength stretched out to us for support and wisdom in a potentially violent political scene. It was not until this incident that we realised that the years of getting on in a quiet way were bearing fruit. We had been about, with prayer and work among all sections of the community—this had been observed. So now we are in the position of seeing that for the basic understanding between peoples and for the development of community relations in this little area the open living of the Christian life has been shown to be influential for unity, peace and good. But it leaves us with much further to go in the same direction since this trouble, with the result that the house is now more of a meeting place than it was before. An inter-faith group of Sikh, Hindu, Muslim and various Christian denominations meets regularly. We are trying to work towards better relations between the young and the rest of the community, notably the police. This has meant that more young people of Asian and West Indian extraction drop in and out.

The interesting part about this is the way the whole openness is tending towards meeting the kind of demand which seems to be made by the circumstances of the present and the future. By that I mean that many of us are by nature a bit shut in, especially in relationships and with people of different social backgrounds or cultures. But when the door of the house is open, then unless you are going to live in revolt or in schizophrenia the door of your mind and your heart must be open also. In that, as in the symbol of the outstretched arms of Christ, it is as well if we grasp that it was on the cross that his heart was opened for love of us. The opening of the mind and heart, as well as the opening of the house and home can be likened to the carrying of the cross daily, to crucifixion and even to death . . . but resurrection follows surely.

12

PEOPLE IN COUNCIL

Before Vatican II the Roman Catholic Church in England used to look at the Church of England, see what was going on, and take it for granted that anything they did was at least a mistake and could easily be heretical. This was especially so when it was clear how much power parish councils made up of lay people had over their clergy. The Catholic priest was normally something of a dictator in *his* parish. Of course, Cardinal Newman had written long ago "On consulting the Laity", but perhaps only a few more university-type laity had ever come across that work.

Then Vatican II came out with its policy in favour of setting up various councils and commissions which would *advise* the bishop and go down sufficiently far in the pecking order to be based on parishes—once more to *advise* the parish priest. The reaction was a widespread non-implementation which reflected the scepticism in some parts and the outright antagonism in others. Some of the bench of bishops in England and Wales told their clergy to set up parish councils; only a few went very far in pursuing the planting and the young growth of such councils. The result was that in many places there was no planting, in others there was no watering and a quick death ensued, in others there was sickly existence, in others the councils did really get off the ground. It was rather like the parable of the sower. Some of Vatican II's word fell by the wayside, a small percentage on rock—quick growth, quick death; the thorns of parochial busy-ness and inbred custom of parish priests accounted for quite a lot of actually living parish councils being stifled. Some fell on good soil and the growth of sharing has been marked.

Like so many new ideas this particular fruit of the Council was looked upon with suspicion in itself, in its purpose and in the imagined difficulty of its planting.

Authority at a point such as this is only good for legislating; implementation is very difficult to enforce beyond keeping an eye on the actual "establishment" of a nominal body. It has to be accepted that much of the slowness in understanding and implementing the Council came from the isolation of the British Isles from the developments of post-war continental Europe. Some inbred conservatism combined with a narrow ecclesiastical education and a suspicion of most ideas coming from beyond the English Channel was enough to encourage caution and feet-dragging. Many of the bishops who took part in the council from these islands were opposed to much of what was first put forward and were slowly helped along to a broader understanding. Some were only ultimately "converted" to acceptance because of loyalty to the Church and the Pope; it can be doubted whether for some there was ever much enthusiasm to implement but rather a sense of duty.

It may be that this is an unfair interpretation, but it is one which crept down from the top to more junior clergy such as myself who gained what knowledge was available from the Press firstly, and later from Council documents as they were published, but seldom felt fired with enthusiasm by local episcopal reaction. This was a very strange period with a very strange atmosphere. Little actually happened in practice but there was so much which at second-hand seemed exciting, liberating and challenging. In international and university circles there was endless discussion, a sense of anticipation, a thrill that a new breath of the Holy Spirit was spreading through the Church. Not least, for some clergy, there was the joy that the laity had been given a "leg up" by the general tenor of the sessions and by individual documents. And it was this kind of feeling which led to a reading or re-reading of Newman and to ready acceptance of the principle of working much more strongly and generally with lay people in the Church. Hence for such clergy the parish council was an obvious method among others for implementing the new emphasis or vision in the Church.

That Southall had a parish council established in St. Anselm's when I arrived was to the credit of a parish priest who though not himself won by the Vatican Council was prepared to let his curates get on with quite a lot of innovation, if the curates were prepared to be fairly forceful in their ideas and enthusiasm. They were. The parish council came into being. Work was done on a constitution, the council itself met and discussed, with the parish priest as president and an elected chairman from the parishioners. The first years were inevitably and rightly settling to the idea, going through teething troubles, and beginning to emerge. The chairman was good, solid, somewhat given to directing the course of discussion. He was definitely "the parish priest's man". At the time, he was the leader of a largely "passive" laity, with small strands of genuine new life springing up through family groups. The parishioners were, for the most part uninterested. For the first elections at which I was present, there were twenty members to be elected and the parish priest could nominate ten others. There were barely more than twenty names proposed and most of them were for re-election. Appeals for new blood achieved practically nothing. When voting took place at a general parish meeting some seventy or eighty out of a parish of about four or five thousand turned out. The three or four who failed to get into the council by ordinary vote crept in by my power of nomination. Given this kind of enthusiasm, the voting numbers and the high percentage of re-election it was difficult to withstand charges of irrelevance and of cliquishness.

The council itself in the following year set about trying to find ways of broadening its image by publicity, not only in the parish newsletter and on the church notice-board, but by opening its meetings to the local press. This opening both to parish observers and to the press was quite a hurdle to jump. A number of councillors felt that our deliberations should be entirely private, even from the parish. After considerable discussion both parish and press were admitted, and I do not think there has been any cause for complaint. The main task however was how to involve more people in volunteering for service and in taking part in elections. A sub-committee studied the problem and took a new approach. It was decided voting should be over a weekend, with the possibility of sick people and house-bound voting on either day from home, if they could not come, but the main voting taking place during the Sunday, with enough leeway for shift workers to take part.

In the event, everything went well. The liturgy of the day was planned so that the two readings and the psalm all spoke of service. We made the adaptation of having the first reading from the Gospel, taking the Last Supper story and Christ's call and witness to service (Jn. 13. 4–5, 12–17). This was followed by the working out of the message of service in the Acts of the Apostles (Acts 6. 1–7), and the homily brought out the relevance to Southall here and now ... noting the calling of those who were prepared to help, the need for volunteers, for interest, for a sense of sharing partnership rather than a "priest-run" parish. The im-mediate application of this occurred in a pause before the Creed. Voting papers and pencils had been given out at the door of the Church, and now all those over eighteen were asked to vote for a limited number of candidates. The papers were then collected and brought up with the offerings and placed on the altar during the rest of the Eucharist. This happened at every celebration that day, and when the votes were finally counted over seven hundred had voted.

The next step, following the counting, was to notify all those who had been on the list and to stir them and others to come to the AGM the next Friday evening. This too was arranged during Mass. The penitential rite was followed in the usual way, then suitable readings. Next came the AGM in curtailed form with the chairman giving a report, a financial report and the president (parish priest) giving his report. On that particular occasion we managed to get the local auxiliary bishop to come to celebrate for and with us, to give a direct link with the wider service of the church through the diocese. On other occasions we have had the local dean and the chairman of the senate of priests ...

because there is always the danger that we become parochial and forget that part of the purpose of our "grassroots" response to consultation in the parochial work of the church is the more effective voice of the local church in the presence of the greater Church, when diocesan, national or international discussions take place and decision are made. It is not easy to persuade a tired shift worker in Southall that it is important for the world Church that he or she should spend time of an evening discussing at parochial level say the election of bishops or the diocesan finances, or even something as small as receiving Holy Communion in the hand. Cynically—and sadly truly—there is serious doubt as to how much listening is done by big brother at the centre. Therefore, a stressing of the link with the centre is a value.

The Eucharist continued with a welcoming of the new and old parish councillors by the bishop, in the name of the diocesan Church. He also left a space for questions and answers from the councillors after giving them an exhortation, along with the rest of the parishioners, to serve and to care. Finally, he led the concelebration of the Mass, which was shared by all the parochial clergy and those parishioners who were able to attend.

The conclusion of the evening was the assembling of the new parish council for a photograph with the bishop, in front of the high altar. The object of this was not just vanity but the production of a photograph for display at the entrance to the church, so that the parishioners would have no excuse for not recognising the parish councillors. Afterwards, the bishop, clergy and parish councillors went into the rectory where, during refreshments, the chairman and officers of the council were elected.

All this is given as an illustration of a possible approach, not a definitive statement of the best way of going about parish council elections. Elections along with content and pattern of work will surely vary from place to place according to the variety of possibilities and demands. A stereotype approach is to be abhorred. We find that practically speaking, there are some modifications every year, and gradually a workable and worthwhile procedure is growing.

What, then, of the work of this council once it is elected? Clearly the mind of the parish clergy, if several, and of the parish priest if a one-horse mission, will be vital. However, to have something which is simply "advisory" is to court disaster, unless there is a very clear discussion of what has been advised with the one who is to take the decisions on implementation—together with his giving reasons for accepting or rejecting the advice. All too often busy men and women come for a serious discussion on an important topic of parochial or larger Church concern, and afterwards, nothing happens, and a genuine frustration and loss of enthusiasm follows. There are two points. The parish priest still technically has the "last word", though his character will affect his openness to suggestion or his defensive or dictatorial attitude. He can kill or vivify. Secondly, it is essential to work in small sub-committee rather than always in council if anything is to get done. The whole council is too large. This is true not merely at parochial level. I myself took part in or suffered the practical demise of our local deanery pastoral council because whatever was put forward by these able, busy and generous peopl, after giving time of an evening to fruitful discussion got stepped on at diocesan pastoral council level. The danger of the "merely advisory" is there with priests' senates as well. I think the only way round it is for the individual in authority, whether bishop or parish priest to be more flexible over an executive function.

We have found that there are crucial areas in a parish system where the absolute power of the parish priest has been used secretly. Canonically he is responsible—but in justice he should share this responsibility. The obvious example, and a very tricky one is finance. Both the raising and the major distribution of income are very much lay affairs. After all, general speaking, the priest is not a wage earner, though I believe he should contribute of his "earnings" as well as of his time to the life of the parish. The main source of money is the ordinary parishioner with the weekly offering. The organisation of offertory promise, covenants and so on is far better done by parishioners, as is the possible financial boost on an annual basis from the pulpit. If a sub-committee of the parish council is responsible, there should be expertise available. But there should also be the opportunity for looking ahead, budgeting and planning. Where there is need or desire for capital expenditure, which will incur a debt, it is the parish which will continue to service that debt even after the parish priest is called to another parish or to God. The parish facing financial responsibility makes the whole financial side much more realistic; discussion of money issues becomes more open, and the publishing of accounts and general discussion of future development helps people to grow both in interest and in shared responsibility for the whole parish. As an example, we recently built a pastoral centre in the parish. Funds were low, because we already had a heavy debt. I told the parish firmly that if they were going ahead, they should make the decision and be prepared to justify it to the central council of administration and to the cardinal . . . as well as taking on any new debt. Owing to our already bad financial state of indebtedness, the council of administration was very doubtful and really did not want to let us go ahead. Things were at crisis point at a particular meeting when our spokesman on finance asked whether there was any way we could influence them to agree. What kind of way, they asked? He suggested that we came back to the meeting next month having raised a new ten thousand pounds. Yes, they said. So the parish council set to work and in the month raised nine thousand, six hundred and sixty pounds!

But finance is not all. In local affairs, dealing with local authorities and so on the Church needs more than a clerical voice. The Parish Council here has accepted that. A "civic awareness" committee has interviewed local candidates for parliament and local council elections, has run a campaign of cleaning up the town, and caused severe upset and much interest by a photographic exhibition on Southall as she is and as she might be. The community relations group have instigated new contact with non-Christian people, helped found a club for Asian women, brought them forward to putting on a mixed boy girl dance for their young people, and so on. Abortive attempts to achieve zoning in the parish were one of the failures of a sub-committee. Probably one of the most active and also most controversial is the liturgy committee, which really has affected and does affect development in the parish.

One of the interesting things to me personally has been the emergence of what might seem dangerous to some . . . the direct challenge to the parish priest on some aspects of his thought or practice . . . liturgy, action with non-Christian communities, commissioning of lay people for the distribution of Holy Communion and so on. I found it interesting and salutary, because it taught me more closely that the development of parish spirit and life would mean (thank God) a more active interest in what was going on, together with a greater desire to share in and be responsible for the state of the parish. This is one aspect that is not always at first clear—the priest in this situation is going to be working much more as one of a team, a partnership and a family. But the latter analogy is only workable provided he realises that as father of the family he accepts the equality of the grown up sons and daughters and does not forever keep them in short trousers and pinafores. It is very stimulating to sit at an open parish council meeting—almost as stimulating as to sit in at a family discussion in which there are teenagers and young adults who love their parents but need to be adult, to have their own opinions and to be free, and who have a lot to receive from their elders—and a lot to give them!

Personally I have no doubt about the value of the parish council, parish pastoral council or whatever it may be called. In addition to any other value it has it is a fine workshop for men and women who have never had the opportunity to be at a meeting, to feel free or be able to speak at a meeting, or to have the courage to express themselves. I can foresee these councils, along with family groups and other outlets, very much including prayer groups, as a wonderful "training ground", apart from their immediate and real importance in themselves. The Catholic participation in unions, local government, social action and all the other numerous possible ways of bringing Christian influence to bear on the world has been lamentably patchy. But it is very heart-warming and hopeful to find the variety of men and women who are prepared to come forward and lay themselves open to learning. We have had three different chairmen of the parish council and each has had his own personal way, background and importance. The first was a shop keeper, the second a painter and decorator, the third an industrial manager worker adviser. To me, the greatness of this is the distribution of talent, background and education . . . and each of them has been a good chairman.

So—the parish council is of value in itself, as a training ground, and as a stimulant and conscience pricker for the clergy. But this is only one aspect of the involvement of the laity of the parish in the whole work of God. It is in its way equally important to find the individual person who says he cannot stand a meeting, but if given an old person to visit would agree to go gladly and regularly. It is equally important to discover the little lady who does not want to be known, but who will wash and iron the altar linen every week . . . so long as she is not roped in and no one knows. We are all of us individual and . . . we have our own funny little ways. In making allowance for these, we can help to release a power for good into the life-blood of the Church.

For instance, out of family groups and house Masses there emerged a "help the Third World" movement which though it has not achieved half as much as those in other parishes, has been quite something for us. Through them, a weekly contribution to a leper rehabilitation colony in India has been set up, and contributes enough to make the difference between the continuance of the work and closure . . . so that the centre not only still flourishes but is now developing its potential. And this led the parish to vote in addition two and a half per cent of its annual income for the Third World. So gradually that sort of caring is developing, through the thinking and discussion of the people in their own neighbourhoods. Other parishes have been far more dramatically successful. But it is not so much the quantity involved as the spirit and sacrifice and thoughtfulness for others which will weigh heavily with God and with our fellow human beings in their distress. Perhaps the main lesson I am trying to draw out is that each parish should look around its own area and then the wider world, trying to assess need and to see where best they can help according to their own origin and way of life.

For a period of time as a development from the parish council there was a parish youth council. The theory was good, and they sent representatives to the parish council. But they had a certain difficulty which was that they were not too happy to have the older group "breathing down their necks". This was quite understandable, but in the long run it led to a situation where there was no real exchange between the two groups, and the youth lost interest and eventually fell apart. This did not prevent them from doing a lot in their own way and their own time, but quite naturally they found it boring and tedious to sit through the ordinary parish council meetings. I often do too! But these are necessary evils, and are not so bad if they are strictly controlled especially over length by the chairman. But there is a very real problem to be faced, lived through and allowed to be fruitful—that is the relationship between young and middle and old, the differing interests, attitudes, and even morality, or perhaps outlook in matters of morals. With the ordinary way in which things develop in a parish there is a danger of watertight compartments being built, which normally mean exclusion of one section from the other. It may well take a conscious effort to keep liaison between the two, and further effort to develop the tension into something constructive for all people. The youth are very much the future. We older ones like myself should live with and enjoy the future in young people, rather than resenting and begrudging their vitality and enthusiasm and sudden insights.

Looking also to the future, one of the general principles

which must be thrashed out is the relation between priest and people in the continuing life and work of a parish. In this, the analogy which springs to mind is that of the secular world. It is as though the priest is the government and the people the civil service. In other words, the priest comes and goes (sometimes it does not seem he goes often or soon enough), while the parishioners, though partly moving, remain the body living permanently in an area, and so in a sense the body which should be responsible for the underlying policy and general continuance. The priest is stimulator, animator—like the government suggesting new policies—while the people live them out and modify them and pay for them. In the past, and really up till now, when a priest has died or retired a new priest arrives like a bolt from the blue, or sometimes like a wet haddock. If however the people are important, it is essential that they should not simply have to wait and see what plan "authority" will have for a successor—a job for an ageing university chaplain, a suitable spot for Bloggs to retire to, a challenge to young so-and-so, or the natural slot for Muggins who is next on the seniority list. It has seemed to me, and I have repeated it publicly to the parish at intervals, that they now know me and the kind of lead or encouragement or wet-blanket effect I have had on various different aspects of parochial life in Southall. It is for them to take a long hard look at what has happened, whether they are with the line or opposed to it, whether they feel things are going the right way or should be changed or even reversed. Further, I have told them that they should be ready to put their views to the diocesan authorities; and be ready *now* for that, because if I drop dead or fall under a train or any other thing which removes me from being parish priest . . . what manner of man would they want to follow me?

If we are really serious about the good of community, the building of the liturgy and the multiple other things, then there is still a long way to go in the breadth of care which is taken in making appointments at all levels. "Grace of state" is all very well as an asset once a person is appointed, but there are other graces also which come before that, especially wisdom and insight on the part of authority and a faculty of listening which is not by any means always used in this vital part of Church living.

One aspect of appointments which may seem at first to be strange is actually taken up from an interpretation of John 3.30—"I must grow smaller". Living and thinking about the posting of clergy and the tenure of appointments, I personally have become clear about two things. Firstly, I do not believe in any younger priest staying too long in the same work. It is important to be long enough in any one place and work to come to know it thoroughly, to make the necessary contacts, and to have the opportunity to achieve something. But a breadth of experience is deepening and strengthening for the future; this rather follows the Newman phrase about frequent change leading to perfection. I had a pattern of change four years, four years, one year, eleven years and now seven. For me and for the job, the one year was too short, the eleven almost too long. I had not got my feet in one year, I was tiring and running out of ideas after eleven years. Here in Southall and getting older, I am thinking in terms of ten years, but may well run out of steam before that. When I was moved after four years from Soho, I hated moving; when moved from Westminster after four years, I was thankful. But both experiences did me good and helped me to grow. I did not want to leave Oxford, but felt it was right to do so. The result was an injection of new life, energy and ideas which certainly boosted me, and I hope revitalised the parish.

One point stands out, and should be considered in training and commitment. In my view—and it is easy to say before encountering the situation—those who are appointed to parishes, even though Canon Law safeguards them in tenure, should make a self-denying ordinance to accept appointment for a limited period. It may be that something like a five year appointment, with a possible five year re-appointment is feasible as a provisional structure, allowing flexibility. And that after ten years, except for special reasons, the priest "in charge" would expect to move somewhere else, and not necessarily as the "priest in charge", but in any suitable role. This whole suggestion depends upon re-thinking the "career" structure of the priest. In my suggestion, the "poverty" of our situation would be the acceptance of the structure by which we did not normally come to a permanence of "my parish, with my feet under my table", but rather pledged ourselves to the insecurity of the pilgrim people with no permanent place to lay our heads. We would have to agree to this and all fellow clergy be prepared to receive and make community with possibly "senior" men who came to join their team.

Finally in this section, it can be seen that all this ties in with references in other places to community building, team work and sharing. It should be seen as an emphasis upon the importance of all parts of the people of God, so that by use of all talents and the development of each one of us in love and service God may be glorified.

13

WHAT MUST I DO?

I want to write something in this book for those who are setting out on the path to priesthood, which at the same time may be useful for those who are already ordained and some way along that same path. Often, because I am now becoming long in the priestly tooth, people ask me to seminaries and theological colleges. I suppose they hope what I have been through or lived out may be of some use to those who are still only "becoming". I also quite frequently have doorbells, letters or phone calls from individual men and women, who say with different degrees of conviction, awe, fear or disbelief: I *think* God is wanting something from me.

Anyone who thinks he has heard the voice of the Lord calling him or her is faced with the "madness" that this call seems to imply. This is not simply a call to priesthood or religious life—it is the general call to be a follower— entering a new depth of living. If the call is specified to priesthood, humanly speaking it would be really nice if you or I had been or was about to be summoned into the "presence" and told by the Lord himself: "As we see it, the best possible course for you, after IQ tests, personality assessments, psychological analysis, together with your interview and your self-expressed opinion is that you should be a priest. And in your priesthood, we promise that you will always get recognition, develop in yourself, find fulfilment and be of use to people, without heartache or frustration."

In fact, the One who calls has said in his lifetime on earth, speaking from the experience of what it is to be a man: "If anyone wants to be a follower of mine, let him renounce himself and take up his cross every day and follow me. For anyone who wants to save his life will lose it; but anyone who loses his life for my sake, that man will save it."

(Lk. 9.23,24. Cf. Matt. 16.24 and Mk. 8.34)

And the prophet who went ahead of him set aside all worldly ambition saying: "He must grow greater, I must grow smaller." (Jn. 3.30)

The One also said to be a would-be follower: "Foxes have holes and the birds of the air have nests, but the Son of Man has nowhere to lay his head." In the same passage, another man said: "Sir, let me go and bury my father first". But the One replied: "Follow me, and leave the dead to bury their dead." (Matt. 8.20–22) Perhaps on the same occasion he met the person who said: "First let me go and say good-bye to my people at home", and replied: "Once the hand is laid on the plough, no one who looks back is worthy of the kingdom of God." (Lk.9.61)

Most of Matthew Chapter 10 is taken up with the ardours, rigours, and persecutions which are the lot of all followers of Jesus Christ. It is small wonder that Dietrich Bonhoeffer wrote on *The Cost of Discipleship*. Perhaps anyone who is feeling the call—whether it is general or specified to priesthood—should read his work and similar writings, from the scriptures right through the more sober and realistic assessments of the lives of the Saints. It would be easy to dismiss these latter as the past highlighted to dazzle the future. The reality is that the hard words of "cross", "suffering", "persecution", and the rest are "for real" in the life of *any* disciple. There is no other way than the way of the Cross . . . this is the expectancy, the rough and tumble of discipleship for any follower, male or female, lay, religious, priest or bishop. It would be blindness and stupidity to try to cover up this demand which is so evident in the life of Christ and the call of his first disciples. But that is not to say that discipleship is simply a ghastly, dreary grind through life. The balancing factor which it is not easy to appreciate until it is lived out is the vigour, joy and fulfilment promised by Christ, because paradoxically he lightens and sweetens the burdens and labours which humanly may seem too wearisome to bear.

Writing generally on holiness for every kind of person, Fr. Jock Dalrymple entitled his book: *Costing Not Less than*

Everything, from a T. S. Eliot poem. I fully accept the universal call to holiness but here I am concerned with priesthood. It is this strain of absoluteness, the call to come away from father and mother, the challenge of selling all to come and follow that has somehow become muted in the general approach to holiness and especially in ordained ministry. Very many lay people lead a more ascetic and devoted life than many a priest. Perhaps it is partly the college life with its routine, its regular meals, regular prayer times and "cushioning" from much of the life of the world, which softens the starkness of Christ's basic call. This softening will be a temptation in any institutional organisation' and leads naturally to the need for periodic re-assessment and renewal. It is particularly difficult not to be softened in the midst of a consumer society with the amazing increase in standards of expectation which touch so many pleasurable aspects of human living. The person "called" by God is not at once immune from self-indulgence. The practice of a standard of ascetic life which differs from the standard of worldly life is a definite part of the training to service in the ordained ministry, more especially when that ministry includes the call to celibacy.

I will always consider myself fortunate to have had the background experience of a home where we were expected to play our part in working in the house, cleaning, cooking etc., as well as being made aware of others outside who had far less than we did. My mother was a great sharer; we picked up some of that from her. We did not live richly, but we had enough. Later, the training of army life, especially on active service on the ground and in the open, made me more aware of the necessities of every day existence, and of the possibility of doing without many of the things which had seemed so essential—a chair to sit on, a bed to sleep in, a table to eat at, running hot and cold water, electric light, a decent lavatory to flush! The same kind of paring away of "essentials" cut down time to be alone and time for sleep, while uncovering the "nakedness" of communal living.

Others have had tougher, less cushioned upbringing and early life. I would not myself have chosen this toughness of war for instance, but by encountering it and living through it, I know in hindsight that it was formative, invaluably so. And this has made me want to encourage others on the way to priesthood to experience some kind of "commando training" as it were, some practice of asceticism, however unpopular that idea may be today. The point is that every one of us has self-indulgent tendencies. It is rather too easy to grow used to having this and that, to expecting certain conditions. If one has never had the opportunity to experience what it is to live with less, it is difficult even to accept the possibility, let alone the Christian demand.

Training should be for real living in the real world, and with the knowledge that it is as a leader of others that the trainee will emerge from the chrysalis stage. But he emerges as a strange mixture of amateur and professional. On the one hand, he will always remain a learner, a listener and an amateur in relationship to the Lord; the Lord does not call us any longer servants; he calls us friends. I hope very much that no one will fall into the trap of being a "professional" friend. There is something about the very nature of friendship which is so individual, so profound and so open to the future that professionalism would hit at the very roots of its being. And this statement is true of the relationship not only to God but to other human persons . . . to treat others professionally as "cases" is to lose the wonder of God's relationship with us. On the other hand, priests are "professional" in a sense that there is and must be training to knowledge of scripture, of dogmatic, moral and pastoral theology, of the liturgy and all the other areas of "expertise" which properly go along with training to carry out a particular "function". It is the balance of these two in our personal commitment which haunts me.

Let me illustrate this haunting fear through a terrifying experience which I once had when giving a retreat to men training for priesthood. In one of my talks I underlined the problem of someone who becomes a "professional" student, moves on to be a "professional" deacon and ends up as a "professional" priest . . . almost drifting through the curriculum of college as one allows oneself to be carried in the flow of a river. My theme was the possibility of drifting into priesthood, because it can be easier at a certain point to go on than to go back, but always doing just the basic essentials rather than giving oneself totally to God and man. Later after saying this, there was a knock at my door and in came a young man. He sat down and began at once: "I am a professional deacon" . . . and then burst into tears. Gradually the story came out . . . he arrived at college . . . he got into a rut, prayer meant nothing, early morning meditation was a drowsy time to kneel or sit through, waiting for Mass to happen, lectures were a bore . . . life in college just went on. Now it appeared he had been made a deacon and was "waiting for priesthood". The things which I had said had suddenly hit him . . . What was it all about? What was he about? Was it easier to go on than to opt out? Was he even convinced that God existed? . . . He said he had intended to be a priest for a number of years, well before coming to college . . . somehow it had become just an inevitable carrying on until ordination, and then . . . And he burst into tears again, because out of the blue the "and then" had hit him as being utterly beyond anything he had catered for. The kind of challenge, demand and sacrifice was out of his range of drifting acceptance, of "creeping vocation". It also gradually came to light that he was held where he was partly from fear that he would upset his parents and let other people down.

I hope this kind of drift is not frequent, but I sometimes wonder and am concerned, when the challenge does not seem to have the combination of the gaunt and compelling, the dreadful and fulfilling, the empty and joysome, the dying and living which Christ put so regularly to his own chosen followers.

Understandably, there are anxieties about the numbers of those who are offering themselves for the priesthood today. But there should be much greater anxiety about those who are rapidly leaving the priesthood. There needs to be really deep study with the help of laicised priests into the causes of seeking a new and further life outside the ordained ministry. Has the expectation not been fulfilled?

Was it a faulty expectation? Is it celibacy that is too hard? Does frustration play a big part in restlessness? Is there ambition, pride, expectation of "fulfilment" involved?

Writing at the present time, it is obvious that there are wide areas of the church where there will be tensions between the ideas and habits of life of the old established parish priest and the newly ordained younger man. Only recently I came across a situation where practically the only form of communication between the parish priest and his assistant was by notes left by the older man at the bottom of the stairs leading to the younger man's room. To move from the warmth of a college grouping into the isolation of such a situation as this is to be immediately open to loneliness, a sense of being cut off from what the training had been about, and even a despair of usefulness in such circumstances.

Given a deep life of prayer, a wisdom and an openness on the part of those responsible for training, there need be no fear of going too far in toughness and expectation. Men are capable of being very generous, though paradoxically they may be very selfish! Authority has the exciting task of bringing out the generosity and absorbing the selfishness in service. If there is a worry about getting too few who will persevere to ordination, this could well be shifted to the fear of getting too few who after ordination will persevere till death! We need to look more carefully at priesthood before we get upset. We may be asking for the wrong response from the wrong people. It could well be that a re-assessment of the goal . . . that is, God's will . . . would clarify the call so that it struck on the ears of fewer but more available disciples. I am not wanting to decry the life and efforts of those already committed. We can open our ears to listen if the word is applicable to us.

The training period, and indeed the life afterwards are both times when problems and temptations and a mingling of happiness and near despair are likely to mix alongside each other. We only grow through this mixture. When Jesus said to the disciples: "Come and follow me", the response was immediate, but after that there were times of argument and doubt and near rebellion among them. Even after the resurrection when Christ was coming and going among them, we find Peter, as it were tired of waiting, saying to the others: "I'm going fishing." (John. 21.3) The nets he had left to follow jesus were still there. He was not doubting or going back on Jesus and his call . . . he was being fully human and filling in the waiting time humanly. Each of us, even deeply entered on our commitment, can be distracted, and so not at first see Jesus when he enters our life openly once more.

It is well that we should establish in our minds the gradual, continuing, development of the disciple. After Pentecost Peter was still developing in his relation to circumcision, in his relation to unclean foods, in his relation to the "pagans". (Cf. Acts. Chs. 10, 11, 15) The end of training is not at ordination but at death, or after any final training the Lord may need to achieve in us beyond the grave.

Peter came to find the very limits of his thought were burst open, and he was continually going out from where he was to somewhere beyond, towards the Omega point, towards the Lord, who as Lord of history stands always ahead of us, beckoning and saying: "Follow me". For Peter this meant in Christ's own words that as he grew older he would be less free than before; and would be led along paths down which he did not want to go. (Jn 21.18)

On the whole, it is easier for the younger generation to change than the older. But there can be deep-seated conservatism and unwillingness to be changed even in the young. How can we train and be trained to be at once rooted in truth and flexible? As I get older I find all my personal weight, age, authority and any other pressure comes out to defend my pet theories or my long established (and often comfortable) habits of life. I remember a fine and revered father of the London Oratory whose stock phrase for any new proposal always was: "It has never been our custom".

With Peter there was circumcision, with us it could be the circumstance and age of baptism. With Peter, the admission of non-Jews was a problem—with us it could be the position of women or our fears about ecumenical activity. Peter had to "think big" when Paul hit his scene. Small-mindedness is always about among us . . . that is, towards new developments, the breaking of fresh ground, being dug out of our comfortable assurance, our ready answer. I almost get fed up with the word signifying the attitude we need—it is openness . . . to the Spirit, to the Church, to mankind. It means stretching our wings and our minds to embrace everyone, not just our faithful flock. I once heard a very good priest who ran a parish in a large, multi-cultural area of sub-urban spread mainly inhabited by Asians and West Indians say simply: "There are no West Indians in my parish." Alas, I'm afraid that meant that no West Indians came into his Church for Mass or the Sacraments! We can so edit our idea of parish or people that some cease to exist . . . for us.

Leaving a blinkered existence, a small world of the baptised and faithful, and being open to the terrifying reality of megalopolis gone-secular, the urban-based priest may have a very different set of problems from the priest in the country. But each has to find the way to preach Christ as he is, wherever he is and to all the people, rich and poor, who are within earshot. So many of these people at least outwardly could not care less about the One we love. The task is great—to live in the midst of indifference, and still to care; to live in materialism and acquisitiveness, and live "poor"; to live among successful, up-and-coming people, and believe and live the unimportance of success; to live only for him and for others, not giving self the first place it so much desires! These kinds of ways of life are kinds of dying. But because they are dyings, they paradoxically bring to life in the man who "dies" a new living, a new alertness to need, suffering, loneliness or poverty. For him homelessness of others hurts, prejudice hitting an "under-dog" hits him; his caring heart grows.

Some of these attitudes are inborn in us but quite an amount can be "acquired" or cultivated through training, praying, listening, and serving. In this "acquiring" there are many different ingredients. The important combinations would seem to be depth and breadth. The tendency to have a superficial look at everything in a course of study often does not leave enough time to look at anything in depth. Yet there has to be room, somehow, for the expertise of the psychiatrist to be involved, alongside the inner knowledge of the man of prayer, the learning and communication of the professor and the down to earth pastoral advice of the man-on-the-streets.

But whatever way training is developed—in smaller groups, in parochially-based experiments, in variety between college and parish, in shortened courses for some and lengthened more academic courses for others—the importance always is the building up of individuals to the ordained ministry which is founded upon a total giving to God, without any restrictions. The call still is very simple and straight: "Come and follow me". In this call there is no promise of thrones to sit upon; the command is to take up the cross daily, and follow.

How can this ideal become part and parcel of the thinking and being of each one who is accepting the challenge? Certainly the deepest and surest way is to become anchored in God in a life or prayer with all that the Spirit may demand in the way of openness, self-giving, poverty and humility. So the training must be geared towards initiative and self-reliance, but also needs to have the strange combination of being able to be alone and being able to live in community. More and more, the decisions in parishes are not taken by the parish priest alone, or even by him in concert with the other clergy. More and more the laity too are becoming involved. This requires new ideas on sharing. At the same time, there is more independence and liberty for the younger priest, which has its liberating side and also its dangers of "creeping secularisation". This has to be backed by intensive personal spiritual growth, as well as the habit of priestly mutual support.

There are many possibilities for learning in and out of the parish from other priests, from night schools, from reading. Much knowledge can be gained from work, from visiting, from house groups, from a liturgy, from discussion with other priests, sisters and lay people, with a special emphasis on married people and women to balance celibate knowledge. There is a possibility of older men continuing their work, while growing in newer ways which do not detract from the past but give new life to their teaching. There are different needs for town and country, for those likely to teach and those who will always be out on the tarmac or at the grass roots. There is a real need for some kind of spiritual commando course which will intensify and deepen the whole basis of our ascetic and spiritual foundation in life.

Somehow, in all this, the priest must get a clear grasp of the fact that he must continue to grow and develop at all levels throughout the rest of his life. There is constant need for spiritual and scripture-theology-pastoral-care refresher courses. And in this, the start is now and not in the future—for those who most badly need renewing at all levels are very often my own age-group and just over and under it. For the dead hand can kill off both the younger clergy, and the faithful, whereas the sight of a spiritually and pastorally alive older man leading on the community is a joy for weary eyes, a cool refreshing draught of love for tired souls.

In this chapter I have emphasised the answering of the call of Christ *to follow*. Clearly being alert to the call is not enough; having once heard the call, a daily act of will is needed to go ahead into the following. In other words, we come into the realm of obedience, the way of life in which each person is trying to live out the prayer of Jesus in the Garden of Gethsemane: "Not my will but thine be done." This life-work is intended to bring the individual human will ever more closely into union with the will of God . . . and in its fulness it really is a life-work, because never in this life do we reach a point when we are no longer facing decisions day by day. All our years, we will be subject to temptation, to choosing self before God's will. That is why the doing is as important as the hearing.

The clearest example apart from Christ himself is the example of Mary. When she was asked to be Mother of

God, she said a simple "Yes". But simple as it may have been, it was also profound enough, real enough for the Holy Spirit to overshadow her and bring forth in and from her the Holy One, Emmanuel, God-with-us. No one can assess how much of a tug it was for Mary to say "yes", but clearly she was immediately open to hearing, and according to the Gospel story it did not take her long to get on with the doing. And so we find Christ her son praising her obliquely for her hearing and doing: "Yea, rather blessed are they who hear the word of God and do it". (Luke 11.28)

I am sure we could sum up obedience to the Lord in that phrase . . . "hearing and doing". From realising that, we can understand better the need for training ourselves as listeners. This is rather like listening to music, gradually becoming sensitive to all the different instruments, to their silence as well as to their sound, so that we can grow more and more in appreciation of a single piece of music. As we come to know it, the music becomes a well-loved friend whose moods and variations we understand. A closer analogy than this is our sensitivity to another human being. Growing intimacy with another person makes it possible to be aware of tones of voice, expressions in the eyes or on the lips, even differences in the way of walking or holding the head. In this kind of relationship of love we can appreciate both the way growth occurs, its variety of speed and slowness, and also the way our will gets caught up in pleasing the will of the other. When all is said and done, obedience to each other's will should be a response ideally not of duty, but of love. So too in our relationship with God who is Love we should respond in kind—did not Christ say: "If you love me keep my commandments"?

With the ear attuned to love, the call is more than ever the simple "follow", and the essential part of "doing" is that every day we get up listening, catch the thread of the voice of God, grasp how to respond to what his will is for us, and then get on with doing it . . .

All the way through, there also runs the thread of choice, with each of us gradually becoming in practice more and more limited in our options—and as the choosing goes on, so we either come closer and closer to the will of God in love, or move away seeking ourselves, consciously or unconsciously.

The rich young man in the Gospel (Mark 10) gives us a good example of growth in sensitivity and choice. Asking what he must do to gain eternal life, he gets the reply that he should keep the commandments, which he says he has already done from childhood. Then there seems to be in him a groping forward, tentative, unsure . . . and Christ comes up with the stark reality . . . "If you would be perfect . . . "—and the young man's choice is suddenly enormously limited, and he cannot bring himself to take the perfect option . . . he goes away sad. But the great thing is that so long as his life lasts on earth, there is still the possibility of going forward again . . . Jesus had looked on him and loved him. Perhaps the young man had mistaken the dutifulness which he showed in following the commandments for the real thing. Challenged by Christ to love, he was not yet ready. It is essential that the training of the priest helps each individual to move from the obedience of duty to the obedience of love. If the individual remains on the line of duty, his work will never "take off ". It is the "madness" of the call that it is a call to love, not a call to duty, so that the demands of love have to be met by love. This takes each of us out of safety and security into "danger". It feels a risky thing to enter love's way because to do so is to give oneself totally, dying to love and so rising to live in love. Security is not of this world, because the call of love is to love "as I have loved you". (Jn.15.12) Then living in his way we will be planted in love, built on love. (Cf Eph.3.17)

This is what I must do!

14

PROLOGUE TO THE FUTURE

This final chapter is put here to end the book with a sense of urgency. Much of what I have written is history as far as I am concerned personally and is "old hat" for those who have been working along the lines of Vatican II. But for some it will be new. The problem facing each and all of us is how we move forward with Christ towards the future kingdom, while preserving all that is good, all that is true. Only if we face God boldly and emptily in prayer, and try to live out the example and teaching of the Lord can we hope to achieve the balance which often seems contradictory— the past giving way to the future, while retaining its substance of goodness.

In the last few years, I have been a member of the joint working party of bishops and priests, religious and lay people about pastoral strategy. The results of our discussion and prayer have appeared in *Church 2000* and *A Time for Building*. We really did work; we spent much time in discussion, prayer, argument and heart-searching. At certain points we influenced one another, at other points we either refused to be influenced or failed to influence! This is the essence of what it is to work in and as a team. We can neither move so quickly as we might wish if we belong to one school of thought, nor so slowly, if we belong to another. If you read the documents, you can say this is "our mind", but it is still impossible to be sure that any one point or even the whole is the exact mind of an individual member. We must live and move as a team, yet while remaining a team, we must also be able to be individual—or we lose our God-given nature, the freedom of the children of God.

As well as being a member of the working party, I have moved round each country of the British Isles, and also Eire, giving talks, retreats, seminars and so on. Beyond that, I have been to parts of Africa, India, the Caribbean, U.S.A. and Europe. I have shared joy and disillusion, horror and excitement, dismay, despair and a great hope: I have met those who felt that they were totally irrelevant to world problems, and those who felt completely happy in maintaining existing parochial concerns. Very frequently visits to the "Third World" left me feeling a sense of tiredness, lethargy and self-centredness in the attitudes of Europe and these islands. The huge variety of the countries of the world and their peoples, the ebullient spirit of young people in young nations, the zest for life and for the future outside our own society are difficult to feel or imagine without the kind of experience I have been fortunate enough to be given.

There is a very difficult Christian-credibility-gap between the "dying" North and West and the "starving" South and East. The former, clutching ever more greedily at world resources, is like some aged alcoholic or drug addict only satisfied with increasing quantities of fuel, drink, food and comfort, and apparently too far gone to understand the injustice to others which must be accepted as just if "we" are to satisfy our addiction. The latter (Africa, Asia, Latin America, the Caribbean) are often so degraded and ill-fed as to be unable to raise the energy for assertion of their rights. But today they are becoming more and more able to voice grievancies, injustices and demands for the involvement of the North and West in their emancipation.

These are generalised statements. Too often they remain so and are disregarded or denied, because the would-be refuters have not "experienced" the reality.

What has our way of living to do with the message of Jesus Christ? Is it—our way of living—Christianity at all? Well, I personally feel bound to ask myself whether I can go on living in "richness", playing about with "peripheral" ecclesiastical concerns, while God's children in other parts of the world die through my selfish greed and disinterestedness, while I make my way in our accepted materialistic society?

Recently, there has been a powerful documentary about world problems called *Five Minutes to Midnight*. It is immediately relevant to starvation. Whether it is relevant to us will be seen by our acceptance or dismissal or simple lack of interest. Anyone who has eyes to see with and ears to hear with can watch the plight of Planet Earth. The strong underlying theme of rich-selfishness and the exploitation of the poor shatters complacency. No ready-made solutions are handed out, but there is the broad lesson for us to learn—that we compound and complete the tragedy if we do not allow a revolution to take place in our minds and hearts which will drastically change our whole way of life.

Because we are "parochially" involved, interested in and concerned with our own local excitements and problems, we consciously or unconsciously insulate ourselves. We must try to be broad enough to "think parish" and "think world". This is not a time when special interest in developing countries can be entrusted to a few zealous people, to a group or sodality. The situation of the world needs to be alive in all of us. But working at home in our islands may give a sense of isolation, with an odd combination of complacency and fear, a tiredness in ourselves and our leadership, at all levels but especially in the higher echelons.

To look at other parts of the world and see hope, adventure and the possibility of growth, in contrast to the drabness of our own scene, is not just a case of the grass seeming greener the other side of the fence. There is much which is not green, but parched and barren, starved to death. But there is also youth and vigour, physical, mental and spiritual. There is a bubbling of the Spirit, an emergence of vision, but one often tinged with a colouring of bitterness and anger. The under-privileged and oppressed are becoming aware in countries distant from our own. This awareness is, from a different angle, even penetrating the parishes and people where we live. It is time for us all to "realise that the cries of the reapers have reached the ears of the Lord of hosts" (James 5.4). The work of the Spirit is all over the place; but at present it is like a spring shooting up in arid burnt-out desert land, creating an oasis. As yet, it is not spreading far into the desert, nor does it seem to be sufficiently strongly received to renew the face of the earth. Among many there is loss of hope, growing inward-looking materialism and even despair, especially in the West. Paradoxically the signs of hope spread as little sparks and thin spirals of smoke in Europe, with greater likelihood of conflagration in other parts of the world. It is time we all realised and accepted the implication of Christ's words: "I have come to bring fire to the earth, and how I wish it were blazing already" (Luke 12.49).

We are at five minutes to midnight. We must open our eyes to the situation . . . as it is now. In order to see properly, we need a spiritual revolution, emptying ourselves so that we may have in us the mind which is in Christ Jesus. As Barbara Ward said some time ago: "The party is over." We cannot in the West continue to live on borrowed time or exploited raw materials of the earth. Preaching Christ, who came as a poor man among us, the whole Church in these islands must take steps to stop living in the encouraged national style . . . on a mortgage. It is people not property, organisations or buildings, the Church is in the world to present to Christ. But our own "Christian" attitude and life-style in the Church today are far more a barometer of the success of exploitation by the mass media than a barometer of our humility, poverty, openness, sharing and love as mirroring the life of Jesus Christ. We have allowed ourselves as a Church and as individuals to be led up the cul-de-sac of worldly possessions and rising standards of living, so that our aims in education and preaching are basically more worldly, selfish and materialistic than Christian.

Change *must* happen in us! We must not put it off now! The change will also have to be drastic. There are many different economic theories and policies, and I am no economist. But Jesus preaches simplicity and austerity, and there is one very clear view which teaches that justice throughout the world will almost certainly entail a sharp re-assessment of economic and social goals, which in turn may well lead to a lowering of our standard of living. It will not be easy to preach such a reduction as being good and necessary and Christian to those who have fought hard all their lives for better conditions for themselves and their children. Yet this is what we have to preach against the consumer world of the West in order to avert even greater tragedy before it is too late—and to set ourselves back once more upon the true Christian path of frugality, justice and peace. Austerity is more Christian than riches. I know the first person I have to tackle is *myself*. But have I enough guts to live austerely, enough guts to preach austerity with the inevitable anger and alienation it will cause? The short answer is "no". The strength will have to come from God.

What I have written before, what I have suggested as ways of living, being and doing are all included in the "programme", but God calls us still further. That is why we need a spiritual revolution . . . NOW! Such a revolution gives a new perspective, a new insight, and so a new heart to set out on an even harder path than before, a path only possible for us because of the presence of Christ with and ahead of us.

Unless the Spirit takes us and moves us, we will mouth platitudes and make plans ineffectively until it is past midnight.

Inevitably, any move forward towards a more living Christianity will cost a great deal personally. It will also provoke fierce charges of stupidity, wrong-mindedness, inhumanity, hypocrisy and even heresy. But if we tackle this by setting our own house in order, we will assuredly have power in the Spirit through prayer to enable change to occur. For this to happen, we must live a more austerely Christian life; we must re-assess our goal in living; we must face the materialist penetration of education, the deadness of parish, deanery and diocesan policy, the general holding back and "conservative" attitude of bishop, priest and people.

We are incarnate. We live *in* the world. We are to leaven the world. But without returning to spiritual sources, the leaven will have no strength. Many of us from every walk of life do not *want* to be stirred to change. Few of us *want* to face austerity or to find the aims of ourselves and our leaders tainted with worldly doctrine. We do not want to admit that education, social action and the distribution of our resources is less than fully Christian . . . can even be anti-Christian as we bolster acquisitiveness and self-seeking through our perhaps unthinking support of the consumer society. Truly it is possible for us to be "neither hot nor cold" . . . we allow ourselves to be processed into the worldly wisdom around us. Only the force of the power of the Spirit can change us.

Facing the issues in church and state, we find them so vast we have a sense of powerlessness. Structure built on structure interweaves with yet another structure. Dismantling, revolutionising, ploughing up in order to allow the breath of the Spirit to enter—it all seems too big, too complicated. So we carry on with the inevitable, sucked into the daily maintenance machine, covering our despair by rationalisation and busy-ness.

Something may be achieved by tinkering with structures at parochial and diocesan levels. Much more will be achieved through personal and community development. God works on individuals and groups. The vision of Vatican II is the local church alive. Local, for the early Church was really local, and comparatively effective because natural difficulties in communication kept groups small. Today we face big differences between city and rural communities. In many high-density areas, even a smaller diocese will remain remote; the only feasible unit for contact and close effectiveness will be "parochial". Here, I am not simply blessing the territorial parish structure as it exists now, but putting forward such small neighbourhood groupings as seem likely to combine together for community and family development. There must be some structure; that structure must at street level be small. How small, in area or numbers will depend on local factors and the good use of all those in the area. Flexibility in size and structure is essential.

Where the locality is taken fully and seriously with the end purpose of spreading the Good News of Jesus Christ, every living soul should be included. All are beloved of God, made for himself and destined for his kingdom. Whether they are of any religious faith or none, they are "in his hand". All structures, organisations and relationships within the "parochial" boundaries should be of potential interest and concern. Inevitably there should and will be commitment to wider groupings of the deanery and diocese churchwise, to other faiths and to the local borough. The local team should have a vital and at the same time effective role in community development at the root-growth level among individuals and in neighbourhoods. The renewal of the Church starts here. Priests and people need freedom, leadership and encouragement to accept this immediate work, and to live on from here in hope. Devolution is of primary importance. In an age of overdeveloped bureaucracy, we must take care not to increase unnecessarily "central services", committees and the number of those who by their work are only marginally in contact with real people.

Naturally, local work is "parochial" in the worst sense if it does not include along with Catholic parishioners the closest possible cooperation with other Christian denominations, and members of other faiths. We cannot be Christian in truth and at the same time ignore or refuse to work with other Godfearing people. Further, we ought to seek ways and means of working with all people of goodwill, believing, unbelieving, agnostic, humanist and even atheistic. For the local church has to be "political" as witness, instigator, challenger, critic and encourager. Our Christianity learned from our leader Jesus Christ is incarnational. We live in real situations where "pie in the sky" reaches nobody except the gullible. To preach Jesus in warm churches to the well-housed while turning a blind eye to homelessness is indecent. This is only an example of the false position we may put the Good News in unless we work away actively to remedy unemployment, poverty, social deprivation, bad working conditions, oppression, personal and marital breakdown, inequality and many other areas of injustice. If it is said this should be a common concern of all human beings, this is right. But how much more should it be the concern of Christians, and those chosen or ordained for Christian leadership. There should be greater priestly concern and awareness, greater priestly involvement with outcasts, "unacceptable" minorities such as addicts, prisoners and ex-prisoners, alcoholics on the one hand and such groups as the Travelling People on the other. The priest can be leader and instigator for justice. He must listen to the voices of his neighbourhood, and interpret them to the Catholics and others in the locality, urging them to action after discussion, thought and general growth in awareness and commitment to the poor of all kinds. In this way he can help the whole people of God to work for a better world of justice and peace.

Vitally important in the British Isles for the living out of peace and justice is the tackling of the largely urban growth of a multi-cultural society. This is not just an "in-phrase". It is a reality which Christians can work in and with constructively—or can leave alone at their peril. We must not ignore the problems of living together, or the benefits. But time *is* running out. Neglect or dismissal of the present racial discrimination, prejudice, inequality and growing unrest will allow the problems to boil over, and further discredit the name of Jesus Christ. We must all work together with special efforts to learn from people of cultures other than our own, whether we are brown, black or white. Positive effort will be needed if we are to make progress in shared living within these islands. We, that is people from differing backgrounds, have a joint responsibility to strive patiently, openly and lovingly at a person-to-person level, as well as in local and central government planning and decision-making. If Christians are not leading in this field we are not worthy of Jesus' name.

In writing here, I am thinking more of the role of the priest, but anyone will see throughout this book that much is applicable to the unordained Christian also. If devolution is necessary for 'the Church', this applies to the duties and functions of the clergy in very practical ways. If, with Jesus Christ, the priest is interested in building up the body, building the whole man, then the priest has to find ways of encouraging growth at all levels—individually (both spiritually and in awareness and responsibility), through group work, allowing parochial pastoral councils to develop, hopefully up to deanery and diocesan level. Without proliferating meetings, he can encourage initiative. If it is thought that counselling is necessary, then brother should help brother at neighbour-level, with more sophisticatedly trained personnel involved where needed, whether this means trained counsellor or priest. When teachers are required to tell children and young people about Jesus Christ, we can certainly train and commission some, but should expect all parents to take on responsibility for their own children, as the baptismal ceremony pledges them to do. And so on . . . the multiplication of apostolic workers beyond the ordained ministry must become a wider and more normal reality. Rather than spreading himself thinly, the priest has to give himself and all he knows and loves to others—that they may go and do the same. This will demand time with individuals and small groups; it will take the discipline of watching others achieve or fail where the priest might feel *he* ought to be working. But our only hope of sufficiently covering the face of the earth is not through multiplication of the ordained priests, but through calling into action all the latent powers of the "priestly people", the *laos*, laity.

This does however bring into question the narrow limits of the present day ordained ministry. Though not scriptural or in keeping with the early practice of the Church the exclusive call to celibacy for the ordained priest has for centuries been the almost universal rule in the Roman Catholic Church. Today, with all the new understandings of sexuality, with the new realisation of the equality of women and the previous "unbalanced" dominance of men in the authority of the Church, new thought leading to the possibility of new practice is emerging in the Church. Here we have a typical instance of what I mentioned at the beginning of this chapter . . . the best of tradition to be kept, the possibility of fresh vision to be admitted. I have already referred to celibacy and I reiterate my personal commitment to it as a valid way of life and one which can be enriching and fulfilling personally and for the whole work of Christ. But I also understand the real problem of welding together as one the two individual vocations of celibacy and priesthood. This is especially important for re-thinking when in the Roman Catholic Church we can see and appreciate the long tradition of the Orthodox Churches, the Church of England and the other Christian denominations with whom we are trying to forge a unity of Christian witness. Their married clergy contribute notably to the preaching and practice of the Good News. The time has come for us to ask whether we are inhibiting this very preaching by our practice!

At the time of writing, the firm stand of the Roman Catholic Church is against ordaining married men. At the same time, the practice is present in other Churches. My plea is that all the scriptural and traditional background be re-studied; that the new insights of world development, equal status of women, the importance of the feminine element in the preaching of the Good News, and all the wider opportunities for spreading Christ's word be squarely faced. I am confident that the future outcome will widen the categories of those who are admitted to priesthood in the ordained sense. There will be much heart-searching; male dominance has to be dethroned . . . by enthroning female equality. For many of us this will hurt; we will try to find scriptural and traditional reasons to uphold male dominance.

The tension becomes even stronger when I need to talk of the situation of those who have already "left the priesthood" to marry, but long to fulfil their priestly functions. Where will we go from here? Will we consider their position, give them hope? In the world view, this may be a small question; in personal agony and desire it can be central and dominant. I am not speaking of those who have left the Church, left God and find all I am writing irrelevant. I am deeply concerned for those who are committed in their minds and hearts to the preaching of the Gospel, but have found some of the requirements for ordained ministry insupportable. I long for them to be freed from the burden of the past, as it is within the power of the Church to do—freed for the future, when a way can be found to use all that they are, all that they could be and all that they want to give.

Much of what I have written links with the ordination of women as much as it does with the question of married priests. I tend to link the two because they raise the issue of the wholeness of the single person and the equality and complementary nature of man and woman in God's world. We all know there are men pledged to celibacy because of priesthood and not particularly for celibacy as such. There are also women pledged to celibacy in large numbers because of religious vow. Some of these women would have been "natural" celibates anyhow, but some are only so as religious sisters "for the kingdom of God", because the two vocations go together. If we are seriously concerned with justice and realising the fulness of the nature God has given to men and women, there is a great deal still to be done in thought and in practice about the status of women. Even lip service does not go far enough at this time; practical application lags behind. Now, I have no authority to be dogmatic; I can only state that as far as I am aware there is no reason in scripture or theology against a woman, who is a true member with man of the "royal priesthood", being ordained to the ministerial priesthood. The argument is traditional. As for how and when ordination might be, here I have what I hope is not just a male hang-up. It seems to me that the immediate development to priesthood for women is unlikely to take place quickly—to say the least. That I think is a realistic statement. But there are plenty of immediate battles and more likely victories in the development of attitudes and practices in the Church, which will break down barriers more quickly than trying to sort out the priesthood issue at once. I hope that we will work strongly and openly in getting our day by day living rightly balanced in this world made by God for men and women to enjoy equally. This will take prayer and patience, humility and mutual trust . . . a series of difficult demands.

And so I come to the last paragraph of *Living Priesthood*. It would seem exciting and challenging to have something new and dramatic to say. Yet the oldest fact is the most exciting, so that paradoxically we can easily pass it by. God loves us! "Yes" we say, and go on with our living. And his love for us is so great that he allows us the freedom to ignore him, or even to go against his love. I know because I have done it in my life, which has been like the history of the children of Israel in the Old Testament—a coming and going in love of God, an effort to serve and a return to selfish sinfulness, until once more the love of Love is overwhelmingly pervading. And that is really what I want to say—Love Him and let Him love you, so that we may all grow to love each other. In this, because we follow Jesus Christ we must experience something of what it is to be "another Christ":

> a thing despised and rejected by men,
> a man of sorrows and familiar with suffering,
> a man to make people screen their faces . . .
>
> (Isaiah 53.3)

This is to be a spur, not an excuse to give up, because our faith in him mirrors the trust he places in us—the trust that we are to build his world towards his now and future kingdom, a kingdom of justice, peace and love. What this means and will mean both in pain and joy is not yet revealed, because each of us is living it now. The important thing is that we do *live* it—and live it in the simple, open attitude of Mary who heard the word of God and did it. Come Lord Jesus!

EPILOGUE

To some his gift was that they should be apostles: to some, prophets: to some, evangelists: to some pastors and teachers: so that the saints together make a unity in the work of service, building up the body of Christ. In this way we are all to come to unity in our faith and in our knowledge of the Son of God, until we become the perfect man, fully mature with the fulness of Christ himself.

Then we shall not be children any longer, or tossed one way and another and carried along by every wind of doctrine, at the mercy of all the tricks men play and their cleverness in practising deceit. If we live by the truth and in love, we shall grow in all ways into Christ, who is the head by whom the whole body is fitted and joined together, every joint adding its own strength, for each separate part to work according to its function. So the body grows until it has built itself up in love. (Eph. 4. 11–16)

Appendix 1

INVOLVEMENT OF RELIGIOUS SISTERS AT SOUTHALL

At a chance meeting in Oxford just after I had been appointed to go to Southall I apparently lit a fuse which exploded down the telephone line shortly afterwards in terms of a nibble which grew to a bite and to reality. (I have described the Oxford Meeting and its outcome in the chapter on Parish Life: Developing Parish Community). I was asked to set out on paper to the Mother Provincial what kind of thing was envisaged for the sisters if they came to work in the area. The letter was as follows:

> The Old Palace
> St. Aldate's,
> Oxford

1 July, 1970.

Dear Mother Eyre,

Tremendous news that you are coming to Southall—i.e. setting up a small house there, if the powers that be on your side agree.

The need is exciting because it includes almost all the problems of megalopolis, secular city etc. I'll put some of them in order:

i. I think the largest single Indian population in the British Isles—very exclusive—basically not christian. Desperate need to be among them and simply to be good and kind and pre-evangelical, living witness of our concern . . . when I was a stranger etc.

ii. Catechetics—desperately short here.

iii. Parents—need to get at parents *where* they are—house visiting, catechetics—house masses.

iv. Social work—a dirth in the parish—need to be concerned with families, marriage breakdowns, housing, unemployment, bad work conditions etc.

v. Liturgy. Real lack of liturgical development and

understanding. Practically no music. Lack of "family Mass".

vi. Bad ecumenical relations. Baptists and Evangelicals opposing RCs joining council of churches. Methodists attacked for being friendly to RCs.

vii. St. Anselm's school. Teaching? English as a second language. Classes sometimes very heavily 'black'.

viii. Percentage in one area of the parish richer and more bourgeois—not keen to mix or mix in.

I am thrilled to go there and chose it as challenging for this day's world. Forgive my haste.

God bless you.

Michael Hollings

After seven or eight months, I was asked to write for the Province of the Society of the Sacred Heart an account of what had developed since their small community was set up in Southall. This account, printed below was written at Easter 1971 and was fitted to the Society's Renewal Chapter's policy document from which the quotations are taken.

Quote : "The chapter experienced, with all the urgency of conversion, the need for A NEW LIFE, a life that must be both fraternal and totally at the service of others, a truly evangelical life".

When I met a sister of the Society of the Sacred Heart at St. Anne's College, Oxford at a summer garden party in June 1970, I had not read these words, and do not even know if at that time they had been written. But clearly, the Society of the Sacred Heart in England had already been feeling the movement of the Spirit which leads to conversion. Was the meeting fortuitous? A calamity and beginning of error for the Society? Or a work of the same Spirit?

The following day when I was rung up by one of the sisters to clarify what I had been suggesting, I took it to be the work of the same Spirit! Was this in any way confirmed? Yes for me it was! In the first place, the community had great difficulty in obtaining a house. They found the one they wanted, and endless things prevented the acquisition. But with great forbearance, they agreed to come and "pig it" in the rectory, pending final agreement on the house. This led to a real trial for them, and a great benefit for them and us in the close form of living and immediacy of contact between priests, rectory set-up and the sisters' community. It was invaluable as a living experience. Also, by the continued housing problem there arose a situation which led to the purchase of a far bigger, better and closer house—a house across the road from the parish church, and as near in distance as it would be to walk from the front entrance to the main block of Digby Stuart College at Roehampton.

Quote : "The Word was made flesh. He lived among us".

"In these times when men constantly question the meaning of life and wonder what the future can hold for such a divided world, surely it is an urgent task for us to show that the Incarnation is NOW, to show Christ's love ourselves; the love of Jesus who lived as a brother of men and who freely gave his life for his friends".

The little Southall community IS living among us—in an ordinary street, in an ordinary road. Immediately they are and they have neighbours; immediately the Incarnation is not only NOW, but HERE. The people of Southall know this, as the ordinary people often knew THE INCARNATION when the Scribes and Doctors did not. They come in—men and women and children—*ordinary* men and women and children. They paint the house, bring in bits of furniture, help wash down the walls, they bring what they have to help the sisters. And then they come for the sisters to help them—they bring the little children to be minded while they go to Sunday Mass; they bring the older children, or let them come to catechism; they come to find a babysitter or ask to borrow a cot. The "young people searching for the meaning of life" may sense the meaning in a small discussion group, or gathered in common and enthusiastically for the drama group in one of the bigger rooms; the older neurotic woman verging on a breakdown is given a bed and a place of peace while she weathers the storm; two college students live and observe the life of the nuns for their college "project"—one a Welsh presbyterian, the other a negress Baptist from U.S.A., the parish priest is driven on sick calls and we talk endlessly on the development of community living and meeting; hopeless men and women drop in for help in housing problems, and go away comforted and sometimes to new homes.

I wonder whether any community in England could say it was more INCARNATE—and because incarnate, a greater Christlike—failure?

Quote: "We must build our communities within, not apart from the world".

The Southall community has moved into a new and difficult concept. It is to BE PART not APART. Fundamentally this begins with prayer. . .

Quote: "We want this new life to be founded, as it always has been, on prayer; it is 'in Christ' that we must build our fraternal communities within, not apart from the world".

The Southall community is *part of* and not *apart from* the community of Southall. As parish priest, I made it clear that there should not be a chapel in the house, however unusual this might seem. The prayer of the people is in St. Anselm's or else in their own homes. They cannot be rich enough to spare one whole room for a chapel, and the priests are occupied in parochial masses in church and house masses in street districts. Difficult as a "nunly" concept? Yes, I'm sure it is. But read again the quote. It is nice to have "our chapel"; but then St. Teresa of Avila notes that when she was hesitating about founding her reform: "The thing that held me back was attachment to *our cell.*" The community of Southall comes together to worship in St. Anselm's; the community of the Society of the Sacred Heart is "building our fraternal communities within, not apart from, the world". Of course, like other family communities, they have house masses, when neighbours are invited to share worship in their home, and they pray together as a community at times they arrange together.

Quote: "It is Christ's own love which urges us to meet the needs of men crushed by a life of subjection and ignorance".

In Southall, the Sacred Heart community is learning to meet the varying needs of the general community of mankind; many of them have been brought about by the unchristian way in which we christians have lived in the past. For instance, the older concepts of dominance and empire have produced benefits no doubt, but they have also produced a problem of immigration which is clearly seen in Southall, and which leads educationally to a situation where in our Catholic primary school there are some 32% "coloured" immigrants, many of whom need remedial treatment (N.B. 32% in 1971. In 1976 the tally is over 60%).

Another "established" concept is the provision of Catholic schools at heavy cost by the Catholic community. I'm sure you have considered this, because you are so much taken up in educational work. But have you considered a situation such as prevails in Ealing Deanery, to which Southall belongs? In Ealing, only 40% of Catholic children are in Catholic schools (1970). Sixty per cent are not in Catholic schools, and only 10% of these receive any religious education. Looking at the population many of whom are West Indian and who need some additional help in ordinary education, and who receive no religious education at present . . . well, what hope have they of growing up "strong and perfect christians and soldiers of Jesus Christ"?

Quote: "Let us work towards the development of a social conscience which impels to action".

Let us take an example or two from Southall . . .

The Elderly are an unduly large proportion in Southall. There are three homes for the elderly and a geriatric hospital. Additionally there are very many older people, living often alone, frequently neglected, poor, in dirty conditions, sometimes rat-ridden. There seems to be poverty, misery and loneliness. Who is doing anything about it? I was tempted to say before the sisters came there was no one. This can't be true, because there are clubs and efforts by Old People's Welfare. But more and regular visits to the elderly have been markedly paying dividends in terms of discovery of new needs, new people being contacted, great joy at the sisters' presence. The CWL runs a club for the elderly of all denominations and none, but the follow-up visiting they cannot do with such regularity as the sisters. The priests take Holy Communion to the house-bound, but they cannot go every day, and we have found bedridden men and women who have been without the sacraments in some cases for years. (1970 1. From 1974 we have had sisters and laity commissioned to distribute Holy Communion).

Housing is a serious and costly problem which is now beginning to be nibbled at. The sisters are becoming a centre to which those in need of accommodation come. Not much of the problem is soluble. But already, with the help of lay people families are being clothed, fed, furnished and even re-housed. The failure rate and cost in time and patience is high. But so are the stakes.

Cathechetics. For the first time in the history of the parish a serious attempt is being made to deal with the high precentage of children in non-catholic schools in an organised catechetical way. In addition to weekly "Sunday school" for different age-groups, there is a slowly growing group of parents who are undergoing initial training in being catechists; one or two have begun teaching small groups of children in their own homes, under guidance, preparing them for Holy Communion. But there should be much more developed planning and growth over the future years, if we are to offset the neglect which concentration on Catholic schools has fostered.

Catholic schooling. But there remains the need to use effectively the educational facilities which exist, and in Southall the Sacred Heart community is helping in this work through one member teaching in St. Anselm's primary school. She also works very effectively with a children's choir and an emerging drama group.

Also under this "social conscience" section, I would like to emphasise that we are only, and in an amateur way, beginning to scratch at problems. From the welfare angle, there has been considerable local opposition, because none of the sisters is considered properly trained or authorised to do welfare work. (Despite this, an untrained sister has now worked six years more and more in the social services area and is now accepted and turned to for help by social services and many others. Courses and paper qualifications do not necessarily make a "social worker" out of anyone; work, care and persevering love do!). There is then a real need if this work is to continue and prosper to train sisters to be in the field of social work, so that they can stand on an equality with secular workers. Amateurism is out for the future, if recognition is required. (I imagine it is quite clear in better known educational fields that a nun cannot, as in the days of old, teach *just because* she is a nun. She *must* be properly qualified. This has taken a long time to learn fully in some orders. We now begin by learning the same painful process for other fields such as social work, catechetics and so on).

Quote : "Each community must establish its own style of life, evaluated in faith in the light of the Gospel".

From the outside, I can see something of the difficulty of the emerging community of Southall. Frankly none of the sisters has lived in this way before. The early training and especially the restricted way of life of the former "lay sisters" provides adjustment problems which are formidable. (1976. In two instances the growth and liberation of ex-lay sisters has been in the words of superiors: "unbelievable" . . . and to me very effective and very beautiful).

There is real danger that the value of the work at Southall may be lost sight of because of the already over-demanding commitment to a very different form of apostolate in big schools and training colleges.

There is real danger that the "new" form of community life, with its greater "democracy" and its plurality of function and fields, its looser "rule of life" and so on may appear dangerous, misguided, and to be brought into line.

(1976. There seems serious danger too that personal "self-fulfilment" in particular fields of work is being given priority in placing sisters, rather than the local need.)

The great hope I have is that the community will be encouraged, allowed liberty, aided in strengthening its future personnel, but that this should be done in consultation with the "sister in charge", and not "out of the blue". Naturally this policy can only work if there is a sense of complete trust, and a real "sense" in the province that this is an apostolic venture of real merit in the true spirit of the forward looking recent general chapter.

Finally, I would like to express my deep gratitude and that of all those who work for God in Southall, together with all God's people here, known and unkown. We keep the Society in our prayers, and we hope you will pray for this part of the field which is now ready for the harvest.

St. Anselm's, Southall
Middlesex.

Holy Saturday, 1971.

MICHAEL HOLLINGS.

Appendix 2

A RECOLLECTION OF PADRE PIO

I hope you have experienced in your life some meeting or awakening of the kind which is the basis for this recollection. If you have not, then I hope that God will in his own time give you such a happening, a death and resurrection, because after it life can never be quite the same again. Never quite the same . . . much fuller and deeper.

My personal experience was encountering Padre Pio.

What follows is not supposed to be accurate in detail, correct in chronology or in any way definitive. It is a personal experience in which I found myself "caught".

I suppose I would not be isolated from the feeling of a good number of people when I first was asked to go down Italy from Rome to meet "the Franciscan friar who has the stigmata, Padre Pio". Part of me said: "Good heavens! That's the man it was suggested I should go and see when I was a soldier in Italy in World War II, and had completely lost all belief. I pooh-poohed the idea then, and I'm not going to be involved in that sort of thing now." Part of me said: "Michael, since then you have come to believe in God again. What is your faith? Do you put limits to what God can do, if he wants?"

In this ambivalence, I went. I have described elsewhere in a now out-of-print book the effect this had on me. [*Hey You!* Burns Oates, 1954.] But as it is out of print, I cannot refer to it, in order to remind myself what I said at that time. So in tranquility, I remember this.

My companion, who had urged me to go with him, told me that Padre Pio had been a sickly sort of young man in the period of World War I. He had been with the Franciscans, had been kept on, despite ill health and, as was normal, got called into the army for war service. He had been invalided out, and came back to his convent, received the stigmata about 1918, and had been there ever since.

Padre Pio was, said my friend, a saint. He, my friend, wanted to ask him about continuing studies for the priesthood, because he was sure Padre Pio would know immediately whether he should or not.

Frankly, I was queasy at the thought of going, because, despite openness in confession, I was still scared somehow that Padre Pio might (almost magically) see evil in me which would preclude my continuing towards the priesthood.

Anyhow . . . we went down there.

Padre Pio had been sent to a convent of the Friars Minor Capuchin at San Giovanni Rotondo, Foggia. This is in the mountainous district which forms the "spur" on the heeled foot of Italy's Adriatic coastline. So we journeyed there to arrive in darkness and chill on a March evening in 1947. That night was spent coldly miserable, shivering on a bed with one blanket, grateful to be woken at 4.30 in the morning to go to Padre Pio's Mass. But this all added to the sense of repulsion and refusal in my body, mind and heart. Waking experience only enhanced this. We went icily through wind and darkness to the convent door, where already at five o'clock people of all sorts were collecting, pressed against the doors, pushing, shoving even hitting each other. Presently the small door was opened, and people surged through, shouting, cursing, rushing, fighting, almost berserk. Inside the church, when we achieved our modest English non-push entry, there was shouting and jostling and crying out.

But we found ourselves moved towards the rear of the altar, to the sacristy, and there only men could come. We stood, and shivered, silently; the small door into the cloister opened, people breathed: "Padre, Padre", and he was there . . .

Yes, he was there, and at once there were two reactions as I recall them now. Firstly, intense disillusion: a little man, shuffling, irritable with those who pressed round too close, a "no-one". And secondly, a relaxation, a peace and a joy: here was a real person with whom I could be myself, as he was himself. What a relief! No need to pose . . . just to be me.

I had spoken no word to him. This was just what he felt like.

The Mass followed. It was long (one hour and a half). It was slow. For part of it, there was an irritation; for part of it, physical pain in kneeling upright. But gradually a sense of rightness, commitment to sacrifice and passion, a suffering born with a serenity and peace which I had never experienced, an acceptance of oneness and sharing both with Christ and humanity which was beyond any limit I had reached.

It was not that there was anything startling or exotic. There was no flowing blood from the wounds, or cries or sighs. I was very much relieved. For me it was a long drawn out penitential exercise, when Padre Pio was caught and held in prayer for five or ten minutes at a time, with a concentration which I was normally far from sharing.

Padre Pio drew to the Mass two or three hundred people at 5 a.m., winter and summer. He had people queuing for his counsel and for sacramental absolution, so that it might take three of four days before your numbered ticket came up. When I knelt before him to lay myself open to God, the beauty and relief was that he was very simple, very ordinary and very reassuring. I went out from the sacristy "open" confessional knowing more truly why penance is spoken of as "an encounter with Christ". It was from this time that I "found" and used the Jesus prayer with meaning; because of the experience, I understood the word of Jesus: More blessed he who has not seen, and has believed . . . but I was happy to have "seen".

When Padre Pio was a young man, he lived in Pietrelcina, in the mountains between Naples and Foggia. His father had to go to America seeking money to help the family finances. His whole background was from the work of the earth, from corn cobs hanging outside the home to dry, from the local parish church, the *contadini*, the fairly common scraping of a living from a land which could be at once beautiful and friendly, yet demanding and sometimes cruel. He knew the Franciscans, he came to love their way.

Early manifestations of his prayer life and spirituality were at Pietrelcina. He seemed "caught" in prayer sometimes, immobile, unheeding. It was near his parental home that he first received the pain of the stigmata without visible sign . . . coming to his mother's call, shaking both hands "as though he was playing a guitar".

Some three years later, when in the choir of the little convent church at San Giovanni Rotondo, he was discovered in prayer, either "caught" or dazed, the now-visible wounds bleeding.

If anyone was to ask me what was perhaps the most striking characteristic of Padre Pio, from the viewpoint of example to the ordinary people of God, I would without hesitation sum it up in the one word: obedience.

From his young days, though completely firm in his determination to seek God in the Franciscans, he submitted to ill-health, to conscription to the Italian Army, to virtual imprisonment without contact with people, after the appearance of the stigmata. More than this, he accepted the command to be examined under anaesthetic, so that his wounds might be "got at", and an attempt made to heal them. He agreed to the wishes of his superiors about writing and moving about, even after he was once more allowed to meet people, when "released" from the claustral confinement of some three or more years.

It is not surprising, if we accept that ultimately all obedience is summed up in the words of Christ about his Mother: "Blessed are they who hear the word of God and keep it." This Padre Pio did, with love, for the will of God is love. St. John of the Cross affirms that love can be repaid by love alone.

There was a further obedience which almost any one of us would have found intolerable, obedience to the will of the People of God who flocked to him, and kept him shut up in the confessional for hour upon hour, each and every day of the week. For him it was on occasions more than his human nature could carry, and he was sharp or even rough, with his peasant-background roughness. People can be and too often are demanding, unfeeling, plain silly or stupid.

Padre Pio had us all, old and young, scrupulous, neurotic, plain, sensible, emotional, mad, simple, sophisticated. You name the variety God's creation; they came. Perhaps before going to San Giovanni, I did not see so clearly why St. Paul in his famous passage on love in I Corinthians begins by saying "love is patient, does not come to an end".

God, in the supremely kind way he has, stretched out his hand to me in the form of a BBC TV producer in the spring before Padre Pio died. Long ago I had accepted I could not afford time or money to visit Padre Pio again. Then the telephone rang, and the producer asked me to go with him and a team to see if it was possible to do a programme on him.

The two or three days I had there were very near the end of his earthly living of patient love. Now he was wheeled into Mass in a chair and sat for the celebration. As he came through to the convent one day, I was presented to him, his eyes gleamed, and then once more took on a "far away" gaze in which it was as though he was looking in not out, absorbed as he so often was at Mass, but now, that absorption taking up more and more of him and more and more of his time.

But he still went on . . . Mass, the confessional, patience, love—life, not love, coming to an end.

It was easy in the homes and hotels round San Giovanni to pick up miraculous tales, to hear stories of minds read, people healed, bilocation, foretelling of the future. Personally, I looked, listened, sieved through the evidence, and was convinced of the authenticity and actuality of a small percentage, along with the "blowing up" of a great number of innocent and ordinary happenings into supernatural manifestations. I have been a frequenter of Lourdes. I know very few cures, comparatively, which have been authenticated in over a hundred years. But I know of almost endless "spiritual" and even "physical" or "mental" favours which have been claimed with lasting joy by an unknown flood of God's ordinary people. The same is in my personal knowledge true of San Giovanni Rotondo, and of the presence of Padre Pio there. Certainly, one of the "physical" miracles due to him, which aided unemployment and the medical treatment of by now thousands of men, women and children, was the "creation" of a huge hospital on the barren hillside above the convent. Much talk and even scandal was rumoured over money sent in for the building and handed directly to the Padre, who stuffed it into his cowl! But the hospital grew and continued its ministry.

Rome was very firm throughout the life of Padre Pio. They disliked "cult"; they imposed restrictions. His Order too kept him strictly to the area of the convent. Many people wrote against him, whispered against him, denounced him.

But still the people came, and without doubt the most wonderful thing in this coming was the mixture, which was always predominantly of the farmers and peasants and workers and very ordinary people of Padre Pio's own stock. Though he touched the highest, he was truly Christlike in that he never lost touch with the lowly. Perhaps he was never happier than when he was sitting in the convent garden in the evening light, chatting with his fellow friars and some of his close friends, chatting of God and economics, of people and politics, of love, service and family life.

This I know. Once you or I have lived a little in the circle of such a man as Padre Pio, life cannot ever be quite the same again, however much we remain selfish and sinful, forgetful and stupid. That is why, in the work of Christ in his world, we need more and more Padre Pios and Mother Teresas, more Taizés and Ionas. Padre Pio would not have been happy that you simply listened and looked, or read this. He would say to you as he said to me: "I will always remember you in my prayers—go away now and seek the Lord's will—and do it."

AFTERWORD

When I had lived twenty-five years as a priest, I wanted to share some of what the experience had meant to me – so I wrote *Living Priesthood*. Now I am nearly forty years ordained and to my surprise the book is still in demand.

About three years ago I was saying to a priest friend at his silver jubilee that the second twenty-five years were better than the first.

I firmly proclaim this as I continue to struggle and rejoice in living priesthood at an older age. One reason for this is that people multiply as life goes on. Some contacts continue, some end – some go away and re-emerge later. I read somewhere that every sentence we use should begin with 'AND'. This is because we come into a story which is only available because we were born; we live from there *and* we add to the story . . . and . . .

I find it joyful, sad, painful and beautiful to meet individuals, pairs, families and groups, getting to know them better, living alongside them, loving and being loved – and then perhaps leaving that particular parish or field of work . . . AND later enjoying a further meeting, when each life has developed for better or worse, richer or poorer, but always has moved on. The priest can touch pre-birth and birth, growth and education, the development of love and vocation, the sacraments of life, the pain and patience and happiness of ordinary daily life. Gradually, he lives with ageing and dying, the bitter-sweet final parting which hates the loss and loves the believed union with the God of love.

There have been many, many changes in the world and in the Church during my lifetime, sometimes going forward so fast that I run breathless to catch up – and fail. But sometimes the very slowness in change combines with a sense of going the wrong way up a moving staircase, to bring frustration.

I see an importance in this frustration. The majority of God's people are pretty powerless and often immobile, confined by circumstance to live in a particular area, work where work is, feel the frustration of being unable to shift the powers that be or to change society or their own special lot. Only a small number are 'upwardly mobile', whether young or older. And it was for these powerless and poor that Jesus came.

Looking back on living priesthood, I realise how different the expectations of the ordinand and then of the priest and even of higher ranking clergy may be. I recognise my own privilege in security, privacy, mobility of working hours and in being in the 'job' I love. I have had a freedom of hours and movement normal only to the privileged classes. I can make time for prayer, for study, for writing, alongside ordinary and extraordinary pastoral work. I have had and still have the opportunity to be present in the most intimate friendships with every kind of person from the dukes and duchesses of the realm to the dukes and duchesses of the road, from babes in arms to aged men and women in terminal care, who need cradling in love – and these from among most of the races of the world and shot through with joy. I have been knocked down and stood up; laughed at, sneered at, accused, cursed, swindled, blackmailed – and I have been praised, cherished, supported, encouraged and loved deeply and lastingly. I move among periods of aridity, hopelessness and despair when everything is colourless and tasteless, to the over-riding sense of peace, joy, hope and trust in the Lord.

I think the greatest wonder in my life is the loving patience of God for me personally, for His Church and for the world which He made and saw and sees as good. While recognising my almost innumerable faults and failings, many entirely wilful, I cannot dwell on them for two reasons. Firstly, I strongly believe that God looks at His people with love and is happy above all to seek out the good and the effort made, the trying, whereas it seems sadly true that many of the Church's pastors put more emphasis on sin and make everyone feel guilty.

As a personal experience, which I only understood fully much later and in hindsight, I realise that I came to ordination largely for my own sake, for my fulfilment, which I sought to achieve through prayer and good works. In fact, I took a lot of time and energy doing God's work for Him, even playing God myself, not relying on Him, often pridefully egocentric. I am sure others have fallen and will fall into the same trap. Well, you can clamber out . . . but only with the help of others and of God.